200 best
Pressure Cooker
recipes

Cinda Chavich

Robert
ROSE

For complete cataloguing information, see page 304.

Disclaimer
The recipes in this book have been carefully tested by our kitchen and our tasters. To the best of our knowledge, they are safe and nutritious for ordinary use and users. For those people with food or other allergies, or who have special food requirements or health issues, please read the suggested contents of each recipe carefully and determine whether or not they may create a problem for you. All recipes are used at the risk of the consumer. Consumers should always consult their pressure cooker manufacturer's manual for recommended procedures and cooking times.

We cannot be responsible for any hazards, loss or damage that may occur as a result of any recipe use.

For those with special needs, allergies, requirements or health problems, in the event of any doubt, please contact your medical adviser prior to the use of any recipe.

Design and Production: Kevin Cockburn/PageWave Graphics Inc.
Proofreader: Sheila Wawanash
Indexer: Gillian Watts
Photography: Colin Erricson and Mark T. Shapiro
Food Styling: Kathryn Robertson and Kate Bush
Prop Styling: Charlene Erricson

Cover image: Chicken Stew with New Potatoes and Baby Carrots (page 146)

We acknowledge the financial support of the Government of Canada through the Book Publishing Industry Development Program (BPIDP) for our publishing activities.

Published by Robert Rose Inc.
120 Eglinton Avenue East, Suite 800, Toronto, Ontario, Canada M4P 1E2
Tel: (416) 322-6552 Fax: (416) 322-6936
www.robertrose.ca

Printed and bound in Canada

4 5 6 7 8 9 FP 17 16 15 14 13 12

Contents

*This book is dedicated to
my grandmother Danita Chavich,
who taught me that
a steamy bowl of homemade soup
spreads a lot of love.*

Acknowledgments

My first thank you is to all the people at Coranco for their co-operation, without which my recipe testers and I would not have been able to develop and refine these recipes. Everything in *200 Best Pressure Cooker Recipes* was tested in the Lagostina Brava Plus and Logica models. They are both first-class pressure cookers, but my real favorite is the Logica, with its handy pressure release valve, easy-opening lid and dual pressure settings. This model is stylish, very versatile and dependable, and it will give you years of great performance in the kitchen.

I would also like to thank my recipe testers, Sue Spicer and Sylvia Kong, for their endless hours of hard work and professional advice. Without their help, this project could not have been completed on time, and with such success.

These recipes were developed and tested in Calgary at an altitude of nearly 3,500 feet. They were then retested at an altitude of 650 feet. We believe that all of the recipes can be prepared with the cooking times as set out in any pressure cooker at any altitude. However, see page 11 for a more detailed description of some of the adjustments you may want to make in certain conditions.

I hope these recipes give you both inspiration and years of enjoyment with pressure cooking.

— *Cinda Chavich*

Introduction

When it comes to naming the kitchen tool of the millennium, my vote goes to the new generation of safe and foolproof pressure cookers.

I am a kitchen gadget junkie, but few of my new acquisitions fully deliver on their promises, and many are relegated to the culinary scrapheap. So when the best kitchen stores began carrying a reportedly foolproof new generation of the old 1950s wonder, the pressure cooker, I was skeptical. I'd heard the horror stories — erupting pots of pea soup and rocketing valves. Who needs to risk life and limb to cook dinner?

But professional curiosity got the better of me. The new pressure cookers are lovely, sleek and shiny stainless steel pots with heavy bottoms and loads of safety devices. Gone is the hissing pressure regulator, bouncing precariously on a jet of steam. In its place, most modern machines have a new regulator and quick-release valve that lets you release the steam instantly, without hauling the hot and heavy monster over to the cold-water tap to cool it down. They have more backup safety mechanisms, so you can't build pressure if the lid isn't properly affixed, or inadvertently clog the main pressure vent and end up with lima beans all over the ceiling.

There really is nothing to fear from this new generation of safe pressure cookers. But that wasn't what hooked me. It was the food. Hands-free risotto, cooked to creamy perfection in 6 minutes. The house filled with the heady aromas of tender beef and red wine stew in half an hour. Almost instant homemade stocks and broths, with all of the infused flavor you'd expect from hours of slow cooking.

Suddenly, I could make healthy meals reminiscent of my grandmother's kitchen in less time than I could sauté a chicken breast.

This is what really makes the pressure cooker indispensable. It's not for all kinds of cooking, but it's a tool that can save you time and energy without compromising quality.

We are eating more beans and whole grains — ethnic dishes like Indian curries and Mexican black bean soup on Wednesdays or daube of lamb with niçoise olives and succulent short ribs for dinner parties. This kind of old-fashioned peasant food is back in style, and that's where the pressure cooker shines. So think about savory stew, coq au vin, or rogan josh tonight. Have a healthy grain pilaf with your grilled fish, or simmer a big pot of bean soup for lunch in less than 15 minutes.

Screw up your courage and crank up your pressure cooker. Once you've served a perfect pot roast after work, you'll be hooked. And you'll never get tired of your new toy. In fact, you won't know what you did without it.

The Essentials of Pressure Cooking

The theory of pressure cooking is simple. By subjecting a sealed pot to heat, pressure builds up inside the unit. This pressure — typically maintained at between 5 and 15 pounds per square inch (psi) — causes the food inside to be cooked at about 250°F (120°C), some 38°F (20°C) hotter than the normal boiling point. The result is that cooking times are significantly reduced. Most foods will cook in one-third the time of conventional boiling or braising.

The evolution of the pressure cooker

It was a French inventor in the 17th century who first screwed a lid firmly onto a cast iron pot to trap steam. He discovered that the steam increased the cooking temperature 15% above the normal boiling point. Nearly 200 years later, another inventive Frenchman perfected a method of preserving food under high pressure and the seeds of home pressure cooking were sown.

Huge home pressure canners were introduced in North America by National Presto Industries in 1915 and, by the 1940s, many manufacturers were selling "pressure saucepans" to busy homemakers.

The early pressure cookers were very straightforward devices, consisting of a heavy pot and lid that was locked on top. The seal was provided by a rubber gasket and the pressure was controlled by a heavy weight that sat loosely on top of a vent pipe in the lid. As steam built up inside the cooker, the pressure would lift the weight slightly, allowing steam to escape. This cycle of pressure build-up and release caused the weight to jiggle and hiss continuously throughout the cooking time — hence the term "jiggle-top" used to describe these old-fashioned cookers.

While the jiggle-top cookers were functional, they also presented some risks. If the steam vent became clogged, the pressure could build to dangerous levels, requiring the cook to place the pot immediately under cold running water to avoid blowing the emergency release plug — and sending food all over the kitchen.

By the 1970s, the popularity of pressure cookers had declined in North America and the microwave oven became the preferred way to cook food quickly. But Europeans rejected this new kind of cooking. And over the next 25 years, European manufacturers like Italy's Lagostina, France's T-Fal and Switzerland's Kuhn Rikon worked to perfect the home pressure cooker with innovations that made them easy and safe to use. Today, while most European households use pressure cookers to prepare food quickly, North Americans are only just beginning to rediscover the benefits of these devices.

The latest generation of pressure cookers feature a stationary pressure regulator, either a fixed weight or spring valve. This system keeps the pressure even by occasionally releasing a burst of steam, and allows the cook to quickly release the pressure in the cooker at the end of the cooking time by pressing a button or flipping a switch. This type of system is less likely to clog than the old weight-valve mechanism, which, because it emits steam constantly, has a much greater chance of getting a piece of food stuck in the vent pipe.

The new cookers also have backup release mechanisms so that it's impossible to have a pressure cooker explosion. While older models were designed with a steam valve or plug that would blow out if excess pressure built up inside the unit (spewing the contents over the kitchen), this isn't possible with the new generation of pressure cookers.

Most have several preventative safety features. When the cooker comes up to pressure, a lid-locking mechanism pops up. This tells you that the unit has reached full pressure and prevents you from opening the lid when the contents are under pressure.

Many cookers also have one or two secondary safety valves — usually on the lid and around the gasket — which are designed to emit steam (not contents) if the main pressure valve malfunctions or becomes clogged with food during cooking.

What to look for in a pressure cooker

The most important thing to remember when buying a pressure cooker is that, as in all things, you get what you pay for. Decide before you shop what is important to you.

The pricier cookers have more bells and whistles, more safety features and heavier bottoms. If you're perfectly comfortable dealing with the jiggle-top technology of bygone years, there are lots of inexpensive pressure cookers available in this category. But if you need a boost to get past the fear of pressure cooking, choose one of the second-generation cookers.

Look for a cooker with a lock that makes the lid impossible to remove when there is any pressure still inside. Find out what kind of backup valve there is to release pressure

if the main valve becomes clogged. In older and less sophisticated models, the valve is simply a rubber plug that will blow out and launch the contents of the cooker into your kitchen. The latest models offer one or more pressure releases that will vent the steam, not the contents, if there is a malfunction in the main pressure valve.

Do your homework (most cooker manufacturers have Internet sites that describe their products). Check out the offerings of as many stores as possible. A number of the new-generation cookers from companies like Lagostina, T-Fal, Kuhn Rikon and Presto are still only sold in specialty kitchen stores or high-end boutiques.

Try opening and closing the pressure cooker. Is it easy to lock the lid in place? Would you feel comfortable opening the cooker when it's extremely hot? Imagine lifting the pressure cooker when it's hot and full of soup or stew. Are the handles comfortable? Will they stay cool?

Look at the pressure release valve. Some release a jet of steam straight into the air, others shoot it out at an angle (saving your ceiling from a moisture bath). If there are two settings or a dial, you can release the steam gradually. Some cookers simply have a metal bale to flip — the steam comes out quickly in all directions and the bale can be very hot. Others require that you push the valve down with your finger (or a wooden spoon) to release the steam — fairly simple, but still time-consuming, since you can't just walk away while the pressure drops.

If you buy a less sophisticated model (without a spring-loaded pressure release valve) you will have to remove the pan from the heat and allow the pressure to reduce naturally, or pick up the hot pressure cooker, take it to the sink and run it under cold water until the heat and steam dissipates.

Do you plan to steam desserts in your cooker? If so, you'll want a model that offers at least two pressure settings — high (13 to 15 psi) and low (5 to 8 psi) — because most cakes and steamed puddings don't rise well when cooked at high pressure. Low pressure is also useful for delicate foods and thick sauces that tend to burn easily.

Choose a cooker that's large enough to accommodate whole roasts — a 6- to 7-quart (6 to 7 L) model is good for most families. A small, skillet-style cooker is good for vegetables and delicate foods that you want to bring to pressure and steam very quickly.

A pressure cooker with a larger cooking surface and good, heavy base will make browning easier and burning less likely. A quality stainless steel surface is easy to clean. Some companies offer pressure cookware sets, with both deep and shallow pans that will accommodate the same pressure lid, as well as regular glass lids so that you can also use the pans for conventional cooking.

What food is best prepared in a pressure cooker?

While the pressure cooker is a wonderfully versatile appliance, it is better for some types of food than others. For example, it is ideal for just about any comfort food — soups, tender stews, pot roasts and creamy risottos. Not only does it give you perfect results, you can cut the usual cooking time down by two-thirds.

Beans, tougher cuts of meat, soups, stews, chiles and grains are also perfect candidates for your pressure cooker.

And don't forget desserts. You will never bake a cheesecake again after you've tried the smooth, creamy versions you can create in your pressure cooker. It also makes wonderful rice pudding, crème caramel and steamed Christmas pudding in a fraction of the time you're used to.

You can also almost instantly cook tender cuts of chicken (breasts are done in only 8 minutes) and perfectly steam fish in the pressure cooker in 3 minutes flat.

Or you can use the cooker as a tool to prep ingredients — dried chickpeas for hummus, beans and whole grains for healthy salads, and cooked fruits for preserves. Beans can be instantly quick-soaked in the pressure cooker, most varieties in less than a minute.

The pressure cooker is perfect for making rich homemade stocks with recycled soup bones and vegetable scraps. Chicken pieces and ribs can be precooked and flavor-infused quickly for finishing on the barbecue. Corn on the cob never touches water when steamed in its own juice on the trivet in less than 2 minutes.

Cooking under high pressure helps to break down the connective tissues in tougher cuts of meat, retains water-soluble nutrients that are normally boiled away, and instantly infuses and mingles flavors in a way that is usually found only in slow-cooked food. And unlike other appliances (like slow cookers), you can brown meats and vegetables in the pan before pressure cooking, adding extra layers of flavor that come from caramelizing sugars.

Adapting conventional recipes for the pressure cooker

Almost any recipe that requires long and slow cooking, simmering, braising or steaming can easily be adapted for pressure cooking. Think of all of your favorite peasant cuisines — from braised Spanish beans and French lamb stews to slow-simmered Indian curries, Asian hot pots, goulash, stroganoff, pot roasts and comforting beef stew. You probably have many favorite family recipes that your mother or grandmother served that could be completed in less than half the traditional time in a pressure cooker.

The high heat and pressure works to instantly tenderize tougher cuts of meat, so you can start to enjoy delicious and inexpensive meals even when you're pressed for time after work. Try recipes using round steak, short ribs, stewing beef, lamb shanks and turkey parts. You'll be amazed at the intense flavor that these cuts can add to everyday meals.

One of the main differences between conventional and pressure cooking recipes is the amount of liquid required. In the pressure cooker, most stews need less than 2 cups (500 mL) broth, stewed tomatoes, coconut milk or other saucy ingredients. Remember that vegetables and meats will release liquid while cooking, about ¼ cup (50 mL) for every 2 cups (500 mL) raw veggies.

Plan to thicken your dishes at the end of the cooking process. I have found that a flour roux used at the start of my favorite Cajun-style stews and gumbos burned in the intense heat of the pressure cooker. The solution: make the roux on the side and whisk it into the stew after the pressure has been released.

Pressure cooking also requires a different approach to using herbs and spices. The high heat of pressure cooking destroys the flavor in delicate herbs, and even the most robust herbs if used fresh. Plan to use dried herbs in your recipes (and

in greater quantities), or add your fresh chopped herbs at the end of cooking.

Steps to successful pressure cooking

Cooking under pressure is easy if you follow a few simple steps.

Browning (where appropriate). While it's not absolutely necessary to brown meats and vegetables before pressure cooking, I heartily recommend it. Most stews, soups and pot roasts benefit greatly from the added flavor that comes with browning and caramelizing sugars before cooking.

Filling. Don't overfill the pressure cooker. Make sure the pot is never more than two-thirds full. If you're cooking beans, rice or grains (which foam up during cooking), make sure the pot is no more than half full. Some cookers have a maximum fill indicator line stamped on the pot. Conversely, be sure you don't underfill the cooker. Consult the manufacturer's instruction booklet to determine the minimum amount of liquid required for pressure cooking in your unit, usually at least ½ to 1 cup (125 to 250 mL).

If you are steaming food on a rack, place a metal trivet or steaming basket inside the unit, add the water and place the food directly on the rack or in a heatproof plate or casserole dish. The trivet or basket is designed to keep the water level below the food you are cooking — so don't add too much water.

Lock the lid. Make sure the lid is properly closed before putting the pressure cooker on the heat. Some pressure cookers have dots or marks you will need to line up before twisting the lid to lock it. With others, you pull a lever across or push a button to activate the lock.

Bring the cooker to full pressure. Get the pressure cooker up to full pressure as quickly as possible by putting it over high heat. If you have a multi-level valve, choose the appropriate "psi" setting. It can take several minutes to achieve full pressure. Use a burner that is no larger than the base of the pot and, if you are cooking with gas, be sure the flame isn't licking up the sides. You can tell when the cooker is up to full pressure in several ways. New models have a button that rises to indicate that pressure has been reached, and will hiss slightly until you reduce the heat. On old jiggle-top models, the weight will begin to jiggle rapidly; reduce the heat immediately or you will have a blow-out.

Reduce heat, just to maintain even pressure. Once the cooker is up to pressure, reduce the heat to low or medium-low. You want to maintain an even pressure during cooking, but you shouldn't hear too much steam escaping (an indication that the heat is too high). With a jiggle-top model, the jiggler should just barely continue to rock, about four or five times a minute. A fixed weight valve should not sputter but may emit a very soft hissing sound, while a spring-valve cooker will be quite silent, with its valve stem rising to the desired level without dropping.

Watch the cooking time. Begin timing when the unit is up to pressure and use an accurate timer (I used the timer on my microwave) to make sure that you release the pressure as soon as the time is up. If you are pressure cooking at high altitudes, you will have to adjust the cooking times. Add about 5% more time for every 1,000 feet (300 m) above sea level. If you find the food is not properly cooked when you remove the lid, lock the lid back in place, bring the pressure cooker back up to full pressure over high heat, reduce heat to low and cook for another 1 or 2 minutes longer. You can also finish the cooking conventionally; this is especially desirable if you want to reduce the cooking liquid to thicken a sauce or stew.

For a convenient list of recommended cooking times for different types of food, see pages 13 to 15.

Release the pressure. When the instructions in a recipe call for releasing the pressure naturally, simply remove the pressure cooker from the heat and wait for the pressure indicator to drop. When the pressure has dissipated, the locking mechanism (on those cookers so equipped) disengages and you can remove the lid. Tilt the lid away from you when opening it. The "natural release" method is best for beans and grains, which can break up and clog the valve if you release the pressure quickly. This method also keeps fragile items like beans intact. It's also good for large pieces of meat (which can toughen), and for soups and stocks, which can spew out when the pressure is released too quickly.

If the recipe calls for releasing the pressure quickly (appropriate for many dishes, and those that might overcook if left under pressure), simply release the pressure valve by pressing the button or flipping the lever. A steady jet of steam will flow out of the machine until all of the pressure has been released. (Be careful; the steam can be hot!) Then the pressure indicator/locking mechanism button will drop and allow you to remove the lid.

If the cooker doesn't have a quick-release valve, you will have to take it to the sink and run cold water over the lid, being careful not to run water into the steam valve, until you hear the locking mechanism release. Some models do not have a locking mechanism to prevent opening the unit while there is still pressure inside. If the lid is removed before all of the pressure has dissipated, the food inside can erupt and burn you. Be careful.

Cleaning the pressure cooker

Read the manufacturer's directions for cleaning your pressure cooker and clean it after every use. Safety devices can fail if the unit is not properly maintained.

Always remove the rubber gasket and clean it with warm soapy water after cooking, then replace it under the rim of the lid. Don't immerse the lid in water or place it in the dishwasher. Remove the jiggle top or spring valve and make sure there is no food clogging the steam vent. You can run water through the vent pipe or use a pipe cleaner to remove any build-up. Look through vent to make sure it's clear every time you close the cover.

Some manufacturers also recommend removing the pressure regulator valve and running it under hot water to clean. Also check the secondary safety valve and clean out any food deposits.

Replace the rubber gasket every year or so. When storing the pressure cooker, store the lid separately or invert it on top to preserve the elasticity of the gasket and eliminate cooking odors.

Troubleshooting

The best source of information about your pressure cooker is the manufacturer. Read the printed material that comes with the cooker for toll-free help lines and websites.

Always follow the manufacturer's instructions. Each pressure cooker works differently and may have unique requirements.

If the cooker begins to hiss loudly during cooking, immediately remove it from the heat. If either or both of the safety release devices engage, turn off the heat and allow the cooker to cool down before removing the lid. Clean all parts well before starting over.

Never leave the pressure cooker unattended. Never deep-fry in the pressure cooker.

Unless you have a new-generation pressure cooker with extra built-in safety systems, avoid cooking applesauce, cranberries, barley, split peas, rhubarb, pasta or cereals — all of which are infamous for clogging up the works.

Sources

If you need more information about pressure cookers, sources include:

Lagostina
1-800-263-4067 • www.lagostina.com

Kuhn Rikon
1-800-662-5882 • 415-461-1048
www.kuhnrikon.com

Mirro Company
1-800-527-7727 • www.mirro.com

T-Fal Canada Inc.
416-297-4131 • www.t-fal.ca

National Presto Industries
1-800-877-0441 • www.gopresto.com

Table of Cooking Times

Vegetables	Cooking time (approx.) *steamed on rack over 1 to 2 cups (250 to 500 mL) boiling water*
Artichoke, medium, trimmed	6 to 8 minutes
Artichokes, small, trimmed	5 to 6 minutes
Asparagus	1 to 2 minutes
Beans, green or yellow	2 to 3 minutes
Beets, small, whole	12 to 14 minutes
Beets, large, whole	20 minutes
Broccoli	2 to 3 minutes
Brussels sprouts	4 minutes
Cabbage, shredded or wedges	2 to 3 minutes
Carrots, sliced or small	4 to 5 minutes
Cauliflower, florets	2 to 3 minutes
Chestnuts (in shell, scored)	6 minutes
Corn, on the cob	3 minutes
Eggplant, cubed	2 to 3 minutes
Kale or other sturdy greens	2 minutes
Potatoes, sliced or cubed (use waxy red potatoes, unless for mashed)	5 to 6 minutes
Potatoes, whole, unpeeled, small to medium	5 to 15 minutes
Potatoes, sweet, cubed	5 minutes
Pumpkin or winter squash	5 to 7 minutes
Rutabagas or turnips, cubed	4 to 5 minutes
Zucchini, sliced	1 minute
Fruit	**Cooking time (approx.)** *cooked with $\frac{1}{2}$ cup (125 mL) water, wine or juice*
Apples, fresh	3 to 4 minutes
Apricots, fresh	2 minutes
Apricots, dried	4 minutes
Figs (dried)	6 minutes
Berries and cherries	0 minutes (bring to pressure and remove from heat)
Peaches, fresh, halved	2 to 3 minutes
Pears, fresh, halved	3 to 4 minutes
Prunes, dried	5 to 6 minutes

Meat and poultry	Cooking time (approx.)	Cooking liquid
Beef, stew meat, cubed	20 to 30 minutes	1 cup (250 mL)
Beef, roast or brisket, 3 lbs (1.5 kg)	35 to 45 minutes	1 to 2 cups (250 to 500 mL)
Beef/veal, shanks	45 minutes	1 cup (250 mL)
Corned beef	50 to 60 minutes	2 to 3 cups (500 to 750 mL)
Beef round steak, $\frac{1}{2}$ inch (1 cm) thick	15 to 20 minutes	1 cup (250 mL)
Beef short ribs	25 minutes	$1\frac{1}{2}$ to 2 cups (375 to 500 mL)
Ham, picnic shoulder, uncooked, 3 lbs (1.5 kg)	30 minutes	2 cups (500 mL)
Ham, slices, uncooked, 1 inch (2.5 cm) thick	12 minutes	1 cup (250 mL)
Pork chops, $\frac{1}{2}$ inch (1 cm) thick	9 minutes	1 cup (250 mL)
Pork shoulder, or butt, roast, 3 lbs (1.5 kg)	40 to 50 minutes	$1\frac{1}{2}$ cups (375 mL)
Pork spare ribs, 2 lbs (1 kg)	15 minutes	1 to 2 cups (250 to 500 mL)
Pork loin roast, 3 lbs (1.5 kg)	30 to 40 minutes	$1\frac{1}{2}$ cups (375 mL)
Lamb, shoulder roast, 3 lbs (1.5 kg)	35 to 40 minutes	1 cup (250 mL)
Lamb, leg roast, 3 lbs (1.5 kg)	35 to 45 minutes	2 cups (500 mL)
Lamb, shoulder, cubed	15 to 20 minutes	1 cup (250 mL)
Chicken, whole, 2 to 3 lbs (1 to 1.5 kg)	20 to 25 minutes	1 cup (250 mL)
Chicken pieces, 2 to 3 lbs (1 to 1.5 kg)	15 to 20 minutes	1 cup (250 mL)
Cornish hens, 2	10 to 12 minutes	1 cup (250 mL)
Duck, pieces	15 minutes	1 cup (250 mL)
Turkey breast, whole, 5 to 6 lbs (2.5 to 3 kg)	35 to 45 minutes	3 cups (750 mL)
Turkey legs and thighs	45 to 55 minutes	3 cups (750 mL)

Grains	Cooking time (approx.) *plus time for natural pressure release*	Water per 1 cup (250 mL) grains *use for jiggle-top models*
Amaranth	4 minutes	$1\frac{1}{2}$ to $1\frac{3}{4}$* cups (375 to 425 mL)
Barley, hulled	35 to 40 minutes	3 cups (750 mL)
Barley, pearl or pot	16 to 20 minutes	3 cups (750 mL)
Buckwheat	4 minutes	$1\frac{3}{4}$ cups (425 mL)
Kamut	40 to 45 minutes	3 cups (750 mL)
Millet	12 minutes	$1\frac{3}{4}$ to 2* cups (425 to 500 mL)
Quinoa	1 minute	$1\frac{1}{2}$ cups (375 mL)
Rice, brown	25 minutes	$1\frac{1}{2}$ to $1\frac{3}{4}$* cups (375 to 425 mL)
Rice, wild	22 to 25 minutes	3 cups (750 mL)
Rice, white	5 to 6 minutes	$1\frac{1}{2}$ to $1\frac{3}{4}$ cups (375 to 425 mL)
Risotto	6 to 7 minutes	$2\frac{1}{4}$ cups (550 mL)
Rye berries	25 to 30 minutes	3 cups (750 mL)
Spelt	35 to 45 minutes	3 cups (750 mL)
Wheat berries	35 to 46 minutes	3 cups (750 mL)

Beans *soaked overnight or pressure-soaked* (*unless otherwise indicated)	Cooking time (approx.) *plus time for natural pressure release*	Water per 1 cup (250 mL) beans *add 1 tbsp (15 mL) vegetable oil*
Adzuki (Japanese brown)	5 to 6 minutes	3 cups (750 mL)
Anasazi	5 to 6 minutes	3 cups (750 mL)
Appaloosa	8 to 10 minutes	3 cups (750 mL)
Baby lima or unsalted butter bean	5 to 6 minutes	3 cups (750 mL)
Black	8 to 9 minutes	3 cups (750 mL)
Black-eyed peas, no soaking*	10 minutes	3 cups (750 mL)
Cannellini (white)	8 to 10 minutes	3 cups (750 mL)
Chickpea (garbanzo)	10 to 15 minutes	3 cups (750 mL)
Christmas lima	6 to 8 minutes	3 cups (750 mL)
Cranberry (barlotto)	6 to 8 minutes	3 cups (750 mL)
Fava	12 to 15 minutes	3 cups (750 mL)
Flageolet	8 to 10 minutes	3 cups (750 mL)
Great Northern	8 to 10 minutes	3 cups (750 mL)
Lentils, brown, no soaking*	10 minutes	Cover by 2 inches (5 cm)
Lentils, French, no soaking*	12 minutes	Cover by 2 inches (5 cm)
Lentils, red, no soaking*	5 minutes	Cover by 2 inches (5 cm)
Lima, large	4 to 6 minutes	3 cups (750 mL)
Navy	4 to 5 minutes	3 cups (750 mL)
Peas, split, no soaking*	8 to 10 minutes	3 cups (750 mL)
Peas, whole	5 to 8 minutes	3 cups (750 mL)
Pigeon peas	5 to 8 minutes	3 cups (750 mL)
Pinto	4 to 6 minutes	3 cups (750 mL)
Rattlesnake	4 to 6 minutes	3 cups (750 mL)
Scarlet runner	8 to 10 minutes	3 cups (750 mL)
Soybean, white	10 to 14 minutes	3 cups (750 mL)
Soybean, black	16 to 18 minutes	3 cups (750 mL)
Tongues of fire	8 to 10 minutes	3 cups (750 mL)

Appetizers

Beef- and Rice-Stuffed Grape Leaves

**Makes about 30
Serves 6 as a
main course**

Sue Spicer, the devoted home economist who helped test many of the recipes for this book, thought that the pressure cooker would be perfect for making one of her favorite Greek appetizers, stuffed grape leaves (or dolmades). She was right. The pressure cooker cuts the cooking time down to 15 minutes (from $1\frac{1}{2}$ hours in the oven), and creates perfectly tender dolmades. This is her delicious recipe, which makes about 30 stuffed leaves. They can be served hot as a main course or at room temperature as an appetizer.

1 lb	lean ground beef	500 g
1 cup	long-grain rice	250 mL
1	roasted red bell pepper, minced	1
1	onion, minced	1
1 cup	beef stock	250 mL
$\frac{1}{3}$ cup	extra-virgin olive oil	75 mL
2 tbsp	finely chopped fresh mint	25 mL
1 tsp	dried tarragon	5 mL
$\frac{1}{2}$ tsp	salt	2 mL
$\frac{1}{2}$ tsp	freshly ground black pepper	2 mL
30	grape leaves (about 1 small jar)	30
2 cups	water	500 mL
2 tbsp	freshly squeezed lemon juice	25 mL

Sauce

2	eggs, beaten	2
1 tbsp	extra-virgin olive oil	15 mL
2 tbsp	freshly squeezed lemon juice	25 mL
2 tsp	Dijon mustard	10 mL
1 tsp	granulated sugar	5 mL

1. In a large bowl, combine beef, rice, red pepper, onion, stock, oil, mint, tarragon, salt and pepper. Drain grape leaves; carefully separate and rinse in cold water. Pat leaves dry. Place any damaged leaves in the bottom of pressure cooker.

2. Arrange leaves, dull side up, on work surface. Place 2 tbsp (25 mL) of filling on each leaf. Fold stem end over filling, turn in the sides and loosely roll, allowing room for rice to expand while cooking.

3. Arrange stuffed leaves in the cooker in layers. Do not pack too tightly. Pour water and lemon juice over leaves.

4. Lock the lid in place and bring the cooker up to full pressure over high heat. Reduce heat to medium-low, just to maintain even pressure, and cook for 15 minutes. Remove from heat and allow pressure to drop naturally. Carefully transfer cooked dolmades to a serving platter.

5. *Sauce:* In a heavy saucepan over low heat, whisk together eggs, oil, lemon juice and mustard; cook, stirring constantly, for about 5 to 10 minutes, until thick. For appetizers, serve sauce in a bowl alongside the stuffed grape leaves for dipping. As a main course, add water as necessary to thin the sauce to pouring consistency and drizzle over dolmades.

● VARIATION

Try the pressure cooking method used here with your favorite recipe for cabbage rolls. It's a winner.

Steamed Pork Ribs with Black Bean Sauce

Serves 4 to 6 as part of a multi-course meal or dim sum party

This yummy dim sum dish works perfectly in the pressure cooker and is a delicious way to start a Chinese feast. Look for bite-sized pork ribs (sometimes called riblets or rib tips) or ask the butcher to cut a rack of spareribs into 1-inch (2.5 cm) strips.

- 7- or 8-inch (18 or 20 cm) heatproof bowl or baking dish (use smaller size if necessary to fit inside pressure cooker)
- Rack or trivet to fit bottom of pressure cooker`

Sauce

2 to 3	cloves garlic, minced	2 to 3
1 tbsp	minced or grated gingerroot	15 mL
1 tbsp	cornstarch	15 mL
1 tsp	granulated sugar	5 mL
¼ cup	Chinese black bean sauce	50 mL
2 tbsp	Chinese rice wine or dry sherry	25 mL
2 tsp	sesame oil	10 mL
2 tsp	Asian chili paste	10 mL
2 lbs	pork spareribs (side ribs), cut into individual 1-inch (2.5 cm) riblets	1 kg
2	green onions, minced	2
1	small hot chile pepper, seeded and minced	1

1. *Sauce:* In a large bowl, combine garlic, ginger, cornstarch, sugar, black bean sauce, rice wine, sesame oil and chili paste.

2. Cut ribs into individual pieces, add to sauce and toss to coat. Cover and refrigerate for at least 1 hour or overnight. Transfer to heatproof bowl.

3. Set rack in the bottom of the pressure cooker. Pour in 2 cups (500 mL) water for steaming. Place bowl on rack. Lock the lid in place and bring the cooker up to full pressure over high heat. Reduce heat to medium-low, just to maintain even pressure, and cook for 15 minutes. Remove from heat and release pressure quickly.

4. Transfer ribs to a platter and sprinkle with green onions and chile pepper. Serve immediately.

Eggplant Caponata

Caponata is the Sicilian version of French ratatouille. Serve it on toasts for an hors d'oeuvre or tossed with hot pasta for a speedy main course.

• TIP

Salting eggplant and rinsing away the brown juices that rise to the surface is necessary to eliminate bitterness. This step is not necessary if you use smaller Japanese eggplants.

1	large purple eggplant, skin on, cut into 1-inch (2.5 cm) cubes	1
2 tsp	salt	10 mL
1 tbsp	packed brown sugar	15 mL
2 tbsp	tomato paste	25 mL
2 tbsp	balsamic vinegar	25 mL
½ cup	extra-virgin olive oil	125 mL
1	onion, chopped	1
1	small red bell pepper, chopped	1
1	small yellow bell pepper, chopped	1
1 cup	canned crushed tomatoes	250 mL
½ cup	air-cured black olives, pitted and chopped	125 mL
2 tbsp	chopped basil	25 mL

1. Toss eggplant with salt; transfer to a colander and let stand for 30 minutes. Rinse and drain well. Pat dry with paper towels.

2. In a bowl, whisk together brown sugar, tomato paste and vinegar; set aside.

3. In the pressure cooker, heat oil over high heat. Add eggplant and sauté for 2 minutes. Stir in onion, red and yellow peppers and tomatoes. Lock the lid in place and bring the cooker up to full pressure over high heat. Reduce heat to medium-low, just to maintain even pressure, and cook for 4 to 5 minutes. Remove from heat and release pressure quickly.

4. Stir to break up eggplant slightly. Stir in reserved tomato paste mixture, olives and basil. Allow to cool. Serve at room temperature or chilled. (It will keep, covered, in the refrigerator for up to 4 days.)

Sun-Dried Tomato Cheesecake

Serve this savory "cheesecake" spread on thin slices of baguette. It makes a pretty addition to an appetizer buffet or cheese tray — cut it into pie-shaped wedges and serve with a cheese knife alongside your favorite ripe Brie.

- 7- or 8-inch (1.5 or 2 L) springform pan (use smaller size if necessary to fit inside pressure cooker)
- Rack or trivet to fit bottom of pressure cooker

Crust

3 tbsp	unsalted butter, softened	45 mL
1/3 cup	dry bread crumbs or crushed onion crackers	75 mL

Filling

1/2 cup	sun-dried tomatoes in oil, drained, oil reserved	125 mL
6	cloves garlic, minced	6
2 tbsp	chopped fresh oregano (or 1 tsp/5 mL dried)	25 mL
3	eggs	3
3 tbsp	all-purpose flour	45 mL
12 oz	cream cheese, softened	375 g
4 oz	goat cheese, softened	125 g
1/4 cup	sour cream or plain yogurt	50 mL
1/2 cup	chopped green onions	125 mL
2 cups	water	500 mL

Topping

1/2 cup	sour cream	125 mL
	Baguette or crackers for serving	

1. *Crust:* Thickly butter bottom and sides of springform pan. Sprinkle bread crumbs inside pan, tilting to coat the sides. Leave excess crumbs on bottom. Wrap outside of pan with foil to seal. Set aside.

2. *Filling:* In a food processor, purée sun-dried tomatoes with 1 tbsp (15 mL) of the reserved oil, garlic, oregano and eggs. Add flour, cream cheese, goat cheese and sour cream; purée until smooth. Stir in green onions. Pour mixture into prepared pan and cover with foil, making sure pan is well sealed.

3. Set rack in bottom of pressure cooker. Pour in water. Fold a 2-foot (60 cm) length of foil several times to make a strip that will be used to remove pan. Center pan on midpoint of strip and fold the ends together to make a handle. Use strip to lower pan into the cooker.

4. Lock the lid in place and bring the cooker up to full pressure over high heat. Reduce heat to medium-low, just to maintain even pressure, and cook for 20 minutes. Remove from heat; let pressure drop naturally for 7 minutes. Release remaining pressure with quick-release valve. Let cheesecake cool in cooker for a few minutes. Using foil handle, lift pan out of cooker onto cooling rack. Remove foil lid. Cheesecake should be set around edges, but still slightly loose in center. If center is still liquid, seal with foil and return to cooker. Lock the lid in place and bring the cooker up to full pressure over high heat. Reduce heat to medium-low, just to maintain even pressure, and cook for 2 minutes longer. When cheesecake is cooked, remove foil. Use a paper towel to mop up any water pooled on top of cake.

5. *Topping:* In a small bowl, whisk sour cream with another 1 tbsp (15 mL) of the reserved oil. Spread over cheesecake, smoothing top. Let cool to room temperature. Refrigerate for at least 8 hours or overnight before serving.

6. With a knife dipped in hot water, cut cheesecake into quarters and present with a cheese knife and sliced baguette.

● **TIPS**

Cheesecake can be wrapped and refrigerated for up to 3 days or frozen for up to 3 months.

Don't discard the oil from your sun-dried tomatoes. It's great for salad dressings or brushing over meat and fish before grilling.

Braised Artichokes with Red Pepper Aïoli

The flavors in this dish remind me of the south of France, where thyme and rosemary grow wild and perfume the air. It makes the perfect first course for a special Mediterranean meal.

● TIP

If you don't have time to roast peppers, use a prepared red pepper spread (such as Gloria brand).

Red Pepper Aïoli

1	clove garlic, minced	1
¼ tsp	salt	1 mL
¼ tsp	freshly ground white pepper	1 mL
Pinch	cayenne pepper	Pinch
1	egg yolk	1
¼ cup	roasted red bell pepper (see tip, at left, for alternative)	50 mL
1 tbsp	freshly squeezed lemon juice	15 mL
⅓ cup	extra-virgin olive oil	75 mL
	Juice of 2 lemons	
4 cups	water	1 L
12	small artichokes	12
2 tbsp	extra-virgin olive oil	25 mL
6	shallots, peeled and halved	6
4	cloves garlic, minced	4
1	sprig fresh rosemary, leaves minced	1
½ tsp	salt	2 mL
½ tsp	freshly ground black pepper	2 mL
½ tsp	dried thyme	2 mL
½ cup	diced fresh or canned tomatoes	125 mL
½ cup	chicken stock	125 mL
⅓ cup	red wine or tomato juice	75 mL
2 tbsp	balsamic vinegar	25 mL

1. *Red Pepper Aïoli:* In a food processor, combine garlic, salt, white pepper, cayenne, egg yolk, red pepper and lemon juice; purée until smooth. With machine running, slowly add oil through the feed tube until the aïoli is thick and emulsified. Refrigerate until ready to serve.

2. In a large bowl, add juice of one of the lemons to water. Cut stems from artichokes, trim tips of leaves and cut each artichoke in half lengthwise. Scoop out choke and place artichoke halves in lemon water to prevent discoloration.

3. In the pressure cooker, heat oil over medium heat. Add shallots and garlic; sauté until they begin to color. Stir in rosemary, salt, pepper, thyme, tomatoes, stock, wine and vinegar. Drain artichokes and add to cooker. Pour remaining lemon juice over top.

4. Lock the lid in place and bring the cooker up to full pressure over high heat. Reduce heat to medium-low, just to maintain even pressure, and cook for 7 minutes. Remove from heat; release pressure quickly.

5. With a slotted spoon, transfer artichokes to a deep serving dish. Boil braising liquid until it's reduced by half. Strain sauce over artichokes and let cool to room temperature. Serve artichokes as a side dish or on individual plates, drizzled generously with the red pepper aïoli.

● TIP

The artichokes are eaten by pulling the leaves off, one by one, then drawing them through your teeth to remove the tender flesh at the base of each leaf. Be sure to supply a dish for leaf discards and finger bowls for this hands-on appetizer.

Pearl Balls with Spicy Soy Dipping Sauce

These little meatballs, encrusted in tender short-grain rice, can be made ahead, then steamed in the pressure cooker when your guests arrive, for speedy Asian-inspired hors d'oeuvres.

- 7- or 8-inch (18 or 20 cm) heatproof plate (use smaller size if necessary to fit inside pressure cooker)
- Rack or trivet to fit bottom of pressure cooker

3	green onions, roughly chopped	3
2	cloves garlic	2
1	1-inch (2.5 cm) piece gingerroot	1
1	can (8 oz/227 mL) water chestnuts, drained	1
1 cup	shredded Chinese (napa) cabbage	250 mL
1 lb	ground pork or chicken	500 g
1	egg, lightly beaten	1
1 tbsp	dark soy sauce	15 mL
1 tsp	sesame oil	5 mL
½ tsp	salt	2 mL
1 cup	short-grain rice (Arborio or sushi rice)	250 mL

Dipping Sauce

¼ cup	dark soy sauce	50 mL
1 tbsp	Asian chili paste	15 mL
1 tbsp	dry white wine or sherry	15 mL
1 tsp	sesame oil	5 mL

1. In a food processor, combine green onions, garlic, ginger, water chestnuts and cabbage; pulse until finely minced. In a bowl, using your hands, mix minced vegetables, pork, egg, soy sauce, sesame oil and salt until well blended. Shape meat mixture into 1-inch (2.5 cm) meatballs. Set aside.

2. Place rice in a bowl and cover with cold water. Stir to release starch, then drain in a fine-mesh sieve. Repeat two to three times, until water is clear. Spread rice on a large plate.

3. Roll meatballs in rice until coated on all sides. Place meatballs on heatproof plate (depending on the size of your pressure cooker, you may have to steam them in batches).

4. Set rack in the bottom of the pressure cooker. Pour in 2 cups (500 mL) water for steaming. Place plate of meatballs on rack. Lock the lid in place and bring the cooker up to full pressure over medium-high heat. Reduce heat to medium-low, just to maintain even pressure, and steam for 20 minutes. Remove from heat and release pressure quickly.

5. *Dipping Sauce:* In a small bowl, combine soy sauce, chili paste, wine and sesame oil.

6. Serve pearl balls hot, with dipping sauce on the side.

● **TIP**

If making meatballs ahead, set on a plate in a single layer, cover with plastic wrap and refrigerate for up to 24 hours.

Moroccan Chicken Meatballs

These meatballs make a nice hot hors d'oeuvre on a party buffet table. Or serve the meatballs and creamy sauce over pasta or instant couscous for a simple family supper.

● **TIP**

For a little more kick, you can increase the cayenne pepper to ½ tsp (2 mL).

1	onion	1
¼ cup	each packed fresh parsley, cilantro and mint leaves	50 mL
1½ lbs	lean ground chicken	750 g
1	egg	1
½ tsp	each ground cumin, sweet paprika and salt	2 mL
¼ tsp	each ground cinnamon and cayenne pepper	1 mL

Sauce

2 tbsp	extra-virgin olive oil	25 mL
1	onion, sliced	1
1	clove garlic, minced	1
2 tbsp	all-purpose flour	25 mL
1	can (28 oz/796 mL) tomatoes, crushed or puréed	1
1	can (10 oz/284 mL) chicken broth, undiluted	1
1 tsp	sweet paprika	5 mL
¼ cup	whipping (35%) cream	50 mL
	Salt and freshly ground black pepper	

1. In a food processor, pulse onion, parsley, cilantro and mint until finely minced. In a bowl, using your hands, combine onion mixture, chicken, egg, cumin, paprika, cinnamon, salt and cayenne. Cover and refrigerate for 1 hour. Shape into 25 small meatballs.

2. *Sauce:* In the pressure cooker, heat oil over medium-low heat. Add onion and garlic; sauté for about 10 minutes or until onion is golden brown and caramelized. Add flour and cook, stirring, for 1 minute. Stir in tomatoes, chicken broth and paprika; bring to a boil. Carefully add meatballs to sauce.

3. Lock the lid in place and bring the cooker up to full pressure over high heat. Reduce heat to medium-low, just to maintain even pressure, and cook for 10 minutes. Remove from heat and release pressure quickly. Gently stir in cream and season to taste with salt and pepper.

Spiced Chickpeas

Here, cooked chickpeas are slowly sautéed with Indian spices until they are golden brown and crisp. This addictive vegetarian snack is great served with beer or cocktails.

1 cup	dried chickpeas	250 mL
1	small onion, peeled	1
1	bay leaf	1
¼ cup	unsalted butter	50 mL
2 tbsp	extra-virgin olive oil	25 mL
1 tsp	minced garlic	5 mL
1 tsp	onion salt	5 mL
1 tsp	ground ginger	5 mL
1 tsp	ground turmeric	5 mL
½ tsp	ground coriander	2 mL
¼ tsp	cayenne pepper	1 mL
1 tbsp	kosher salt	15 mL

1. Soak chickpeas overnight in water to cover or use the quick pressure-soak method (page 208). Drain.

2. In the pressure cooker, combine chickpeas, 4 cups (1 L) water, onion and bay leaf. Lock the lid in place and bring the cooker up to full pressure over high heat. Reduce heat to medium-low, just to maintain even pressure, and cook for 15 minutes. Remove from heat; allow pressure to drop naturally. Drain chickpeas well; discard onion and bay leaf.

3. In a small pot over medium heat or in a bowl in the microwave, melt butter; stir in olive oil and garlic. In a large bowl, toss the chickpeas with the garlic mixture. Combine the onion salt, ginger, turmeric, coriander and cayenne; sprinkle spice mixture over chickpeas and toss to coat.

4. Spread chickpeas in a single layer on one or two large rimmed baking sheets. Bake in a preheated 400°F (200°C) oven for 5 to 10 minutes until brown and crisp, shaking the pan or stirring the peas often so that they brown evenly and don't burn. Transfer to a large bowl; toss with kosher salt.

5. Serve chickpeas hot or at room temperature. To reheat, spread on a rimmed baking sheet and bake in a preheated 350°F (180°C) oven for 5 to 10 minutes.

Hummus

This Mediterranean
spread is perfect with
warm triangles of pita
bread or veggies for
dipping.

● VARIATION

*This is a good, basic
recipe for hummus.
When you want a change
in flavor and color, try
adding ½ cup (125 mL)
roasted red pepper or
½ cup (125 mL) chopped
parsley (or even roasted
garlic) before puréeing
the mixture.*

1 cup	dried chickpeas	250 mL
1 tsp	ground cumin	5 mL
1 tsp	salt	5 mL
¼ cup	extra-virgin olive oil	50 mL
¼ cup	tahini paste (sesame seed paste)	50 mL
2 tsp	sesame oil	10 mL
	Juice of 2 large lemons	
3	cloves garlic, minced	3
¼ cup	warm water (approx.)	50 mL

1. Soak chickpeas overnight in water to cover or use the quick pressure-soak method (page 208). Drain.

2. In the pressure cooker, cover chickpeas with at least 1 inch (2.5 cm) water. Lock the lid in place and bring the cooker up to full pressure over high heat. Reduce heat to medium-low, just to maintain even pressure, and cook for 15 minutes. Remove from heat and release pressure quickly. Drain.

3. In a food processor, combine chickpeas, cumin, salt, olive oil, tahini, sesame oil, lemon juice and garlic; purée until smooth. If mixture seems too dry, add enough of the warm water as necessary to thin. Serve immediately with warm pita bread or refrigerate.

Black Olive and Lentil Purée

This assertive combination, with roots in the Mediterranean, is great for scooping up with toasted pita bread to start an Italian- or Greek-inspired dinner. A little crumbled goat cheese or feta makes a nice addition.

● TIP

If desired, you can replace the anchovy paste with 1 tsp (5 mL) Asian fish sauce.

1 cup	brown or green lentils, rinsed	250 mL
2	cloves garlic, minced	2
1 tsp	extra-virgin olive oil	5 mL
½ cup	dry-cured black olives, pitted	125 mL
1 tbsp	dried oregano	15 mL
2 tsp	anchovy paste	10 mL
½ tsp	Asian chili paste	2 mL
¼ cup	extra-virgin olive oil	50 mL
3 tbsp	freshly squeezed lemon juice	45 mL
	Salt and freshly ground black pepper	
2 tbsp	chopped fresh flat-leaf (Italian) parsley	25 mL
	Crumbled goat cheese or feta cheese (optional)	
	Toasted pita bread	

1. In the pressure cooker, combine 4 cups (1 L) water, lentils, garlic and the 1 tsp (5 mL) olive oil. Lock the lid in place and bring the cooker up to full pressure over high heat. Reduce heat to medium-low, just to maintain even pressure, and cook for 10 minutes, until very tender. Remove from heat and allow pressure to drop naturally. Drain, reserving cooking liquid. Set aside.

2. In a small saucepan, combine ½ cup (125 mL) of the cooking liquid, olives, oregano, anchovy paste and chili paste; bring to a boil over medium heat. Reduce heat and simmer until liquid has evaporated. Remove from heat and let cool slightly.

3. In a blender or food processor, purée olive mixture, the ¼ cup (50 mL) olive oil and the lemon juice.

4. In a bowl, combine lentils and olive purée, whisking to break up the lentils a little and combine well. Season to taste with salt and pepper. Cover and refrigerate for at least 2 hours, to let the flavors meld, or for up to 24 hours. Just before serving, stir in parsley and top with feta, if desired. Serve with pita toasts.

Fava Bean Purée

Scoop this savory spread up with pita triangles or chips, or roll it up in pita breads for a Middle Eastern snack.

● TIPS

Za'atar is a spice mixture found in Middle Eastern groceries. Along with the herbs and spices, it has a strong citrusy note that comes from dried sumac berries. If you can't find it, substitute ¼ tsp (1 mL) each dried thyme, dried marjoram or oregano, ground cumin, salt and ground lemon pepper or grated lemon zest.

If you prefer a chunkier spread, you can mash the cooked beans in a bowl instead of using a food processor to purée them. Then simply mix in the remaining ingredients by hand.

¼ cup	extra-virgin olive oil, divided	50 mL
1	small onion, chopped	1
2	cloves garlic, crushed	2
½ tsp	ground cumin	2 mL
1 cup	split peeled dried fava beans	250 mL
2 tbsp	chopped fresh flat-leaf (Italian) parsley	25 mL
1 tsp	salt	5 mL
1 tsp	za'atar (see tip, at left)	5 mL
2 tbsp	freshly squeezed lemon juice	25 mL
2 tsp	sesame oil	10 mL
	Additional extra-virgin olive oil	
	Paprika	
	Pita bread triangles or pita chips	

1. In the pressure cooker, heat half the olive oil over medium heat. Add onion and sauté for 10 minutes, until starting to brown. Add garlic and cumin; sauté for 2 minutes. Stir in 3 cups (750 mL) water and fava beans.

2. Lock the lid in place and bring the cooker up to full pressure over medium-high heat. Reduce heat to medium-low, just to maintain even pressure, and cook for 20 minutes. Remove from heat and release pressure quickly. Drain, reserving cooking liquid.

3. In a food processor, purée beans, adding a little of the cooking liquid if necessary to make a smooth mixture. Add parsley, salt, za'atar, the remaining olive oil, lemon juice, and sesame oil; process until well combined.

4. Spread purée in a large dish, drizzle with olive oil and dust with paprika. Serve with pita triangles.

White Bean Dip

With the addition of olive oil, garlic and chiles, the humble white bean becomes a zesty dip.

● TIP

For a slightly more Mediterranean version, substitute dried thyme for cumin and chopped basil for cilantro. Gently heat the dip to warm it, then mix in a few ounces of crumbled goat cheese or feta cheese and serve with pita wedges.

¾ cup	dried white beans, such as Great Northern or navy beans	175 mL
2	cloves garlic	2
3 tbsp	freshly squeezed lemon juice	45 mL
⅓ cup	extra-virgin olive oil	75 mL
2 tsp	ground cumin	10 mL
1½ tsp	chili powder	7 mL
Pinch	hot pepper flakes	Pinch
3 tbsp	minced fresh cilantro	45 mL
	Salt and freshly ground black pepper	

1. Soak beans overnight in water to cover or use the quick pressure-soak method (page 208). Drain.

2. In the pressure cooker, cover beans with at least 1 inch (2.5 cm) water. Lock the lid in place and bring the cooker up to full pressure over high heat. Reduce heat to medium-low, just to maintain even pressure, and cook for 12 to 13 minutes for Great Northern beans or 8 to 9 minutes for navy beans. Remove from heat and allow pressure to drop naturally. Drain beans and rinse under cold running water to cool them quickly.

3. In a food processor, drop cloves of garlic through feed tube with machine running to chop. Add beans, lemon juice, olive oil, cumin, chili powder and hot pepper flakes; purée until smooth.

4. Fold in cilantro and season to taste with salt and pepper. Serve with taco chips or fresh vegetables.

Dhal Dip with Pappadums

This is the perfect starter for an Indian meal. Serve the spicy split-pea spread with crispy pappadums and sliced peppers, green beans and zucchini sticks for dipping. Or spread it on a pita and top with grilled vegetables for an exotic vegetarian wrap.

● **TIP**

To puff pappadums, fry them in hot oil for a few seconds or cook them in the microwave for about 45 seconds. You can buy large round pappadums or tiny cocktail-sized crackers.

1 tbsp	extra-virgin olive oil	15 mL
1 tsp	unsalted butter	5 mL
1	small onion, chopped	1
2 tsp	minced gingerroot	10 mL
1	clove garlic, minced	1
1	serrano pepper, seeded and minced	1
½ tsp	garam masala	2 mL
¼ tsp	ground turmeric	1 mL
½ tsp	dry mustard	2 mL
1 cup	dried yellow split peas	250 mL
¼ cup	plain yogurt or sour cream	50 mL
2 tbsp	chopped cilantro	25 mL

1. In the pressure cooker, heat oil and butter over medium heat. Add onion, ginger, garlic and serrano; sauté until soft. Stir in garam masala, turmeric and dry mustard; cook for 1 minute or until spices are fragrant. Stir in split peas and 2 cups (500 mL) water.

2. Lock the lid in place and bring the cooker up to full pressure over high heat. Reduce heat to medium-low, just to maintain even pressure, and cook for 8 minutes. Remove from the heat; allow pressure to drop naturally. Transfer to a bowl.

3. Stir dhal until cooled and thickened. Whisk in yogurt until mixture is smooth; stir in cilantro. Serve with pappadums for dipping.

Chunky Greek Eggplant and Pepper Spread

Use crostini or pita chips to scoop up this addictive condiment. Serve it alongside bowls of olives and fresh cheese, drizzled with olive oil, for a meze meal.

2	large purple eggplants	2
1 tbsp	sea salt	15 mL
¼ cup	extra-virgin olive oil	50 mL
3	cloves garlic, chopped	3
1	onion, cut into slivers	1
1	red bell pepper, cut into slivers	1
1	yellow bell pepper, cut into slivers	1
1 tsp	dried oregano	5 mL
2 tsp	balsamic vinegar	10 mL
1 tsp	Asian chili paste or hot pepper sauce	5 mL
	Salt and freshly ground black pepper	
	Crostini or pita chips	

1. Remove green caps from eggplants and discard. Without peeling, slice eggplants into small slivers, 1 to 2 inches (2.5 to 5 cm) long and about ⅛ inch (0.25 cm) wide (you should have about 3 cups/750 mL). Place in a bowl, cover with cold water and stir in salt. Let stand for 30 minutes. Drain well, pressing out any bitter brown juice.

2. In the pressure cooker, heat oil over medium heat. Add garlic and onion; sauté for 10 minutes, until starting to brown. Add eggplant and sauté for 5 minutes. Stir in red and yellow peppers and ½ cup (125 mL) water.

3. Lock the lid in place and bring the cooker up to full pressure over medium-high heat. Reduce heat to medium-low, just to maintain even pressure, and cook for 20 minutes. Remove from heat and allow pressure to drop naturally.

4. Remove the lid and stir in oregano. Return cooker to medium heat and boil for 5 to 10 minutes, or until most of the excess moisture has boiled away and the oil rises to the top. Remove from heat and stir in vinegar and chili paste. Season to taste with salt and pepper. Serve with crostini.

Southern Caviar

Black-eyed peas are fast to cook and don't require presoaking. This "caviar" makes a tasty appetizer to scoop up with your favorite tortilla chips or to serve salad-style at an outdoor barbecue or picnic. Pass a pitcher of margaritas.

1 cup	dried black-eyed peas, rinsed and drained	250 mL
3	green onions, chopped	3
1	large clove garlic, minced	1
½ cup	finely chopped red bell pepper	125 mL
2 tbsp	minced canned or pickled jalapeño pepper	25 mL
½ tsp	ground cumin	2 mL
2 tbsp	freshly squeezed lime juice	25 mL
2 tbsp	extra-virgin olive oil	25 mL
	Salt and freshly ground black pepper	
2 tbsp	chopped fresh cilantro	25 mL

1. Place peas in the pressure cooker and add at least 4 cups (1 L) cold water, or enough to cover beans by 1 inch (2.5 cm). Lock the lid in place and bring the cooker up to full pressure over high heat. Reduce heat to medium-low, just to maintain even pressure, and cook for 8 minutes. Remove from heat and allow pressure to drop naturally. Drain well.

2. In a bowl, combine peas, green onions, garlic, red pepper, jalapeño, cumin, lime juice and olive oil. Season to taste with salt and pepper. Let stand at room temperature for 30 minutes to let the flavors meld (or refrigerate for up to 24 hours; return to room temperature before serving). Stir in cilantro just before serving.

Soups

Carrot and Coriander Soup

Here's the perfect way to start a dinner party, or just use up your fall crop of carrots: a smooth, colorful soup, creamy, yet low in calories.

¼ cup	unsalted butter	50 mL
1	onion, chopped	1
1	clove garlic, minced	1
½ cup	chopped celery	125 mL
1 tbsp	minced gingerroot	15 mL
1½ lbs	carrots, chopped	750 g
¼ cup	chopped fresh cilantro stems (save the leaves)	50 mL
1 tsp	ground coriander	5 mL
½ tsp	curry powder	2 mL
5 cups	chicken stock (approx.)	1.25 L
1 tsp	freshly squeezed lemon juice	5 mL
	Sea salt	
1 tbsp	chopped fresh cilantro leaves	15 mL

1. In the pressure cooker, melt butter over medium heat. Add onion, garlic, celery and ginger; sauté for 5 minutes, until softened and fragrant. Add carrots, cilantro stems, coriander and curry powder; sauté for 5 minutes. Stir in chicken stock.

2. Lock the lid in place and bring the cooker up to full pressure over medium-high heat. Reduce heat to medium-low, just to maintain even pressure, and cook for 10 minutes. Remove from heat and release pressure quickly. Let cool slightly.

3. Working in batches, transfer soup to a blender or food processor and purée until smooth (or use an immersion blender in the cooker). Return soup to cooker and reheat over medium heat, thinning with a little stock or water if necessary. Stir in lemon juice and season to taste with salt.

4. Ladle into soup bowls and garnish with cilantro leaves.

Curried Cauliflower Soup

The spices and small red lentils combine to give this soup a lovely golden color and a hearty texture. If you have a couple of cups of leftover cooked rice, stir it in for an even more substantial soup.

4	cloves garlic, peeled	4
1	1-inch (2.5 cm) piece gingerroot, peeled	1
1	onion, chopped	1
1/4 cup	water	50 mL
2 tbsp	canola oil	25mL
1 tsp	ground cumin	5 mL
1 tsp	ground coriander	5 mL
1 tsp	ground turmeric	5 mL
1/4 tsp	cayenne pepper	1 mL
2 cups	chopped cauliflower	500 mL
4 cups	chicken stock or water	1 L
1/2 cup	red lentils	125 mL
	Salt, freshly ground black pepper and freshly squeezed lime juice	

1. In a blender, combine the garlic, ginger, onion and water and purée to a paste. Set aside.

2. Heat the oil in the pressure cooker over medium-high heat, add the cumin, coriander, turmeric and cayenne and cook together for 30 seconds. Add the cauliflower and reserved onion paste and cook, stirring, for 5 minutes longer, until the onions begin to brown.

3. Add the stock and lentils to the pot. Lock the lid in place and bring the cooker up to full pressure over high heat. Reduce heat to medium-low, just to maintain pressure, and cook for 8 minutes. Let the pressure drop naturally.

4. Season to taste with salt, pepper and a squeeze of lime juice.

Creamy Tomato Soup

You'll never go back to canned tomato soup after tasting this fresh, creamy made-from-scratch version. Garnish with homemade croutons and fresh basil (for a fancy meal) or serve it every day with soda crackers or combined with leftover rice. With a small grilled cheese sandwich on the side, this makes a comforting weekday family meal. Kids love it!

● **TIP**

To make quick work of chopping the fresh vegetables, combine them in a food processor and pulse until finely chopped. You can also chop the tomatoes by whirling them in the food processor.

¼ cup	unsalted butter	50 mL
3	cloves garlic, finely chopped	3
2	stalks celery, finely chopped	2
1	onion, finely chopped	1
1	small red bell pepper, finely chopped	1
1	can (14 oz/398 mL) tomatoes, chopped, with juice	1
4 cups	chicken stock	1 L
3 tbsp	tomato paste	45 mL
2 tsp	dried basil	10 mL
½ cup	whipping (35%) cream	125 mL
	Salt and freshly ground black pepper	

1. In the pressure cooker, melt butter over medium heat. Add garlic, celery, onion and red pepper; sauté for 10 minutes, until onions start to brown. Stir in tomatoes with juice, chicken stock, tomato paste and basil.

2. Lock the lid in place and bring the cooker up to full pressure over medium-high heat. Reduce heat to medium-low, just to maintain even pressure, and cook for 8 minutes. Remove from heat and release pressure quickly.

3. Stir in cream, return to medium heat and simmer for 5 minutes, until thickened. Season to taste with salt and pepper.

Caramelized Onion Soup

Serves 6

When they're in season, use sweet Vidalia onions for this classic soup. It's the perfect way to start a fancy steakhouse-style dinner. It also makes a toasty après-ski snack.

- Baking sheet

4 tbsp	extra-virgin olive oil	60 mL
6	large white or red onions, thinly sliced	6
4	cloves garlic, minced	4
6 cups	beef stock	1.5 L
1 cup	dry red wine or port	250 mL
2 tsp	brown sugar	10 mL
½ tsp	dried thyme	2 mL
	Salt	

Toasts

½	baguette	½
1 cup	shredded Gruyère or Emmental cheese	250 mL

1. In the pressure cooker, heat oil over medium heat. Add onions and sauté for about 20 minutes, until starting to brown and caramelize. Add garlic and sauté for 5 minutes. Stir in stock, wine, brown sugar and thyme.

2. Lock the lid in place and bring the cooker up to full pressure over medium-high heat. Reduce heat to medium-low, just to maintain even pressure, and cook for 8 minutes. Remove from heat and allow pressure to drop naturally. Season to taste with salt.

3. *Toasts:* Meanwhile, preheat oven to 400°F (200°C). Slice baguette on the diagonal into ½-inch (1 cm) slices and arrange on baking sheet. Top each slice with cheese. Bake for 5 to 10 minutes, until cheese is bubbly and toasts are beginning to brown.

4. Place a toast in the bottom of each shallow soup plate and ladle soup over and around it. (Or simply perch a piece of toast on the rim of each bowl or float one in each bowl.)

Wild Mushroom and Potato Bisque

There's very little cream in this elegant mushroom soup; it gets its smooth texture from potatoes. Make it without chicken stock for a vegetarian version. To speed things up even more, use the food processor to mince the vegetables and mushrooms.

● **TIP**

If you have the time to prepare homemade stock, try the one on page 283.

1 tbsp	extra-virgin olive oil	15 mL
2	cloves garlic, minced	2
1	small onion, minced	1
12 oz	Yukon gold potatoes (or other yellow-fleshed variety) peeled and grated	375 g
1	small tomato, seeded and chopped	1
1 cup	finely chopped wild and domestic mushrooms (brown, oyster, shiitake, portobello, morels, cèpes, etc.)	250 mL
4 cups	chicken stock or vegetable stock (see tip, at left)	1 L
1	bay leaf	1
¾ tsp	minced fresh thyme	4 mL
½ cup	whipping (35%) cream	125 mL
	Salt and freshly ground black pepper	

1. In the pressure cooker, heat oil over medium heat. Add garlic and onion; sauté for about 5 minutes or until soft. Add potato, tomato and mushrooms; cook, stirring, for about 5 minutes longer or until mushrooms begin to give up their moisture. Stir in the stock, bay leaf and thyme.

2. Lock the lid in place and bring the cooker up to full pressure over high heat. Reduce heat to medium-low, just to maintain even pressure, and cook for 5 minutes. Release pressure quickly.

3. Discard bay leaf. Stir in cream and heat through. Using a potato masher, break up potatoes to thicken the soup, if necessary, or use an immersion blender to purée if you prefer a smoother soup. Season to taste with salt and pepper.

Winter Mushroom and Barley Soup

There's nothing delicate about this vegetarian soup — the portobello mushrooms and barley provide plenty of hearty flavor. For a richer (but non-vegetarian) soup, use beef or chicken broth instead of water.

2 tbsp	unsalted butter	25 mL
1 tbsp	extra-virgin olive oil	15 mL
1	large onion, halved and sliced	1
2	stalks celery, chopped	2
1	carrot, chopped	1
2 tsp	minced garlic	10 mL
1	bay leaf	1
1	portobello mushroom cap, chopped	1
8 oz	mixed fresh mushrooms, sliced	250 g
½ cup	pearl or pot barley	125 mL
6 cups	water	1.5 L
2 tbsp	vermouth or brandy	25 mL
2 tsp	salt	10 mL
¼ tsp	freshly ground black pepper	1 mL
	Chopped fresh parsley	

1. In the pressure cooker, heat butter and oil over medium heat. Add onion and sauté for 5 minutes or until softened. Stir in celery, carrot, garlic and bay leaf; cook, stirring, for 10 minutes or until onion begins to turn golden.

2. Add portobello and mixed mushrooms; cook for 5 minutes, until they release their moisture. Stir in the barley, water, vermouth, salt and pepper.

3. Lock the lid in place and bring the cooker up to full pressure over high heat. Reduce heat to medium-low, just to maintain even pressure, and cook for 20 minutes. Remove from heat and allow pressure to drop naturally.

4. Discard bay leaf and adjust seasoning with salt and pepper to taste. Serve immediately, sprinkled with parsley.

Mushroom and Wild Rice Soup

Serves 6

This is a good way to combine indigenous ingredients such as wild rice and mixed forest mushrooms in an elegant soup for a fall dinner. The evaporated milk makes it creamy but light.

• TIP

Use a nice mix of mushrooms, including white and brown mushrooms and wild mushrooms such as chanterelles and morels.

¾ cup	wild rice	175 mL
1½ cups	water	375 mL
¼ cup	unsalted butter	50 mL
3	stalks celery, finely chopped	3
1	onion, finely chopped	1
1 lb	mushrooms (see tip, at left), chopped	500 g
3 tbsp	all-purpose flour	45 mL
4 cups	chicken stock	1 L
1	can (12 oz or 370 mL) evaporated milk	1
	Salt and freshly ground black pepper	
1 tbsp	chopped fresh dill	15 mL

1. In the pressure cooker, combine wild rice and water. Lock the lid in place and bring the cooker up to full pressure over high heat. Reduce heat to medium-low, just to maintain even pressure, and cook for 20 minutes. Remove from heat and allow pressure to drop naturally. Transfer rice to a bowl and set aside.

2. Wipe cooker clean. Add butter and melt over medium heat. Add celery and onion; sauté for 5 minutes, until softened. Add mushrooms and sauté until they begin to release their liquid. Stir in flour. Gradually stir in chicken stock. Return wild rice to the cooker.

3. Lock the lid in place and bring the cooker up to full pressure over high heat. Reduce heat to medium-low, just to maintain even pressure, and cook for 3 minutes. Remove from heat and allow pressure to drop naturally.

4. Stir in evaporated milk and season to taste with salt and pepper. Stir in dill.

Creamy Beer Chowder

Serve this comforting soup to start a fall meal of hearty bratwurst sausages and braised red cabbage.

2	carrots, chopped	2
1	leek, white part only, chopped	1
1	stalk celery, chopped	1
1 cup	chopped onion	250 mL
2 tbsp	unsalted butter	25 mL
3	yellow-fleshed potatoes, peeled and cubed	3
1	bottle (12 oz/341 mL) dark beer	1
3 cups	chicken stock	750 mL
2 tsp	sweet paprika	10 mL
½ cup	whipping (35%) cream	125 mL
	Salt and freshly ground black pepper	
	Chopped fresh parsley	

1. In a food processor, combine carrots, leek, celery and onion; pulse until finely chopped.

2. In the pressure cooker, melt butter over medium heat. Add chopped vegetables and sauté for 5 minutes, until softened and fragrant. Stir in potatoes, beer, chicken stock and paprika.

3. Lock the lid in place and bring the cooker up to full pressure over medium-high heat. Reduce heat to medium-low, just to maintain even pressure, and cook for 10 minutes. Remove from heat and allow pressure to drop naturally.

4. Stir in cream, return to medium heat and simmer for 5 minutes, until slightly thickened. Using a potato masher, crush some of the potatoes to thicken the soup. Season to taste with salt and pepper.

5. Ladle into shallow soup bowls and garnish with a little parsley.

Chilean Potato Soup

This recipe is based on a soup I enjoyed at a Nuevo Latino restaurant in Vancouver's trendy Gastown district. Thanks to chef/owner Stuart Irving of Cobre for the inspiration.

1 tbsp	extra-virgin olive oil	15 mL
3	cloves garlic, minced	3
1	large onion, chopped	1
1	yellow bell pepper, chopped	1
1	red bell pepper, chopped	1
1 tsp	ancho chile pepper powder	5 mL
1 tsp	saffron threads, crushed	5 mL
4 cups	chicken stock	1 L
2 cups	water	500 mL
¼ cup	cornmeal	50 mL
1 lb	baby potatoes (unpeeled), chopped	500 g
2 tbsp	chopped fresh cilantro	25 mL
	Salt and freshly ground black pepper	
	Freshly squeezed lemon juice	

1. In the pressure cooker, heat oil over medium-high heat. Sauté garlic and onion for 5 minutes, until starting to brown. Add yellow and red peppers, chile powder and saffron; sauté for 2 minutes. Stir in chicken stock, water, cornmeal and potatoes.

2. Lock the lid in place and bring the cooker up to full pressure over high heat. Reduce heat to medium-low, just to maintain even pressure, and cook for 10 minutes. Remove from heat and release pressure quickly.

3. Using a potato masher, roughly mash potatoes into the soup (or use an immersion blender to partially purée the soup). Stir in cilantro and season to taste with salt and pepper. Sprinkle with lemon juice.

Spicy Sweet Potato Soup

Serves 4

This soup is creamy, rich and smooth — but has hardly any added fat. The gorgeous orange color makes it the perfect prelude to a fall supper.

● TIP

Garam masala is a spice mixture that's available at Indian groceries and in the spice sections of larger supermarkets. If it's not available, substitute your favorite curry powder.

1 tbsp	extra-virgin olive oil	15 mL
2	cloves garlic, minced	2
1	onion, chopped	1
3 cups	chicken stock	750 mL
2 cups	chopped peeled sweet potatoes	500 mL
1	small potato, peeled and chopped	1
2	carrots, chopped	2
1	ancho chile pepper, stem and seeds removed	1
1½ tsp	garam masala	7 mL
	Salt	

1. In the pressure cooker, heat oil over medium heat. Add garlic and onion; sauté for 5 minutes or until soft. Stir in stock, sweet potatoes, potato, carrots, and ancho chile.

2. Lock the lid in place and bring the cooker up to full pressure over high heat. Reduce heat to medium-low, just to maintain even pressure, and cook for 12 minutes. Remove from heat and release pressure quickly.

3. Purée soup with an immersion blender or in a food processor until creamy and smooth. Stir in garam masala and season to taste with salt.

Thai Green Curry and Sweet Potato Soup

For an even spicier version of this flavorful Asian soup, use a Thai red curry paste instead of the green variety. Both are available in jars or packets at Asian markets or the Asian food section of many large supermarkets.

● **TIP**

To make this soup into a substantial vegetarian meal, ladle it over cooked egg or rice noodles.

2 tbsp	vegetable oil	25 mL
3	red, yellow or orange bell peppers, cut into slivers	3
2	cloves garlic, minced	2
1	large onion, slivered	1
1 tbsp	Thai green curry paste	15 mL
2	sweet potatoes, peeled and cubed	2
1	can (14 oz/398 mL) unsweetened coconut milk	1
¼ cup	water	50 mL
1 tsp	freshly squeezed lemon or lime juice	5 mL
1 cup	snow peas or green beans, cut into 1-inch lengths	250 mL
1 tbsp	chopped cilantro	15 mL

1. In the pressure cooker, heat oil over medium heat. Add bell peppers, garlic and onion; sauté for 5 minutes. Stir in curry paste and cook for 1 minute. Add sweet potatoes, coconut milk, water and lemon juice.

2. Lock the lid in place and bring the cooker up to full pressure over medium-high heat. Reduce heat to medium-low, just to maintain even pressure, and cook for 3 minutes. Remove from heat and release pressure quickly.

3. Stir in snow peas, cover and cook (not under pressure) for 2 to 3 minutes or just until vegetables are tender-crisp. Stir in cilantro before serving.

Beet and Vegetable Borscht

Serves 8

This is an old-fashioned soup, brought to North America by immigrants from the Ukraine, Romania and other parts of Eastern Europe. For a vegetarian version, replace beef stock with water.

1 tbsp	unsalted butter	15 mL
2	cloves garlic, minced	2
1	large onion, minced	1
3 cups	cubed peeled potatoes (preferably a waxy red variety)	750 mL
1 cup	chopped carrots	250 mL
3 or 4	beets, unpeeled, with 1 inch (2.5 cm) of tops intact	3 or 4
4 cups	shredded red cabbage	1 L
8 cups	beef stock or water	2 L
1	can (14 oz/398 mL) tomatoes, crushed, with juices	1
1 tbsp	balsamic or red wine vinegar	15 mL
	Salt	
	Freshly ground black pepper	
	Paprika	
2 tbsp	chopped fresh dill	25 mL
½ cup	sour cream	125 mL
2 tbsp	all-purpose flour	25 mL

1. In the pressure cooker, melt butter over medium heat. Add garlic and onion; sauté for about 5 minutes or until onion starts to brown. Stir in potatoes and carrots; sauté for 3 minutes. Add beets, cabbage, stock and tomatoes.

2. Lock the lid in place and bring the cooker up to full pressure over high heat. Reduce heat to medium-low, just to maintain even pressure, and cook for 10 minutes. Remove from heat and allow pressure to drop naturally.

3. Transfer beets to a bowl and let cool slightly. Slip off skins, discard tops, and cut into cubes. Return beets to the soup and stir in the balsamic vinegar. Simmer for 10 minutes. Season to taste with salt, pepper and paprika. Stir in dill.

4. In a small bowl, whisk together sour cream and flour; stir into hot soup. Cook, stirring, for about 5 minutes or until hot (but not boiling) and slightly thickened. Serve immediately.

Root Vegetable Soup

Flavorful root vegetables are available at all times of the year for this creamy, elegant soup, which is deceptively low in fat. If you're using dried dill, add it before pressure cooking.

● TIP

For a spicy garnish to this (or any other) creamy soup, place 3 dried ancho chiles in a bowl and add boiling water to cover; soak for 30 minutes. Drain, remove stems and seeds, and purée chiles with ¼ cup (50 mL) chicken stock until smooth. Combine with enough low-fat sour cream to make a smooth sauce. Pour the sauce into a squeeze bottle and use to garnish soups with decorative swirls or simply drizzle it from a spoon. Use the ancho cream to finish this soup, bean soup, pumpkin soup or other creamy concoctions for a blast of chili flavor.

2 tsp	vegetable oil or unsalted butter	10 mL
1	clove garlic, minced	1
1 cup	chopped onions	250 mL
3 cups	chicken stock	750 mL
1	potato, peeled and chopped	1
¾ cup	chopped carrots	175 mL
¾ cup	peeled chopped sweet potato	175 mL
½ cup	chopped parsnip	125 mL
2 tbsp	chopped fresh dill (or 2 tsp/10 mL dried)	25 mL
	Salt and freshly ground white pepper	

1. In the pressure cooker, heat oil over medium heat. Add garlic and onion; sauté for about 5 minutes or until tender. Add stock, potato, carrot, sweet potato and parsnip.

2. Lock the lid in place and bring the cooker up to full pressure over high heat. Reduce heat to medium-low, just to maintain even pressure, and cook for 7 minutes. Remove from heat and release pressure quickly.

3. In a food processor or with an immersion blender, purée vegetables with some of the cooking liquid until smooth. Return purée to the pot and stir to mix with the remaining liquid. Bring to a boil. Stir in dill and season to taste with salt and white pepper just before serving.

Pumpkin Soup

Start your next Thanksgiving meal with this classic seasonal soup. Use evaporated milk instead of cream to help keep the fat content low, but without compromising the creamy texture or taste.

● TIPS

If you don't have fresh pumpkin, use 2 cups (500 mL) canned pumpkin purée (not pumpkin pie filling) and add it when you purée the soup in the food processor.

For an elegant garnish, artfully drizzle a little ancho cream (see tip, page 50) over each serving using a plastic squeeze bottle.

¼ cup	unsalted butter	50 mL
2	large onions, chopped	2
1	stalk celery, chopped	1
2	leeks, white parts only, chopped	2
3	large carrots, chopped	3
3	large potatoes, chopped	3
6 cups	chicken stock	1.5 L
2 cups	cubed peeled fresh pumpkin or canned pumpkin purée (see tip, at left)	500 mL
1½ cups	whipping (35%) cream or evaporated milk	375 mL
	Salt and freshly ground black pepper	
2 tbsp	unsalted butter	25 mL
¼ cup	chopped green onion	50 mL
¼ cup	chopped parsley	50 mL

1. In the pressure cooker, melt ¼ cup (50 mL) butter over medium heat. Add onions and celery; sauté for 5 minutes. Add leeks, carrots and potato; cook, stirring, for another 5 minutes. Stir in stock and pumpkin.

2. Lock the lid in place and bring the cooker up to full pressure over high heat. Reduce heat to medium-low, just to maintain even pressure, and cook for 8 minutes. Remove from heat and release pressure quickly. Let cool slightly.

3. In a food processor, purée solids with some of the cooking liquid until smooth. Return purée to cooker and stir in cream. Heat through but don't boil. Season to taste with salt and pepper; whisk in the 2 tbsp (25 mL) butter until melted. Stir in green onions and parsley. Serve immediately.

Bajan Pumpkin Soup

Serves 8

This is my version of a creamy — and spicy — pumpkin soup I enjoyed in Barbados. It's a little more exotic than the usual, and a beautiful, rich color.

3 tbsp	unsalted butter	45 mL
1	onion, chopped	1
2	cloves garlic, chopped	2
1	red bell pepper, chopped	1
1	hot chile pepper (preferably Scotch bonnet), seeded and minced	1
1 lb	calabaza or butternut squash, peeled and cubed	500 g
2 cups	chopped peeled sweet potatoes	500 mL
4 cups	chicken stock	1 L
1 tbsp	Caribbean curry powder	15 mL
¼ tsp	ground nutmeg	1 mL
2 to 3	sprigs fresh thyme	2 to 3
1 cup	coconut milk	250 mL
	Salt and freshly ground black pepper	
2	green onions, finely chopped	2
½ tsp	fresh thyme leaves	2 mL

1. In the pressure cooker, melt butter over medium heat. Add onion and sauté for 5 minutes, until softened. Add garlic, red pepper, chile pepper and squash; sauté for 5 minutes. Add sweet potatoes, chicken stock, curry powder, nutmeg and thyme sprigs to taste.

2. Lock the lid in place and bring the cooker up to full pressure over high heat. Reduce heat to medium-low, just to maintain even pressure, and cook for 15 minutes. Remove from heat and release pressure quickly. Let cool slightly. Discard thyme sprigs.

3. Working in batches, transfer soup to a blender or food processor and purée until smooth (or use an immersion blender in the cooker.) Return soup to cooker and bring to a simmer. Add coconut milk and heat through. Season to taste with salt and pepper.

4. Ladle into bowls and sprinkle each serving with green onions and thyme leaves.

Spanish Vegetable Soup

Serves 4 to 6

This hearty, comforting combination of winter vegetables was inspired by a classic soup served in Spain's Catalonia region. For a full meal in a bowl, serve it over slices of toasted country bread rubbed with olive oil and garlic.

4 tbsp	extra-virgin olive oil, divided	60 mL
6	cloves garlic, chopped	6
2	Spanish onions, chopped	2
1	large leek, white part only, chopped	1
1	red bell pepper, chopped	1
1	large tomato, chopped	1
3 cups	chopped cabbage	750 mL
3 cups	water or vegetable stock	750 mL
1 tsp	paprika	5 mL
1	sprig fresh thyme (or 1 tsp/5 mL dried thyme)	1
1	bay leaf	1
	Salt and freshly ground black pepper	
4 to 6	½-inch (1 cm) thick slices from a slim baguette	4 to 6
	Extra-virgin olive oil	
2	cloves garlic, halved	2

1. In the pressure cooker, heat 3 tbsp (45 mL) of the oil over medium-low heat. Add chopped garlic, onions and leeks; sauté for 10 minutes, until softened. Stir in red pepper and tomato; sauté for 5 minutes. Stir in cabbage, water, paprika, thyme and bay leaf.

2. Lock the lid in place and bring the cooker up to full pressure over high heat. Reduce heat to medium-low, just to maintain even pressure, and cook for 15 minutes. Remove from heat and release pressure quickly. Discard thyme and bay leaf. Season to taste with salt and pepper and stir in the remaining olive oil.

3. Meanwhile, preheat broiler. Brush bread with olive oil and broil until golden.

4. Rub toast with the cut side of the halved garlic and set each piece in a shallow soup plate. Ladle soup over toast.

Moroccan Harira Soup with Chickpeas

Serves 4

The chile pepper gives this tomato-based soup a little zing. Choose a Scotch bonnet pepper for a spicier version.

½ cup	dried chickpeas	125 mL
2 tbsp	extra-virgin olive oil	25 mL
1	large onion, chopped	1
1	chopped jalapeño or Scotch bonnet pepper (the latter is hotter)	1
½ cup	chopped celery	125 mL
1 tsp	ground ginger	5 mL
1 tsp	ground turmeric	5 mL
½ tsp	ground cinnamon	2 mL
½ tsp	crumbled saffron (optional)	2 mL
½ tsp	freshly ground black pepper	2 mL
4 cups	water	1 L
3 cups	chopped tomatoes or 1 can (28 oz/796 mL) crushed tomatoes	750 mL
1	can (10 oz/284 mL) beef broth, undiluted	1
¾ cup	green or brown lentils	175 mL
3 tbsp	freshly squeezed lemon juice	45 mL
	Lemon slices	

1. Soak chickpeas overnight in water to cover or use the quick pressure-soak method (page 208). Drain.

2. In the pressure cooker, heat oil over medium heat. Add onion, jalapeño and celery; sauté for about 5 minutes or until soft. Stir in ginger, turmeric, cinnamon, saffron and pepper; cook for 1 minute until fragrant. Stir in chickpeas, water, tomatoes, broth, lentils and lemon juice, making sure cooker is no more than half full.

3. Lock the lid in place and bring the cooker up to full pressure over high heat. Reduce heat to medium-low, just to maintain even pressure, and cook for 20 minutes. Remove from heat and allow pressure to drop naturally. Serve garnished with lemon slices.

Classic Navy Bean Soup

This is a classic combination: chunky white beans and ham. For a change of pace, stir about 1 cup (250 mL) chopped spinach or sorrel leaves into the soup just before serving.

2 cups	dried white navy beans	500 mL
1	meaty ham bone or smoked pork hock (about 1 lb/500 g)	1
4	whole black peppercorns	4
1	bay leaf	1
6 cups	water	1.5 L
1 tbsp	extra-virgin olive oil	15 mL
2	large carrots, chopped	2
1	large onion, chopped	1
1	stalk celery, chopped	1
1	clove garlic, minced	1
1	small potato, peeled and cubed	1
	Salt and freshly ground white pepper	

1. Soak beans in water to cover overnight or use the quick pressure-soak method (page 208). Drain.

2. In the pressure cooker, combine beans, ham bone, peppercorns, bay leaf, water and oil. Lock the lid in place and bring the cooker up to full pressure over high heat. Reduce heat to medium-low, just to maintain even pressure, and cook for 10 minutes. Remove from heat and allow pressure to drop naturally. Discard bay leaf and peppercorns.

3. Remove ham bone from the soup and let cool slightly. Remove any meat from the bone and chop into bite-size pieces. Discard the bone. Return the meat to the soup and add carrots, onion, celery, garlic and potato.

4. Lock the lid in place and bring the cooker up to full pressure over medium-high heat. Reduce heat to medium-low, just to maintain even pressure, and cook for 10 minutes. Remove from heat and allow pressure to drop naturally.

5. Remove 1 to 2 cups (250 to 500 mL) of the soup to a blender or food processor and purée until smooth (or use an immersion blender in the cooker to partially purée the soup). Return purée to the pot to thicken the soup. Season to taste with salt and white pepper.

Mexican Pinto Bean Soup

Hearty and filling, this soup is the perfect antidote to a case of the mid-winter blues.

1 cup	dried pinto beans	250 mL
2	cloves garlic	2
1	large onion, halved	1
1 tbsp	vegetable oil	15 mL
2 tbsp	extra-virgin olive oil or vegetable oil	25 mL
	Salt and freshly ground black pepper	
⅓ cup	whipping (35%) cream	75 mL
	Grated Monterey Jack cheese, cilantro sprigs and diced avocado	

1. Soak beans overnight in water to cover or use quick pressure-soak method (page 208). Drain.

2. In the pressure cooker, cover beans with at least 1 inch (2.5 cm) water. Add 1 clove garlic, half the onion and the 1 tbsp (15 mL) vegetable oil. Lock the lid in place and bring the cooker up to full pressure over high heat. Reduce heat to medium-low, just to maintain even pressure, and cook for 10 minutes. Remove from heat and release pressure quickly. The beans should be very soft. If not, lock the lid in place and return to full pressure; cook for 2 to 3 minutes longer. Remove from heat and release pressure quickly. Drain beans, reserving cooking liquid.

3. In a food processor, purée bean mixture, adding some of the reserved liquid as necessary to make smooth.

4. Meanwhile, mince remaining onion and garlic. In a large pot, heat the 2 tbsp (25 mL) oil over medium heat. Add onion and garlic; sauté for about 5 minutes or until golden. Add puréed bean mixture to the pot along with enough of the reserved liquid to make a smooth soup.

5. Bring to a boil and simmer for 10 minutes. Season to taste with salt and pepper. Add cream and simmer until thickened and smooth. Serve individual bowls of soup topped with a handful of cheese, a few cubes of avocado and a sprig of cilantro.

Tuscan Greens and Beans Soup

This traditional Italian recipe makes a hearty, rustic soup for chilly afternoons, with all of the ingredients for a full meal.

2 cups	dried white beans	500 mL
¼ cup	extra-virgin olive oil	50 mL
3	large leeks, white and pale green parts only, thinly sliced	3
4	plum (Roma) tomatoes, seeded and chopped	4
3	cloves garlic, minced	3
8 cups	chicken stock or water	2 L
1	bay leaf	1
3 cups	chopped spinach, arugula or beet greens	750 mL
1 tbsp	balsamic vinegar	15 mL
1 tsp	Asian chili paste	5 mL
2 to 3 tsp	minced fresh rosemary	10 to 15 mL
	Salt and freshly ground black pepper	

1. Soak beans in water to cover overnight or use the quick pressure-soak method (page 208). Drain.

2. In the pressure cooker, heat oil over medium heat. Add leeks and sauté for 10 minutes, until softened. Add tomatoes and garlic; sauté for 2 minutes. Add beans, chicken stock and bay leaf.

3. Lock the lid in place and bring the cooker up to full pressure over high heat. Reduce heat to medium-low, just to maintain even pressure, and cook for 12 minutes. Remove from heat and allow pressure to drop naturally. Test the beans; if they're not completely tender, return the cooker to full pressure and cook for 2 minutes. Remove from heat and allow pressure to drop naturally. Discard bay leaf.

4. Add spinach and stir until wilted. Stir in balsamic vinegar and chili paste. Season to taste with rosemary, salt and pepper.

Spicy Mixed Bean and Barley Soup

Serves 6

This chunky vegetarian soup is perfect when you have a lot of different peas, beans and lentils to use up. Use the legumes called for in the recipe, or substitute whatever beans you have on hand.

● **TIP**

For a hearty lunch, serve this soup with a biscuit or slice of homemade bread.

1 cup	mixed dried beans (red, white, black, pinto, black-eyed peas)	250 mL
½ cup	pearl or pot barley	125 mL
¼ cup	green or yellow split peas	50 mL
¼ cup	red lentils	50 mL
2 tsp	ground cumin	10 mL
2 tsp	dried oregano	10 mL
1	bay leaf	1
1	small dried chile pepper, crumbled, or ½ tsp (2 mL) hot pepper flakes	1
1 tsp	chili powder	5 mL
5 cups	cold water	1.25 L
2	cloves garlic, minced	2
1	stalk celery, chopped	1
1	onion, minced	1
1	can (14 oz/398 mL) tomatoes, chopped, with juices	1
	Salt and freshly ground black pepper	
2 tbsp	chopped parsley	25 mL

1. Soak beans overnight in water to cover or use the quick pressure-soak method (page 208). Drain.

2. In the pressure cooker, combine beans, barley, split peas, lentils, cumin, oregano, bay leaf, chile pepper, chili powder, water, garlic, celery, onion and tomatoes. Lock the lid in place and bring the cooker up to full pressure over high heat. Reduce heat to medium-low, just to maintain even pressure, and cook for 20 minutes. Remove from heat and allow pressure to drop naturally. The beans and barley should be very tender. If not, lock the lid in place and bring to full pressure; cook for 5 minutes longer. Allow pressure to drop naturally.

3. Discard bay leaf. Season to taste with salt and pepper; stir in parsley.

Barley and Lentil Chowder with Kale

Serves 6 to 8

This simple, stick-to-your-ribs winter soup is a perfect choice when it seems like the cupboard is almost bare. It's peasant cuisine at its best: inexpensive, but delicious and loaded with healthy ingredients.

2 tbsp	extra-virgin olive oil	25 mL
1½ cups	chopped onions	375 mL
1 cup	chopped carrots	250 mL
1 cup	chopped rutabaga	250 mL
4	cloves garlic, minced	4
10 cups	chicken stock or water	2.5 L
3 cups	chopped kale (or other winter greens, such as Chinese (napa) cabbage)	750 mL
½ cup	pearl barley	125 mL
½ cup	green lentils	125 mL
1 tsp	dried thyme	5 mL
½ tsp	dried sage	2 mL
1	large bay leaf	1
2 tsp	Worcestershire sauce	10 mL
1 tbsp	chopped fresh flat-leaf (Italian) parsley	15 mL
	Salt and freshly ground black pepper	

1. In the pressure cooker, heat oil over medium heat. Add onion and sauté for 5 minutes, until softened. Add carrots and rutabaga; sauté for 10 minutes, until vegetables start to brown and caramelize. Add garlic and sauté for 1 minute. Add chicken stock, kale, barley, lentils, thyme, sage, bay leaf and Worcestershire sauce.

2. Lock the lid in place and bring the cooker up to full pressure over high heat. Reduce heat to medium-low, just to maintain even pressure, and cook for 20 minutes. Remove from heat and allow pressure to drop naturally. Stir in parsley and season to taste with salt and pepper.

Lentil Soup with Bulgur

This healthy Middle Eastern soup is said to be the perfect cure for a hangover. It's also a great way to take the chill off a winter afternoon.

3 tbsp	extra-virgin olive oil	45 mL
1	large onion, minced	1
2	cloves garlic, minced	2
1 tbsp	hot paprika	15 mL
6 cups	chicken stock (approx.)	1.5 L
1 cup	red lentils	250 mL
¼ cup	long-grain white rice	50 mL
2 tbsp	tomato paste	25 mL
¼ cup	bulgur	50 mL
1 tbsp	dried mint	15 mL
	Salt and freshly ground black pepper	
	Lemon wedges	

Topping

2 tbsp	extra-virgin olive oil	25 mL
1 tsp	dried mint	5 mL
½ tsp	hot paprika	2 mL

1. In the pressure cooker, heat oil over medium heat. Add onion and sauté for 5 minutes, until softened. Add garlic and paprika; sauté for 2 minutes. Stir in chicken stock, lentils, rice and tomato paste.

2. Lock the lid in place and bring the cooker up to full pressure over medium-high heat. Reduce heat to medium-low, just to maintain even pressure, and cook for 10 minutes. Remove from heat and allow pressure to drop naturally.

3. Stir in bulgur and mint. Set the lid on top and let stand for 10 minutes to rehydrate the bulgur. Stir in a little more stock or water if the soup seems too thick. Season to taste with salt and pepper.

4. *Topping:* Meanwhile, in a bowl, combine oil, mint and paprika.

5. Ladle soup into shallow soup bowls and drizzle each serving with some of the topping. Pass lemon wedges for diners to squeeze over their soup, if desired.

Greek Lentil Soup with Dill

This is a typical Lenten dish in Greece: a simple vegetarian soup that transcends the sum of its parts. The olive oil gives the meatless soup the necessary richness, so use a bold, spicy extra-virgin oil for this dish. Sprinkle each bowl with a little crumbled feta for authenticity, or serve with slices of bread, slathered with creamy, ripe cheese, and a few black olives.

● **TIP**

Use a food processor to finely chop the onions and purée the tomatoes.

¼ cup	extra-virgin olive oil	50 mL
2	cloves garlic, minced	2
1	large onion, finely chopped	1
1	can (19 oz/540 mL) tomatoes, with juice, puréed (or 1 can plain tomato sauce)	1
1	dried hot chile pepper, crumbled (optional)	1
4 cups	chicken stock	1 L
¾ cup	brown or green lentils	175 mL
2 tbsp	chopped fresh dill, divided	25 mL
1 tbsp	balsamic vinegar	15 mL
	Salt and freshly ground black pepper	
	Crumbled feta cheese (optional)	
	Additional chopped fresh dill (optional)	

1. In pressure cooker, heat oil over medium heat. Add garlic and onions; sauté for 5 minutes, until softened. Add tomato purée, chile pepper (if using), chicken stock, lentils, half the dill and balsamic vinegar.

2. Lock the lid in place and bring the cooker up to full pressure over high heat. Reduce heat to medium-low, just to maintain even pressure, and cook for 8 minutes. Remove from heat and allow pressure to drop naturally. Season to taste with salt and pepper. Just before serving, stir in the remaining dill.

3. Ladle into shallow soup bowls and garnish with feta and more dill, if desired.

Pasta Fazool

Is it a soup you eat with a fork — or a pasta dish to eat with a spoon? Either way, pasta fazool (or, strictly speaking, fagioli) makes a delicious one-pot meal. Add a loaf of bread, a jug of wine, and an après-ski crowd.

● TIPS

For the pasta, try penne, small rotini or orecchiette.

If you like, you can replace the pancetta with an equal amount of prosciutto.

1½ cups	dried white cannellini beans	375 mL
3 tbsp	extra-virgin olive oil	45 mL
2	stalks celery, chopped	2
1	large onion, chopped	1
1	carrot, chopped	1
4 oz	pancetta, finely chopped	125 g
1 tbsp	chopped garlic	15 mL
1 tbsp	chopped fresh rosemary	15 mL
1 tsp	dried basil	5 mL
¼ tsp	hot pepper flakes	1 mL
1	can (14 oz/398 mL) plum (Roma) tomatoes, chopped	1
3 cups	chicken stock	750 mL
1½ cups	dried short pasta	375 mL
	Salt and freshly ground black pepper	
	Extra-virgin olive oil, rosemary sprigs and shards of Parmesan cheese	

1. Soak beans overnight in water to cover or use the quick pressure-soak method (page 208). Drain.

2. In the pressure cooker, heat oil over medium heat. Add celery, onion, carrot, pancetta and garlic; sauté until onion starts to brown. Stir in beans, rosemary, basil, hot pepper flakes, tomatoes and stock.

3. Lock the lid in place and bring the cooker up to full pressure over high heat. Reduce heat to medium-low, just to maintain even pressure, and cook for 15 minutes. Remove from heat and allow pressure to drop naturally. The beans should be very soft and starting to break down. If not, return to full pressure and cook for 1 to 2 minutes longer. Remove from heat and allow pressure to drop naturally.

4. Stir in pasta and simmer, uncovered, for 5 to 7 minutes or until pasta is tender. Season to taste with salt and pepper. Serve in deep soup bowls. Garnish individual servings with a drizzle of olive oil, a sprig of rosemary and a few shards of Parmesan cheese.

Ham and Split Pea Soup

Split peas and red lentils reduce to a purée when cooked. This can clog the pressure valve of a jiggle-top pressure cooker, so be careful! If you own this type of cooker and hear loud hissing noises during cooking, remove it from the heat and quickly release pressure by running cold water over the lid. Check for any food clogging the vent, wash the lid thoroughly, then return it to the pot and continue cooking. Always allow the pressure to come down naturally when cooking these legumes to avoid clogging the pressure valve. In newer models of cookers, there are several backup safety systems to automatically release pressure if there is a clog in the primary valve system, so cooking these kinds of foods is no longer a problem.

1 tbsp	unsalted butter or vegetable oil	15 mL
2	cloves garlic, minced	2
1	onion, chopped	1
1 lb	dried split peas (about 2 cups/500 mL)	500 g
2	carrots, diced	2
½ tsp	dried thyme	2 mL
8 oz	smoked ham or lean back bacon, finely diced	250 g
6 cups	chicken stock	1.5 L
4 cups	water	1 L
2 cups	dry white wine	500 mL
½ cup	brown rice	125 mL
1	package (10 oz/300 g) frozen green peas, thawed, or equal amount of fresh garden peas, in season, cooked	1
	Salt and freshly ground black pepper	

1. In the pressure cooker, melt butter over medium heat. Add garlic and onion; sauté for about 5 minutes or until tender. Stir in split peas, carrots, thyme, ham, stock, water, wine and brown rice.

2. Lock the lid in place and bring the cooker up to full pressure over high heat. Reduce heat to medium-low, just to maintain even pressure, and cook for 10 minutes. Remove from heat and allow pressure to drop naturally for 10 minutes, then release any remaining pressure.

3. Stir in green peas and season to taste with salt and pepper. Bring soup to a boil and serve immediately. Or chill overnight and reheat the next day — the soup will be even more flavorful.

Red Bean and Ukrainian Sausage Soup

Serves 8

Brought to North America by Ukrainian immigrants over a century ago, smoky garlic ham sausage is a prairie staple.

● TIP

If you can't find a good, garlicky ham sausage, substitute kielbasa in this hearty soup. For an even spicier version, choose chorizo.

1½ cups	dried red kidney beans	375 mL
2	jalapeño peppers, chopped	2
1	large onion, chopped	1
8 oz	smoked Ukrainian ham sausage, chopped (see tip, at left, for alternative)	250 g
1	bay leaf	1
1 tbsp	chili powder	15 mL
1 tsp	dried oregano	5 mL
½ tsp	freshly ground black pepper	2 mL
¼ tsp	cayenne pepper	1 mL
3 cups	beef stock	750 mL
1	can (14 oz/398 mL) plum tomatoes, crushed	1
½ cup	tomato sauce	125 mL
2 tbsp	packed brown sugar	25 mL

1. Soak beans in water to cover overnight or use the quick pressure-soak method (page 208). Drain.

2. In the pressure cooker, add water to cover beans by at least 1 inch (2.5 cm). Lock the lid in place and bring the cooker up to full pressure over high heat. Reduce heat to medium-low, just to maintain even pressure, and cook for 12 minutes. Remove from heat and allow pressure to drop naturally. Drain beans and set aside.

3. Wipe pressure cooker clean and place over medium-high heat. Add jalapeño peppers, onion, sausage, bay leaf, chili powder, oregano, black pepper and cayenne; cook, stirring, for 8 minutes or until the onions are soft. Stir in stock, tomatoes, tomato sauce, brown sugar and drained beans.

4. Lock the lid in place and bring the cooker up to full pressure over high heat. Reduce heat to medium-low, just to maintain even pressure, and cook for 20 minutes. Remove from heat and allow pressure to drop naturally. Discard bay leaf before serving.

Caribbean Pepper Pot Soup (Callaloo)

Callaloo is a hearty soup found on islands throughout the Caribbean. This version is thickened with fresh okra and seasoned with salt beef. It's a homey, if slightly exotic, way to get your greens.

● TIP

If you can't find traditional salt beef, substitute fresh corned beef (not canned) and omit the soaking step.

8 oz	salt beef	250 g
2 tbsp	canola oil	25 mL
1 cup	chopped onion	250 mL
1 lb	spinach, chopped	500 g
8 oz	kale, callaloo or other winter greens, stems trimmed, chopped	250 g
4	cloves garlic, minced	4
1 lb	okra, stems removed and pods sliced	500 g
1 lb	sweet potatoes, peeled and cubed	500 g
1	Scotch bonnet pepper, seeded and minced (or Asian chili paste)	1
1	can (14 oz/398 mL) coconut milk	1
5 cups	chicken stock or water	1.25 L
2 tbsp	freshly squeezed lime juice	25 mL
1 tsp	dried thyme	5 mL
2	cans (each 6 oz/170 g) crabmeat, drained and shells picked out	2
4	green onions, chopped	4
	Freshly ground black pepper	

1. Soak salt beef in cold water for 24 hours, draining and refilling water at least once, to remove excess salt. Chop beef into small cubes and set aside.

2. In the pressure cooker, heat oil over medium heat. Add onion and sauté for 5 to 10 minutes, until softened. Add spinach, kale and garlic; sauté for 10 minutes, until greens are wilted and cooked down. Stir in okra and sauté for 10 minutes, until no longer sticky. Add beef, sweet potatoes, Scotch bonnet pepper, coconut milk, chicken stock, lime juice and thyme.

3. Lock the lid in place and bring the cooker up to full pressure over high heat. Reduce heat to medium-low, just to maintain even pressure, and cook for 20 minutes. Remove from heat and release pressure quickly.

4. Stir in crabmeat and green onions, return to medium heat and simmer for 5 minutes. Season to taste with pepper.

Cajun Black Bean and Sausage Gumbo

This hearty soup has an almost stew-like consistency. Serve it as a main course with cornbread and beer or, as here, ladle it over hot cooked rice in deep soup plates.

2 cups	dried black turtle beans	500 mL
7 cups	water	1.75 L
½ cup	vegetable oil	125 mL
½ cup	all-purpose flour	125 mL
2 lbs	spicy Italian sausage, casings removed, meat crumbled	1 kg
6	cloves garlic, minced	6
4	onions, chopped	4
4	stalks celery, chopped	4
1	red bell pepper, chopped	1
2 tsp	dried thyme	10 mL
4 cups	chicken stock	1 L
3 tbsp	Worcestershire sauce	45 mL
½ cup	minced fresh parsley	125 mL
½ cup	chopped green onions	125 mL
	Salt and freshly ground black pepper	
3 cups	cooked white rice	750 mL
½ cup	seeded chopped tomato	125 mL

1. Soak beans overnight in water to cover or use the quick pressure-soak method (page 208). Drain.

2. In the pressure cooker, combine beans and water. Lock the lid in place and bring the cooker up to full pressure over high heat. Reduce heat to medium-low, just to maintain even pressure, and cook for 10 minutes. Remove from heat and allow pressure to drop naturally. Drain beans and set aside.

3. Wipe cooker clean and heat oil over medium-low heat; sprinkle in flour and cook, stirring constantly, until the roux turns the color of peanut butter, about 12 minutes. (Be careful — this gets very hot and burns easily.) Reduce heat to low. Stir in sausage, garlic, onions, celery, red pepper and thyme; cook, stirring, for about 10 minutes or until vegetables are very tender. Stir in beans, stock and Worcestershire sauce.

4. Lock the lid in place and bring the cooker up to full pressure over high heat. Reduce heat to medium-low, just to maintain even pressure, and cook for 8 minutes. Remove from heat and allow pressure to drop naturally. Stir in green onions and parsley; season to taste with salt and pepper.

5. Using a large spoon or ice cream scoop, place a big mound of rice in the center of each soup plate. Ladle soup around the rice. Garnish with chopped tomato.

● **TIP**

Bean soups like this gumbo are a great place to experiment with new heirloom bean varieties. The flavor and color of different beans are showcased in soups and can change the character of the dish significantly. Look for varieties such as Black Nightfall or Rio Zape pinto beans. You can even combine different beans in soups and stews — just make sure they're all about the same size and age.

Scotch Broth

This is a classic Scottish dish, one of those old-fashioned, hearty soups that are perfect for serving on a winter day.

● TIP

Next time you bone a leg of lamb, save the bones and brown them. Use in this recipe along with the meat to give the soup a rich color and flavor. Remove bones from soup before serving.

2 tsp	vegetable oil	10 mL
3	stalks celery, diced	3
1	onion, diced	1
1 lb	boneless lamb shoulder or shank, trimmed of fat and finely chopped	500 g
8 cups	chicken stock or cold water	2 L
2 cups	carrots, cut into small dice	500 mL
2 cups	turnips, cut into small dice	500 mL
1 tsp	freshly ground black pepper	5 mL
½ tsp	dried thyme	2 mL
2 tsp	minced garlic	10 mL
1	bay leaf	1
1 cup	pearl barley	250 mL
	Salt	

1. In the pressure cooker, heat oil over medium heat. Add celery and onions; sauté for about 8 minutes or until soft. Add lamb, in batches, and brown on all sides. Return lamb and accumulated juices to cooker. Stir in stock, carrots, turnips, pepper, thyme, garlic and bay leaf. Stir in barley.

2. Lock the lid in place and bring the cooker up to full pressure over high heat. Reduce heat to medium-low, just to maintain even pressure, and cook for 22 minutes. Remove from heat and allow pressure to drop naturally.

3. Season to taste with salt. Discard bay leaf before serving.

Homestyle Chicken Noodle Soup

Serves 4 to 6

This hearty version of old-fashioned chicken noodle soup has lots of healthy veggies and chunks of tender chicken. It's a meal in a bowl!

1 tbsp	extra-virgin olive oil	15 mL
1 tbsp	unsalted butter	15 mL
1	onion, chopped	1
2	stalks celery, chopped	2
2	carrots, chopped	2
1 lb	boneless skinless chicken breasts or thighs, cut into small cubes	500 g
4 cups	chicken stock	1 L
2 cups	water	500 mL
½ tsp	dried thyme	2 mL
1	bay leaf	1
	Salt and freshly ground black pepper	
1 cup	fresh or frozen peas	250 mL
1 cup	small egg noodles	250 mL
1 tbsp	chopped fresh parsley	15 mL

1. In the pressure cooker, heat oil and butter over medium-high heat. Add onion and sauté for 5 minutes, until starting to brown. Add celery and carrots; sauté for 2 minutes. Add chicken, chicken stock, water, thyme and bay leaf. Season to taste with salt and pepper.

2. Lock the lid in place and bring the cooker up to full pressure over high heat. Reduce heat to medium-low, just to maintain even pressure, and cook for 8 minutes. Remove from heat and release pressure quickly.

3. Return to medium heat and bring to a boil. Add peas and noodles; simmer, stirring occasionally, for 5 to 7 minutes, or until noodles are tender. Sprinkle with parsley.

Nuevo Latino Chicken and Rice Soup

This chunky soup is so thick it's almost a stew — similar to the homey soups served throughout Central and South America.

● **TIP**

If you can find sour (Seville) oranges, substitute 2 tbsp (25 mL) sour orange juice for the lemon juice. Sour oranges are usually available only in January or February.

3	cloves garlic	3
1	onion, roughly chopped	1
1	red or yellow bell pepper, roughly chopped	1
3	plum (Roma) tomatoes, chopped	3
2 tbsp	freshly squeezed lemon juice	25 mL
1 tsp	dried oregano	5 mL
2 tbsp	extra-virgin olive oil	25 mL
1½ lbs	boneless skinless chicken thighs, cut into ¾-inch (2 cm) chunks	750 g
4 oz	chorizo sausage (about 1 sausage), chopped	125 g
1 cup	long-grain brown rice	250 mL
1 tsp	sweet or hot paprika	5 mL
½ tsp	ground turmeric	2 mL
4 cups	chicken stock	1 L
2 cups	water	500 mL
1	can (12 oz/341 mL) sweet corn, drained	1
¼ cup	chopped pitted black olives (dry-cured or niçoise)	50 mL
2 tbsp	chopped fresh cilantro	25 mL
	Salt and freshly ground black pepper	

1. In a food processor, combine garlic, onion and red pepper; pulse until evenly chopped. Add tomatoes, lemon juice, and oregano; pulse until chunky.

2. In the pressure cooker, heat oil over medium-high heat. Add vegetable mixture and cook, stirring occasionally, for about 10 minutes, until fragrant and starting to brown. Add chicken and sauté for 5 minutes, until chicken is browned on all sides. Stir in chorizo, rice, paprika and turmeric; sauté for 2 minutes. Stir in chicken stock and water.

3. Lock the lid in place and bring the cooker up to full pressure over high heat. Reduce heat to medium-low, just to maintain even pressure, and cook for 18 minutes. Remove from heat and allow pressure to drop naturally.

4. Stir in corn and return to medium heat until corn is heated through. Add olives and cilantro, season to taste with salt and pepper, and serve immediately, in deep soup bowls.

● **TIP**

No cilantro? Substitute 1 tbsp (15 mL) Indian coriander chutney, a condiment that's similar to basil pesto, but made with puréed cilantro.

African Sweet Potato and Peanut Soup

Serves 6 to 8

Bright orange sweet potatoes give this spicy, exotic soup a vibrant color and rich, creamy texture, while crunchy peanut butter adds a subtle but unique flavor. Serve this healthy soup with bread for a full meal.

2 tbsp	extra-virgin olive oil	25 mL
4	cloves garlic, minced	4
1	large onion, chopped	1
1	red or green bell pepper, chopped	1
1 lb	boneless skinless chicken breasts, chopped	500 g
1 tbsp	grated gingerroot	15 mL
2 tsp	sweet paprika	10 mL
1	sweet potato, peeled and cubed	1
1	baking potato, peeled and cubed	1
1 cup	corn kernels	250 mL
4 cups	chicken stock	1 L
1 cup	tomato juice	250 mL
1 tsp	salt	5 mL
1 tsp	Asian chili paste (or ½ tsp/2 mL cayenne pepper)	5 mL
⅓ cup	crunchy peanut butter	75 mL
2	green onions, finely chopped	2

1. In the pressure cooker, heat oil over medium heat. Add garlic, onion and red pepper; sauté for about 10 minutes, until softened. Add chicken, ginger and paprika; sauté for 5 minutes, until chicken is browned on all sides. Stir in sweet potato, potato, corn, chicken stock, tomato juice, salt and chili paste.

2. Lock the lid in place and bring the cooker up to full pressure over medium-high heat. Reduce heat to medium-low, just to maintain even pressure, and cook for 10 minutes. Remove from heat and allow pressure to drop naturally.

3. Stir in peanut butter. Serve immediately, garnished with green onions.

Meat

Perfect Pot Roast

Use beef rump or round roast in this flavorful pot roast recipe, a classic comfort food. You can also substitute bison, a popular new red meat that is ultra-lean and raised without growth hormones and antibiotics. The braising makes it tender, and the puréed vegetables add richness to the gravy without extra fat. And it's done in less than an hour!

● **TIP**

Try serving this with steamed new potatoes instead of the egg noodles.

¼ cup	all-purpose flour	50 mL
½ tsp	salt	2 mL
¼ tsp	freshly ground black pepper	1 mL
1	3½-lb (1.75 kg) beef braising roast	1
3 tbsp	vegetable oil or extra-virgin olive oil	45 mL
1	large tomato, chopped	1
1 cup	diced onions	250 mL
1 cup	diced carrots	250 mL
½ cup	diced celery	125 mL
1 cup	beef stock	250 mL
1 cup	dry red wine	250 mL
2 tbsp	all-purpose flour, whisked with 2 tbsp (25 mL) cold water	25 mL
1 lb	wide egg noodles, cooked and tossed with unsalted butter	500 g
	Minced fresh thyme or oregano	

1. In a plastic bag, combine ¼ cup (50 mL) flour with salt and pepper. Add roast and shake to coat all sides with flour. Discard excess flour mixture.

2. In the pressure cooker, heat oil over medium-high heat and brown roast well on all sides. Transfer to plate. Set aside.

3. Add tomato, onions, carrots and celery to pan; sauté until lightly browned. Place roast on top of vegetables. Pour in stock and wine.

4. Lock the lid in place and bring the cooker up to full pressure over high heat. Reduce heat to medium-low, just to maintain even pressure, and cook for 45 minutes. Remove from heat and release pressure quickly.

5. Transfer roast to a platter and tent with foil to keep warm. In a blender or food processor, purée vegetables and stock. Return to pot and slowly whisk in flour mixture. Bring to a boil; reduce heat and simmer, stirring, until gravy is thickened, about 5 minutes. Season gravy with salt and pepper to taste. Season to taste with thyme or oregano. Arrange egg noodles around roast on platter and drizzle with gravy.

Italian-Style Pot Roast with Pasta

This makes a hearty meal on a winter evening. Serve the sauce with whole-grain penne pasta or small cheese-filled tortellini, and pass the Parmesan.

3 lb	boneless beef round or rump roast	1.5 kg
	Salt and freshly ground black pepper	
2 tbsp	extra-virgin olive oil	25 mL
3	cloves garlic, chopped	3
2	stalks celery, chopped	2
2	carrots, chopped	2
1	large onion, sliced	1
1	can (14 oz/398 mL) tomatoes, chopped, with juice	1
1 cup	beef stock	250 mL
½ cup	dry red wine	125 mL
1 tbsp	chopped fresh rosemary	15 mL
2 tbsp	tomato paste	25 mL
¼ cup	chopped fresh flat-leaf (Italian) parsley	50 mL
12 oz	short pasta, cooked and drained	375 g
	Freshly grated Parmesan cheese	
	Additional chopped fresh rosemary	

1. Season roast on all sides with salt and pepper. In the pressure cooker, heat oil over medium-high heat and brown roast on all sides. Remove roast and set aside.

2. Add garlic, celery, carrots and onion to the cooker and sauté for 5 minutes, until vegetables soften. Stir in tomatoes with juice, beef stock, wine, rosemary and tomato paste. Return roast and any accumulated juices to the pot.

3. Lock the lid in place and bring the cooker up to full pressure over medium-high heat. Reduce heat to medium-low, just to maintain even pressure, and cook for 1 hour. Remove from heat and release pressure quickly.

4. Remove roast from the cooker and let cool slightly before cutting into thick slices. Arrange down the center of a warm platter and tent with foil to keep warm.

5. Add pasta to the sauce, return to medium heat and simmer, uncovered, for 5 minutes. Serve pasta and sauce alongside the roast, topped with Parmesan and rosemary.

Slow-Roasted Beef Brisket

This spicy beef pot roast is delicious served with creamy horseradish mashed potatoes, egg noodles, or chopped and folded into big flour tortillas.

● **TIPS**

Chipotle chiles are jalapeños that have been roasted over a fire until they are deeply smoked. You can buy them in cans from Mexico in adobo sauce, or dried for reconstituting in warm water.

Look for chipotles in specialty or gourmet grocery stores (or in the produce sections of well-stocked supermarkets) or substitute 2 tsp (10 mL) Asian chili paste mixed with a few generous drops of liquid smoke.

2 tbsp	packed brown sugar	25 mL
½ tsp	ground cumin	2 mL
2	chipotle peppers in adobo sauce	2
3 tbsp	extra-virgin olive oil, divided	45 mL
2 tbsp	tomato paste	25 mL
1	beef brisket, about 3 lbs (1.5 kg), trimmed	1
1	large onion, sliced	1
3	cloves garlic, minced	3
1	can (14 oz/398 mL) Mexican-style stewed tomatoes	1
1 tbsp	Worcestershire sauce	15 mL
½ tsp	salt	2 mL
¼ tsp	freshly ground black pepper	1 mL

1. In a small bowl, mash brown sugar, cumin, chipotle peppers, 1 tbsp (15 mL) of the olive oil and tomato paste to form a smooth paste. In a zippered plastic bag or shallow dish, coat brisket with paste. Seal or cover and let stand at room temperature for 1 hour or refrigerate overnight.

2. Meanwhile, in the pressure cooker, heat remaining oil over medium-low heat. Add onions and cook, stirring, for about 10 minutes or until golden brown. Add garlic and cook for 2 minutes longer. Stir in the tomatoes, Worcestershire sauce, salt and pepper; simmer, uncovered, for 5 minutes. Place marinated brisket in sauce. Drizzle with any remaining marinade and spoon a little of the tomato sauce over top.

3. Lock the lid in place and bring the cooker up to full pressure over high heat. Reduce the heat to medium-low, just to maintain even pressure, and cook for 1 hour. Remove from heat and allow pressure to drop naturally for about 10 minutes, then release any remaining pressure quickly.

4. Transfer brisket to a warmed platter and tent with foil to keep warm. Bring sauce to boil; reduce heat and simmer for about 10 minutes or until reduced and thickened. Slice brisket thinly against the grain (or shred) and serve with the sauce.

Barbecue Beef on a Bun

This is a perfect meal for any summer party crowd. It can be precooked quickly in the pressure cooker early in the day, then finished on the barbecue during the party. Set out some old washtubs filled with beer and ice, and serve some coleslaw and potato salad on the side for a real cowboy experience. Yee-Ha!

1	beef brisket, about 3 lbs (1.5 kg)	1
3	cloves garlic, minced	3
1	large onion, minced	1
1	chipotle pepper in adobo, chopped, or 1 jalapeño pepper, chopped, and 1 tsp (5 mL) liquid smoke	1
½ cup	packed brown sugar	125 mL
1	bottle (12 oz/341 mL) dark beer	1
1 cup	ketchup	250 mL
2 tbsp	Dijon mustard	25 mL
1 tbsp	chili powder	15 mL
1 tbsp	dried basil	15 mL
1 tsp	ground cumin	5 mL
	Worcestershire sauce	
	Salt and freshly ground black pepper	
	Crusty onion rolls	

1. Trim fat from brisket and roll into an evenly shaped roast, tying at intervals. Season to taste with salt and freshly ground black pepper. Place brisket in the pressure cooker.

2. In a bowl, whisk together garlic, onion, chipotle, brown sugar, beer, ketchup, mustard, chili powder, basil, cumin and Worcestershire sauce; pour over top of meat.

3. Lock the lid in place and bring the cooker up to full pressure over high heat. Reduce heat to medium-low, just to maintain even pressure, and cook for 45 minutes. Remove from heat and release pressure quickly. Transfer brisket to a plate. Cover and refrigerate. Skim as much fat from the sauce as possible and simmer for 30 minutes to reduce and thicken. Set aside.

4. Just before serving, place roast on a preheated barbecue over medium-low heat and cook for 15 minutes, until slightly charred and smoky, turning frequently.

5. Slice brisket thinly, or shred; mix in some of the reserved barbecue sauce and pile on a bun. You can also make this in advance and reheat the meat in the sauce. Serve with beans, coleslaw and potato salad or baked potatoes on the side.

Jigg's Dinner

Traditionally, Jigg's dinner, an East Coast specialty, is simmered for hours on the stovetop on Sundays, but this version for the pressure cooker is fast enough for everyday dining.

● **TIPS**

For traditional Pease Pudding (often served alongside Jigg's Dinner), soak 1 cup (250 mL) yellow split peas overnight. Drain and tie in a cloth pudding bag, leaving room for the peas to expand. Cook in the pot along with the beef and remove before cooking the vegetables.

Leftover broth makes a good base for a hearty beef and barley soup. Refrigerate or freeze for later use.

4 lbs	salted (corned) beef brisket or salt beef short ribs	2 kg
	Cold water	
1 lb	potatoes, peeled and cubed	500 g
2	large carrots, chopped	2
1	small rutabaga, cubed	1
1	onion, sliced	1
1	small green cabbage (uncored), cut into wedges	1
1	parsnip, sliced	1

1. Place beef in a large pot, fill pot with cold water and soak beef overnight in the refrigerator. Drain. (If your beef is particularly salty, you may need to change the water once or twice while soaking.)

2. Transfer beef to the pressure cooker and add enough fresh cold water to cover by about 1 inch (2.5 cm). Lock the lid in place and bring the cooker up to full pressure over high heat. Reduce heat to medium-low, just to maintain even pressure, and cook for 45 minutes. Remove from heat and allow pressure to drop naturally.

3. Meanwhile, preheat oven to 200°F (100°C). Remove beef from the cooker, place on an ovenproof platter, cover loosely with foil and place in warm oven.

4. Add potatoes, carrots and rutabaga to the cooker. Lock the lid in place and bring the cooker up to full pressure over medium heat. Cook for 5 minutes. Remove from heat and release pressure quickly.

5. Add onion, cabbage and parsnip to the cooker. Lock the lid in place and bring the cooker up to full pressure over medium heat. Cook for 5 minutes. Remove from heat and release pressure quickly.

6. Slice the beef and arrange on the platter. Using a slotted spoon, lift vegetables from the broth and arrange around the meat. Spoon some of the broth over top.

Rouladen

Serve this classic German dish with spaetzle noodles or roasted potatoes, sautéed red cabbage and beer.

● TIP

You can usually find steak thinly sliced for rouladen at a German butcher or any larger supermarket meat counter. Otherwise, substitute tenderized minute steaks.

4	beef rouladen (sliced bottom round steak, pounded thin)	4
	Salt and freshly ground black pepper	
2 tbsp	grainy mustard	25 mL
4	strips back bacon, halved	4
4	green onions, chopped	4
4	dill pickles, quartered lengthwise	4
1 tbsp	unsalted butter	15 mL
1 tbsp	extra-virgin olive oil	15 mL
1 cup	beef stock	250 mL
½ cup	dry red wine	125 mL
1 tbsp	cornstarch, dissolved in 2 tsp (10 mL) cold water	15 mL

1. Lay beef on a work surface, season with salt and pepper and slather with mustard. Arrange bacon along bottom half of meat and top with green onions and pickles. Roll meat up jellyroll-style and secure with toothpicks.

2. In the pressure cooker, heat butter and oil over medium-high heat and brown rolls lightly on all sides. Add beef stock and wine.

3. Lock the lid in place and bring the cooker up to full pressure over medium-high heat. Reduce heat to medium-low, just to maintain even pressure, and cook for 15 minutes. Remove from heat and release pressure quickly. Remove beef to a warm platter.

4. Whisk the cornstarch solution into the cooking liquid and simmer over medium heat, stirring, for 1 to 2 minutes, until sauce is thickened. Drizzle sauce over meat.

Round Steak Louisiana-Style

In Louisiana, this rich braised steak is called grillades and is often made with veal. The pressure cooker quickly tenderizes cuts like round steak, making this a fast and inexpensive meal. Thicken the sauce after it's cooked with a light roux made of softened butter and flour, then serve steaks and sauce over grits or rice. Stir in fresh parsley and chopped green onions at the end for color and fresh flavor.

4 lbs	inside or outside round steaks, about ½ inch (1 cm) thick, all visible fat removed	2 kg
8 oz	double-smoked bacon	250 g
	Vegetable oil	
3	cloves garlic, minced	3
1½ cups	chopped green bell peppers	375 mL
1 cup	chopped onions	250 mL
¾ cup	chopped celery	175 mL
2 cups	chopped tomatoes	500 mL
1 tsp	dried thyme	5 mL
1 cup	water	250 mL
1 cup	dry red wine	250 mL
2 tsp	salt	10 mL
2	bay leaves	2
½ tsp	freshly ground black pepper	2 mL
½ tsp	cayenne pepper	2 mL
2 tbsp	Worcestershire sauce	25 mL
¼ cup	all-purpose flour	50 mL
¼ cup	unsalted butter, softened	50 mL
1 cup	chopped green onions	250 mL
2 tbsp	chopped parsley	25 mL

1. Place meat between two sheets of waxed paper and, using a meat mallet, pound to ¼-inch (0.5 cm) thickness. Cut into serving-size pieces.

2. In the pressure cooker over medium-high heat, cook bacon until crisp. Crumble and set aside. Add steaks in batches and brown on both sides, adding oil as necessary to prevent burning. Transfer to a bowl. Set aside.

3. Reduce heat to medium. Add garlic, green pepper, onions and celery; sauté for about 5 minutes or until softened. Add tomatoes and thyme; cook for 3 minutes longer, until tomatoes are starting to break down. Stir in water and wine. Return meat to cooker with accumulated juices, salt, bay leaves, pepper, cayenne and Worcestershire sauce.

4. Lock the lid in place and bring the cooker up to full pressure over high heat. Reduce heat to medium-low, just to maintain even pressure, and cook the meat for 15 minutes. Remove from heat and release pressure quickly. The meat should be fork-tender. If not, return to full pressure and cook for 3 to 4 minutes longer. Remove from heat and release pressure quickly.

5. Transfer meat to a warmed serving platter and tent with foil to keep warm. Discard bay leaves. In a small bowl, mash flour with butter to form a smooth paste. Whisk into sauce and simmer, stirring, for about 5 minutes or until thickened. Stir in chopped green onions. Pour sauce over steak and garnish with reserved crumbled bacon and parsley.

● TIP

For those who like their steak extra spicy, pass the Louisiana hot pepper sauce.

Spicy Beef and Beer Stew

Sweet, spicy and savory, this is beef stew with an attitude. Add a crusty loaf of French bread and it's a meal.

2	cloves garlic, minced	2
¼ cup	packed brown sugar	50 mL
1 tsp	ground cumin	5 mL
1 tsp	salt	5 mL
½ tsp	freshly ground black pepper	2 mL
¼ tsp	ground cinnamon	1 mL
5 lbs	boneless beef chuck steak, cut into large chunks	2.5 kg
2 tbsp	vegetable oil	25 mL
2	large onions, cut into wedges	2
1	green bell pepper, cut into chunks	1
1	bottle (12 oz/341 mL) dark beer	1
2	tomatoes, diced, or 3 tbsp (45 mL) tomato paste	2
1 tsp	hot pepper flakes	5 mL
10	small new potatoes, halved	10
16	baby carrots	16
2 tbsp	all-purpose flour, whisked with 2 tbsp (25 mL) cold water (optional)	25 mL

1. In a large bowl, combine garlic, 1 tbsp (15 mL) of the brown sugar, cumin, salt, black pepper and cinnamon. Add beef cubes and stir to coat. Cover and refrigerate for 1 hour.

2. In the pressure cooker, heat oil over medium-high heat; brown meat, in batches. Return browned meat to cooker. Add onion and green pepper; sauté for 5 minutes. In a bowl, combine beer, diced tomato, hot pepper flakes and remaining brown sugar; pour into cooker. Stir in potatoes and carrots.

3. Lock the lid in place and bring the cooker up to full pressure over high heat. Reduce the heat to medium-low, just to maintain even pressure, and cook for 35 minutes. Remove from heat and release pressure quickly.

4. If desired, whisk in flour mixture and bring to a boil; reduce heat and simmer, stirring, for about 5 minutes or until thickened.

Beef Steak Stroganoff

This is a classic and comforting combination: tender minute steaks with a creamy mushroom sauce. Serve extra sauce over buttered egg noodles or mashed potatoes.

● **VARIATION**

This method also works well for pork or chicken cutlets.

4	minute steaks (about 1 lb/500 g total), pounded to tenderize	4
	Salt and freshly ground black pepper	
½ cup	all-purpose flour	125 mL
2 tsp	Hungarian paprika	10 mL
3 tbsp	extra-virgin olive oil	45 mL
1	onion, slivered	1
½ cup	dry white wine	125 mL
8	large shiitake mushrooms, sliced	8
2	cloves garlic, minced	2
¾ cup	beef stock or water	175 mL
¼ cup	sour cream	50 mL
1 tbsp	chopped fresh parsley, divided	15 mL

1. Season steaks on both sides with salt and pepper. On a plate, combine flour and paprika. Dip steaks in flour, coating well, then use a meat mallet to pound the flour into the surface of the meat. Reserve the excess flour.

2. In the pressure cooker, heat oil over medium heat and brown steaks on both sides. Remove steaks and set aside.

3. Add onion and wine to the cooker and stir up any browned bits. Sauté until onion is softened. Add mushrooms and garlic; sauté until mushrooms begin to brown. Return steaks and accumulated juices to the cooker, spooning some of the mushrooms and onions over the meat. Pour in beef stock.

4. Lock the lid in place and bring the cooker up to full pressure over medium-high heat. Reduce heat to medium-low, just to maintain even pressure, and cook for 12 minutes. Remove from heat and release pressure quickly. Remove steaks to a platter and keep warm.

5. In a bowl, combine sour cream and 1 tbsp (15 mL) of the reserved flour. Stir into the braising liquid in the pot and bring to a boil over medium heat. Reduce heat and simmer, stirring, for 5 minutes, until smooth and slightly thickened. Season to taste with salt and pepper and stir in half the parsley. Pour sauce over steaks and garnish with the remaining parsley.

Panang Beef Curry Bowls

Serves 4

Serve this spicy curry over rice noodles in deep bowls for a fast and authentic Southeast Asian meal.

● TIPS

Look for Thai curry pastes — both green and red — in small tubs at Asian supermarkets. That's also the best place to find canned coconut milk and fresh lemongrass.

If you can't find lemongrass, you can use 2 tsp (10 mL) grated lemon zest instead.

Prepare about 4 cups (1 L) of the rice noodles.

Serve lime wedges on the side to squeeze over each bowl.

1½ lbs	beef stew meat, trimmed and sliced	750 g
2 to 3 tbsp	Thai red curry paste, divided	25 to 45 mL
2 tbsp	extra-virgin olive oil	25 mL
1	Japanese eggplant, diced	1
1	red bell pepper, cut into ½-inch (1 cm) squares	1
1	clove garlic, minced	1
1	2- to 3-inch (5 to 7.5 cm) piece lemongrass, finely minced	1
1 cup	coconut milk (regular or light)	250 mL
½ cup	chicken stock	125 mL
1 tbsp	granulated sugar	15 mL
1 tbsp	crunchy peanut butter	15 mL
2 tsp	fish sauce (nam pla)	10 mL
1 tbsp	cornstarch, dissolved in 1 tbsp (15 mL) cold water	15 mL
	Hot cooked wide rice noodles	
1 tbsp	chopped roasted peanuts	15 mL
1 tbsp	chopped fresh cilantro	15 mL

1. In a bowl, combine beef and 1 tbsp (15 mL) of the curry paste. Set aside.

2. In the pressure cooker, heat oil over medium-high heat. Add eggplant and sauté until beginning to brown. Add beef and sauté for 5 minutes, until browned. Stir in 1 tbsp (15 mL) curry paste, red pepper, garlic, lemongrass, coconut milk, chicken stock, sugar, peanut butter and fish sauce.

3. Lock the lid in place and bring the cooker up to full pressure over high heat. Reduce heat to medium-low, just to maintain even pressure, and cook for 10 minutes. Remove from heat and release pressure quickly.

4. Whisk in the cornstarch solution and bring to a simmer over medium heat. Simmer, stirring, for 1 minute, until thickened. Adjust flavor with more curry paste, if desired.

5. Divide rice noodles among deep bowls and ladle curry over top. Sprinkle with peanuts and cilantro.

Bombay Beef

Serve this spicy beef stew with rice or naan bread and your favorite vegetable. To save time, you can substitute ¼ cup (50 mL) coriander chutney (available at Indian groceries) for the cilantro, serrano chili and lemon juice paste, but you may not achieve the brilliant green color that makes this simple curry stand out.

1½ lbs	beef stew meat, trimmed of excess fat	750 g
3	onions	3
4	cloves garlic, minced	4
1	dried chile pepper, crushed	1
1	1-inch (2.5 cm) piece of ginger, minced	1
1 tsp	ground turmeric	5 mL
1 tsp	salt	5 mL
½ tsp	saffron threads, crumbled	2 mL
2 tbsp	canola oil	25 mL
¼ cup	ground almonds	50 mL
2	serrano peppers, seeds removed	2
½ cup	cilantro leaves	125 mL
1 tbsp	freshly squeezed lemon juice	15 mL
½ tsp	garam masala	2 mL

1. Place the meat in a bowl. Cut the onions in half, lengthwise, then slice into thin slivers. Add to the meat in the bowl, along with the garlic, dried chile pepper, ginger, turmeric, salt and saffron.

2. Heat the oil in the pressure cooker over high heat. When it's hot, add the meat mixture. Cook, stirring, until spices are fragrant and meat and onions are beginning to brown. Reduce heat if necessary to prevent spices from burning.

3. Add ¾ cup (175 mL) water, lock the lid in place and bring the cooker up to full pressure over high heat. Reduce the heat to medium-low, just to maintain even pressure, and cook for 25 minutes. Reduce the pressure quickly. Remove the lid, stir in the ground almonds and continue to boil over medium heat for 10 minutes or until sauce is reduced and thickened.

4. Meanwhile, in a blender, combine the serranos, cilantro, lemon juice and 2 tbsp (25 mL) water. Blend until smooth. When the sauce is thick, add the cilantro purée and cook together for 3 minutes. Sprinkle with garam masala.

Chinese Red-Cooked Beef

When Chinese cooks braise red meat in a sweet soy and wine sauce, they call it "red cooking." The key ingredients in this aromatic mixture are star anise, cinnamon and black pepper, the dark spices that give this tender beef its depth of flavor. It's also a delicious combination for braising pork or chicken. Serve with white rice and stir-fried broccoli or bok choy.

● **TIP**

Use a vegetable peeler to cut long strips of orange zest.

1 tbsp	canola oil	15 mL
3 lbs	beef short ribs or shank, on the bone	1.5 kg
4	cloves garlic	4
1	2-inch (5 cm) piece gingerroot, sliced	1
1	dried red chile pepper (or 1 tsp/5 mL hot pepper flakes)	1
8	whole black peppercorns	8
2	whole star anise	2
1	cinnamon stick (about 2 inches/5 cm)	1
1 cup	water	250 mL
½ cup	Chinese cooking wine	125 mL
⅓ cup	dark soy sauce	75 mL
¼ cup	granulated sugar	50 mL
	Zest of 1 orange, in long strips	
1 tbsp	cornstarch, dissolved in 1 tbsp (15 mL) cold water	15 mL

1. In the pressure cooker, heat oil over medium-high heat and quickly sear short ribs on all sides. Stir in garlic, ginger, chile pepper, peppercorns, star anise, cinnamon, water, wine, soy sauce, sugar and orange zest.

2. Lock the lid in place and bring the cooker up to full pressure over medium-high heat. Reduce heat to medium-low, just to maintain even pressure, and cook for 40 minutes. Remove from heat and release pressure quickly. Remove ribs to a platter and keep warm (alternatively, you can finish the ribs by searing them quickly on a hot barbecue grill).

3. Strain the sauce and skim off excess fat. Return to the cooker, whisk in the cornstarch solution and bring to a boil over medium heat. Reduce heat and simmer, stirring, for 2 minutes, until smooth and nicely thickened. Drizzle sauce over ribs.

Beef Short Ribs in Barbecue Sauce

This is the best — and fastest — way to cook lean beef short ribs or big meaty side ribs. These cuts are actually more flavorful than tender cuts such as T-bone steaks; it's a revelation when you can make these cuts tender, too.

● TIPS

The sauce in this recipe is also good for marinating flank steak before barbecuing.

If you can't buy boneless beef short ribs, use 4 lbs (2 kg) bone-in ribs and remove the bones yourself or have your butcher debone them.

1 tbsp	vegetable oil	15 mL
2 to 3 lbs	boneless beef short ribs or big beef side ribs	1 to 1.5 kg
2	cloves garlic, minced	2
1	onion, minced	1
¼ cup	packed brown sugar	50 mL
1 tsp	freshly ground black pepper	5 mL
1	can (14 oz/398 mL) tomato sauce	1
½ cup	chili sauce	125 mL
½ cup	strong coffee	125 mL
½ cup	beef stock	125 mL
1 tbsp	Worcestershire sauce	15 mL
1 tbsp	light (fancy) molasses	15 mL
1 tsp	liquid smoke	5 mL
1 tsp	hot pepper sauce	5 mL

1. In the pressure cooker, heat oil over medium-high heat. Add ribs in batches and cook for about 15 minutes or until browned. Transfer ribs to a bowl; set aside. Discard any excess fat.

2. Reduce heat to medium. Add garlic and onion; sauté for about 3 minutes, until soft. Add brown sugar, pepper, tomato sauce, chili sauce, coffee, stock, Worcestershire sauce, molasses, liquid smoke and hot pepper sauce; simmer for 15 minutes, scraping up any browned bits from bottom of cooker. Return ribs to cooker along with any accumulated juices.

3. Lock the lid in place and bring the cooker up to low pressure over medium-high heat. Reduce heat to medium-low, just to maintain even pressure, and cook for 25 minutes. Remove from heat and release pressure quickly.

4. Simmer, uncovered, for another 10 minutes, basting often, until ribs are glazed and sauce is thickened. Serve ribs along with lots of horseradish, beans and baked potatoes.

Five-Spice Short Ribs

Look for meaty boneless short ribs for this simple recipe. The five-spice powder — an exotic mix of star anise, cloves, cinnamon, fennel seed and Szechuan peppercorns — makes it a perfect match for braised baby bok choy or broccoli and steamed rice.

1 tsp	extra-virgin olive oil	5 mL
2 lbs	lean boneless beef short ribs	1 kg
1	onion, slivered	1
1 tbsp	minced gingerroot	15 mL
1 tsp	minced garlic	5 mL
1 tsp	Asian chili paste (approx.)	5 mL
1 cup	beef stock	250 mL
2 tbsp	brown sugar	25 mL
2 tbsp	soy sauce	25 mL
1 tsp	five-spice powder	5 mL
1	cinnamon stick (about 2 inches/5 cm)	1
1 tbsp	cornstarch, dissolved in 1 tbsp (15 mL) cold water (optional)	15 mL
3	green onions, cut into 1-inch (2.5 cm) slivers	3

1. In the pressure cooker, heat oil over medium-high heat and brown short ribs on all sides. Add onion and sauté until starting to brown. Stir in ginger, garlic and chili paste; sauté for 1 minute. Stir in beef stock, brown sugar, soy sauce, five-spice powder and cinnamon.

2. Lock the lid in place and bring the cooker up to full pressure over medium-high heat. Reduce heat to medium-low, just to maintain even pressure, and cook for 35 minutes. Release pressure quickly and remove the lid. Simmer for 10 minutes, until sauce has thickened and meat is very tender. Remove ribs to a platter and keep warm.

3. Skim any excess fat from the sauce and discard cinnamon stick. If desired, whisk in the cornstarch solution and simmer, stirring, for 2 minutes, until thickened. Adjust flavor with more chili paste, if desired. Pour sauce over ribs and garnish with green onions.

Sloppy Joes

This is a speedy version of the old family favorite: a beefy sauce spooned over toasted crusty buns, then eaten with a knife and fork. The meat sauce is also delicious on hot dogs, for a home-style version of ballpark chili dogs.

● VARIATION

To turn this spicy meat sauce into a speedy bowl of chili, just stir in 2 cups (500 mL) drained and rinsed cooked or canned red or white beans at the end of step 3 and simmer until heated through. Wrap in whole wheat tortillas with chopped tomatoes, avocado slices, lettuce and shredded cheese for a fast, healthy supper.

1 tbsp	canola oil	15 mL
1	large onion, chopped	1
1 lb	extra-lean ground beef	500 g
1	red or yellow bell pepper, chopped	1
2 tbsp	chili powder (hot or mild)	25 mL
1 tsp	ground cumin	5 mL
1 tsp	dried oregano	5 mL
¾ cup	dark beer	175 mL
½ cup	chili sauce or ketchup	125 mL
2 tbsp	Dijon mustard	25 mL
Dash	Worcestershire sauce	Dash
2	large green onions, chopped	2
6	crusty buns, halved and toasted	6
	Shredded Cheddar cheese	

1. In the pressure cooker, heat oil over medium-high heat. Add onion and sauté for 10 minutes, until starting to brown. Add ground beef and sauté for 10 minutes, until no longer pink. Stir in red pepper, chili powder, cumin and oregano.

2. In a bowl, whisk together beer, chili sauce, mustard and Worcestershire sauce. Add to the cooker and stir to combine.

3. Lock the lid in place and bring the cooker up to full pressure over medium-high heat. Reduce heat to medium-low, just to maintain even pressure, and cook for 10 minutes. Release pressure quickly and remove the lid. If necessary, simmer for 1 to 2 minutes to thicken the sauce. Stir in green onions.

4. Spoon Sloppy Joe mixture over toasted buns and top with shredded cheese.

Swedish Meatballs

This classic combination is a hit with adults and kids alike. Serve the creamy sauce over lots of wide egg noodles.

1	slice whole wheat bread	1
½ cup	milk	125 mL
1 lb	extra-lean ground beef	500 g
8 oz	ground pork	250 g
1	egg	1
1	small onion, minced	1
1 tsp	dried dillweed	5 mL
½ tsp	salt	2 mL
¼ cup	unsalted butter	50 mL
¼ cup	all-purpose flour	50 mL
1	can (10 oz/284 mL) beef broth, diluted with equal amount of water	1
½ cup	whipping (35%) cream	125 mL
	Salt and freshly ground black pepper	
	Cooked egg noodles	
2 tbsp	chopped fresh dill	25 mL

1. In a large bowl, soak bread in milk until absorbed. Using your hands, break up bread; mix in beef and pork. Stir in egg, minced onion, dried dill and salt. Form into ¾-inch (2 cm) balls. Set aside.

2. In the pressure cooker, melt butter over medium-high heat; stir in flour until moistened. Gradually whisk in beef broth and water. Bring to a simmer. Carefully transfer meatballs to sauce.

3. Lock the lid in place and bring the cooker up to full pressure over medium-high heat. Reduce heat to medium-low, just to maintain even pressure, and cook for 10 minutes. Remove from heat and release pressure quickly. Stir in cream and simmer until sauce is creamy and thick. Season to taste with salt and pepper. Serve over cooked egg noodles, sprinkled with fresh dill.

Porcupine Meatballs

This is my version of an old family classic — very simple, but very satisfying.

1 lb	regular ground beef (or half beef and half pork)	500 g
1	small onion, minced (about ½ cup/125 mL)	1
1	clove garlic, minced	1
½ cup	long-grain white rice	125 mL
1 tsp	salt	5 mL
¼ tsp	freshly ground black pepper	1 mL
2 tbsp	extra-virgin olive oil	25 mL
1	large onion, slivered	1
½	red bell pepper, chopped	½
½	green bell pepper, chopped	½
2 cups	tomato juice or tomato vegetable cocktail	500 mL
2 tbsp	Worcestershire sauce	25 mL
1 tsp	Asian chili paste	5 mL

1. In a bowl, combine ground beef, minced onion, garlic, rice, salt and pepper. Form into 8 large meatballs. Set aside.

2. In the pressure cooker, heat oil over medium heat. Add slivered onions and sauté for 10 minutes, until starting to brown. Stir in red and green pepper.

3. In a bowl, whisk together tomato juice, Worcestershire sauce and chili paste. Arrange meatballs over onions and peppers and pour the tomato juice mixture over top.

4. Lock the lid in place and bring the cooker up to full pressure over medium-high heat. Reduce heat to medium-low, just to maintain even pressure, and cook for 15 minutes. Release pressure quickly and remove the lid. Simmer for 10 minutes, until sauce is thickened. Serve meatballs with sauce spooned over top.

Osso Buco

You can make this classic Italian dish with veal or lamb shanks. Ask the butcher to cut the shanks into 1½-inch (4 cm) slices. Serve the osso buco with saffron-flavored risotto (see recipe, page 231) or over creamy polenta flavored with Parmesan; add a robust red wine and you've got a rustic but elegant meal.

¼ cup	all-purpose flour	50 mL
½ tsp	salt	2 mL
¼ tsp	freshly ground black pepper	1 mL
4	slices veal or lamb shanks, about 1½ inches (4 cm) thick	4
8	thin slices pancetta or smoked bacon	8
2 tbsp	extra-virgin olive oil	25 mL

Sauce

2	stalks celery, minced	2
2	cloves garlic, minced	2
1	carrot, shredded	1
1	onion, minced	1
1	portobello mushroom, cut into strips (or substitute other flavorful varieties like shiitake, cèpes, etc.)	1
1 tsp	dried thyme	5 mL
1	bay leaf	1
1 tsp	fresh or dried rosemary, minced	5 mL
1	bulb fennel, finely chopped, or ½ tsp (2 mL) fennel seed	1
1 cup	dry red wine	250 mL
1 cup	tomato sauce	250 mL
	Salt and freshly ground black pepper	

Gremolata

¼ cup	chopped fresh flat-leaf (Italian) parsley	50 mL
2	cloves garlic, minced	2
¼ tsp	salt	1 mL
	Grated zest of 1 lemon	

1. In a plastic bag or bowl, combine flour with salt and pepper. Add veal and toss to coat. Wrap each piece in a slice of pancetta. Discard excess flour. In the pressure cooker, heat oil over medium-high heat. Add veal in batches and cook until browned. Transfer to a plate. Set aside.

2. Add celery, garlic, carrot, onion and mushroom to cooker; sauté for 2 minutes. Stir in thyme, bay leaf, rosemary, fennel, wine and tomato sauce, scraping up any browned bits from bottom of cooker. Nestle veal in sauce; pour in any accumulated juices.

3. Lock the lid in place and bring the cooker up to full pressure over high heat. Reduce heat to medium-low, just to maintain even pressure, and cook for 15 minutes. Remove from heat and release pressure quickly. Transfer veal to a serving platter and tent with foil to keep warm. Discard bay leaf. If desired, simmer sauce, uncovered, to thicken. Season to taste with salt and pepper. Pour over veal.

4. *Gremolata:* In a small bowl, combine parsley, garlic, salt and lemon zest. Sprinkle on top of veal and serve with soft polenta.

● **TIP**

While gremolata is a classic condiment for osso buco, it's also perfect for sprinkling over grilled fish or shrimp. Make a point of buying flat-leaf (Italian) parsley — it has a more pronounced flavor than the more common curly variety because it contains more essential oils.

Greek-Style Braised Lamb Shoulder

Serves 4

Start this recipe the night before to make sure the marinade infuses its flavors throughout the lamb. The perfect side dishes are boiled or roasted new potatoes and green vegetables like steamed beans or broccoli, lightly dressed with lemon and olive oil. Or try serving this tender lamb with steamed green beans and Roasted Garlic Risotto with Asiago, (see recipe, page 233).

3½ to 4 lb	boneless lamb shoulder roast	1.75 to 2 kg
	Grated zest and juice of 1 lemon (about 3 tbsp/45 mL juice)	
3	cloves garlic, minced	3
1 tsp	dried oregano	5 mL
½ tsp	freshly ground black pepper	2 mL
¼ cup	Dijon mustard	50 mL
1 cup	chopped onions	250 mL
3	bay leaves	3
2	cloves garlic, whole	2
1 tbsp	dried rosemary	15 mL
1 tsp	yellow mustard seeds	5 mL
1 cup	water	250 mL

1. Trim fat and sinew from the lamb and cut it into large, serving-size pieces. In a large bowl or sealable plastic bag, combine lemon zest and juice, minced garlic, oregano, pepper and mustard; add lamb and stir or toss to coat. Cover or seal and refrigerate overnight.

2. In the pressure cooker, combine onions, bay leaves, whole garlic, rosemary and mustard seeds. Add lamb and marinade. Pour in water.

3. Lock the lid in place and bring the cooker up to full pressure over high heat. Reduce heat to medium-low, just to maintain pressure, and cook for 18 minutes. Remove from heat and release pressure quickly. The lamb should be very tender. If not, return to full pressure and cook for 2 to 3 minutes longer, depending on doneness. Remove from heat and release pressure quickly.

4. Remove meat from cooking juices and serve on a warm platter, surrounded with boiled or oven-roasted potatoes and vegetables.

Braised Lamb with Barley

Serves 4

This comforting combination features one tender lamb shank per person, served with barley alongside. Steamed green beans make a nice side dish.

• TIPS

For the best results, use a food processor to finely chop the vegetables.

This technique also works well for braising whole turkey legs on the bone. Just remove the skin and bones before serving the chunks of tender dark meat with the barley.

4	small lamb shanks (about 3 lbs/1.5 kg total), trimmed	4
	Salt and freshly ground black pepper	
3 tbsp	extra-virgin olive oil	45 mL
1	large onion, finely chopped	1
3	cloves garlic, minced	3
2	stalks celery, finely chopped	2
1	large carrot, finely chopped	1
2 tbsp	tomato paste	25 mL
1 tsp	dried thyme	5 mL
½ tsp	sweet paprika	2 mL
1 cup	pearl barley	250 mL
2½ cups	beef or chicken stock	625 mL
½ cup	dry red wine	125 mL
1 tbsp	brown sugar	15 mL
1 tbsp	chopped fresh parsley, divided	15 mL

1. Season lamb on all sides with salt and pepper. In the pressure cooker, heat oil over medium-high heat and brown the lamb on all sides. Remove lamb and set aside.

2. Add onion to the cooker, stirring up any browned bits, and sauté for 5 minutes, until softened. Add garlic, celery and carrot; sauté for 2 minutes, until fragrant. Stir in tomato paste, thyme and paprika. Stir in barley, beef stock, wine and brown sugar. Return lamb and any accumulated juices to the pot.

3. Lock the lid in place and bring the cooker up to full pressure over medium-high heat. Reduce heat to medium-low, just to maintain even pressure, and cook for 30 minutes. Remove from heat and allow pressure to drop naturally. The lamb should be fork-tender. If not, return to full pressure and cook for another 5 minutes. Remove from heat and allow pressure to drop naturally. Remove lamb to a warm platter.

4. If necessary, return cooker to medium heat and simmer for 5 to 10 minutes to reduce the liquid. Stir in half the parsley and season to taste with salt and pepper. Spoon barley around lamb and sprinkle with the remaining parsley.

Spanish Lamb Stew Braised in Rioja

This is a wonderful way to use an inexpensive cut of lamb. Start this dish the day before you plan to serve it, so that the meat has plenty of time to marinate.

3 lbs	boneless lamb shoulder, cut into 2-inch (5 cm) chunks	1.5 kg
1 cup	Rioja or other dry, fruity red wine, divided	250 mL
5	cloves garlic, minced, divided	5
	Leaves from 1 sprig of rosemary, minced	
½ tsp	salt	2 mL
¼ tsp	freshly ground black pepper	1 mL
¼ cup	all-purpose flour	50 mL
3 tbsp	extra-virgin olive oil	45 mL
1	large onion, chopped	1
1 tbsp	sweet Spanish or Hungarian paprika	15 mL
1	bay leaf	1
1	can (14 oz/398 mL) plum tomatoes, chopped	1
½ cup	beef stock or chicken stock	125 mL
½ cup	roasted red bell pepper, chopped	125 mL

1. In a sealable plastic bag, combine lamb, ½ cup (125 mL) of wine, 3 cloves of the garlic and rosemary; seal bag and refrigerate overnight.

2. Drain lamb, reserving marinade. Pat dry with paper towels. In a large bowl, toss lamb with salt and pepper, then with flour, coating well; discard excess flour. In the pressure cooker, heat oil over medium-high heat. Add lamb in batches and cook until browned.

3. Return browned lamb to cooker. Add remaining garlic, onion and paprika; cook, stirring, for 5 minutes. Add remaining wine, bay leaf, tomatoes, stock and reserved marinade.

4. Lock the lid in place and bring the cooker up to full pressure over high heat. Reduce heat to medium-low, just to maintain even pressure, and cook for 20 minutes. Remove from heat and release pressure quickly. Discard bay leaf. If desired, simmer sauce, uncovered, to thicken. Stir in roasted pepper.

Steamed Pork Ribs with Black Bean Sauce (page 20)

Dhal Dip with Pappadums (page 34)

Thai Green Curry and Sweet Potato Soup (page 48)

Bajan Pumpkin Soup (page 52)

Cajun Black Bean and Sausage Gumbo (page 66)

Perfect Pot Roast (page 74)

Beef Steak Stroganoff (page 83)

Braised Lamb with Barley (page 95)

Pork Loin Chops with Red Cabbage and Apples (page 108)

Pork Wraps with Green Tomatoes and Ancho Chiles (page 116)

Whole "Roasted" Chicken with Lemon, Garlic and Herbs (page 126)

Chicken Stew with New Potatoes and Baby Carrots (page 146)

Lamb Curry with Lentils

This is a mild, South Asian–style curry, flavored with coconut milk and thickened with red lentils. Serve it with lots of basmati rice, and a dish of steamed cauliflower or carrots on the side.

1 tbsp	vegetable oil	15 mL
2 lbs	boneless lamb shoulder, fat removed, cut into 2-inch (5 cm) pieces	1 kg
1 cup	chopped onions	250 mL
2	cloves garlic, crushed	2
2 tsp	minced gingerroot	10 mL
2 tsp	curry powder	10 mL
1 tsp	salt	5 mL
¼ tsp	ground cumin	1 mL
¼ tsp	ground cloves	1 mL
¼ tsp	ground cardamom	1 mL
¼ tsp	freshly ground black pepper	1 mL
½ cup	diced tomatoes	125 mL
¼ cup	red lentils	50 mL
1 cup	unsweetened coconut milk	250 mL
½ cup	beef stock	125 mL
1 tbsp	freshly squeezed lemon juice	15 mL
¼ cup	chopped fresh cilantro or parsley	50 mL
4 cups	hot cooked basmati rice	1 L

1. In the pressure cooker, heat oil over medium-high heat. Add lamb in batches and cook until browned. Transfer to a bowl. Set aside.

2. Reduce heat to medium. Add onion, garlic, ginger, curry powder, salt, cumin, cloves, cardamom and pepper; sauté 2 minutes or until fragrant. Add tomatoes; cook for 1 minute. Stir in lentils, coconut milk, beef stock, lemon juice and lamb, with any accumulated juices.

3. Lock the lid in place and bring the cooker up to full pressure over high heat. Reduce heat to medium-low, just to maintain even pressure, and cook for 15 minutes. Remove from heat and release pressure quickly. Stir in cilantro. Serve over rice.

Lamb Tagine with Prunes

This stew is mildly exotic, a combination of spices and tender lamb with colorful vegetables and dried fruits. It's even better when reheated the next day, after all the flavors in the sauce have had a chance to marry.

1 tsp	ground cinnamon	5 mL
¾ tsp	ground coriander	4 mL
½ tsp	ground cardamom	2 mL
½ tsp	ground cumin	2 mL
½ tsp	ground ginger	2 mL
½ tsp	garlic powder	2 mL
½ tsp	salt	2 mL
¼ tsp	freshly ground black pepper	1 mL
¼ tsp	crushed saffron threads	1 mL
¼ tsp	cayenne pepper	1 mL
2 lbs	boneless lamb shoulder	1 kg
3 tbsp	extra-virgin olive oil	45 mL
6	carrots, cut into thick slices	6
1	large onion, chopped	1
4	cloves garlic, chopped	4
1	large yellow bell pepper, cubed	1
1	large red bell pepper, cubed	1
1 tbsp	chopped gingerroot	15 mL
15	prunes, pitted and quartered (about 1 cup/250 mL)	15
½ cup	raisins or currants	125 mL
2 cups	chicken stock	500 mL
1 tbsp	tomato paste	15 mL
1 tbsp	liquid honey	15 mL
	Grated zest of 1 lemon	
2 tbsp	freshly squeezed lemon juice	25 mL
1 tbsp	cornstarch, dissolved in 1 tbsp (15 mL) cold water	15 mL
3 tbsp	chopped fresh parsley	45 mL
1 cup	whole-grain couscous, cooked	250 mL

1. In a small bowl, combine cinnamon, coriander, cardamom, cumin, ginger, garlic powder, salt, black pepper, saffron and cayenne.

2. Cut lamb into 1-inch (2.5 cm) cubes, trimming off as much fat and sinew as possible. Place lamb in a large non-reactive glass or stainless steel bowl, sprinkle with spice mixture and rub spices into the meat. Cover and refrigerate for at least 1 hour or overnight.

3. In the pressure cooker, heat oil over medium heat and, working in batches, brown lamb. Remove lamb and set aside.

4. Add carrots and onion to the cooker and sauté for 5 minutes, until starting to brown and caramelize. Stir in garlic, yellow pepper, red pepper and ginger. Return lamb and any accumulated juices to the pot and stir in prunes, raisins, chicken stock, tomato paste, honey, lemon zest and lemon juice.

5. Lock the lid in place and bring the cooker up to full pressure over high heat. Reduce heat to medium-low, just to maintain even pressure, and cook for 20 minutes. Release pressure quickly and remove the lid. The lamb should be fork-tender. If not, return to full pressure and cook for another 5 minutes. Release pressure quickly and remove the lid. Whisk in the cornstarch solution and simmer, stirring, for 5 minutes, until thickened. Stir in parsley. Serve over hot couscous.

● **TIP**

Couscous is extremely easy to make — just remember the 2:1 rule: twice as much water as couscous. Start with salted water or chicken broth, bring to a boil in a saucepan, stir in the couscous, remove from heat and let stand, covered, for 5 to 10 minutes. Fluff with a fork and serve. You can also enrich your couscous with spices or flavorings such as butter or olive oil, raisins, sautéed onions or finely chopped fresh parsley. Couscous makes a speedy side dish for grilled meats or fish.

Saag Lamb

This tender lamb curry with a silky spinach sauce is a favorite dish at many Indian restaurants. Marinate the lamb overnight for the best flavor. Serve with basmati rice or naan bread and vegetables.

● **TIPS**

Instead of the Asian chili paste, you could use ¹/₂ tsp (2 mL) cayenne pepper.

You can replace the garam masala with ¹/₄ tsp (1 mL) each ground cinnamon, cardamom, cloves and turmeric.

4	cloves garlic, chopped	4
2	onions, chopped, divided	2
2 tbsp	minced or grated gingerroot	25 mL
¹/₂ cup	plain yogurt	125 mL
1 tsp	Asian chili paste	5 mL
2 lbs	boneless lamb shoulder, trimmed and cut into 2-inch (5 cm) pieces	1 kg
2 tbsp	canola oil	25 mL
1 tbsp	ground coriander	15 mL
1 tsp	ground cumin	5 mL
2	packages (each 10 oz/300 g) frozen chopped spinach, thawed	2
¹/₄ cup	tomato paste	50 mL
1 tsp	salt	5 mL
¹/₄ cup	finely chopped fresh cilantro	50 mL
¹/₄ cup	whipping (35%) cream	50 mL
1 tsp	garam masala (see tip, at left)	5 mL

1. In a blender or food processor, purée garlic, half the onions, ginger, yogurt and chili paste.

2. Place lamb in a bowl and pour in purée, stirring to coat. Cover and refrigerate for at least 3 hours or overnight.

3. In the pressure cooker, heat oil over medium-high heat. Add the remaining onions and sauté until starting to brown. Add coriander and cumin; sauté for 1 minute.

4. Drain the lamb, reserving the marinade. Add the meat to the pot and sauté until no longer pink. Stir in the reserved marinade, spinach, tomato paste and salt.

5. Lock the lid in place and bring the cooker up to full pressure over medium-high heat. Reduce the heat to medium-low, just to maintain even pressure, and cook for 30 minutes. Remove from heat and release pressure quickly. The lamb should be fork-tender. If not, return to full pressure and cook for another 5 to 10 minutes. Remove from heat and release pressure quickly. Stir in cilantro, cream and garam masala.

Lamb Rogan Josh

This is a classic Indian curry that's perfect for a party. Use lean lamb (or substitute beef) and marinate overnight for layers of deep, rich flavor. Serve the tender lamb curry with golden Indian Rice Pilau, seasoned with cinnamon, turmeric and cardamom (see recipe, page 226).

● TIPS

You can use $1/2$ tsp (2 mL) ground cinnamon instead of the cinnamon stick.

For a pretty finish, garnish with cilantro springs.

2 lbs	lean lamb shoulder, trimmed and cut into chunks	1 kg
$1/2$ cup	plain yogurt	125 mL
4	green cardamom pods	4
1	small cinnamon stick	1
2 tsp	paprika	10 mL
1 tsp	each ground turmeric, coriander and cumin	5 mL
$1/2$ tsp	cayenne pepper	2 mL
2 tsp	garam masala	10 mL
2 cups	canned tomatoes	500 mL
2	cloves garlic, peeled	2
1	large onion, chopped	1
1	2-inch (5 cm) piece gingerroot	1
3 tbsp	vegetable oil	45 mL
1 cup	water	250 mL
2 tbsp	chopped fresh cilantro	25 mL

1. In a bowl, toss lamb with yogurt. In a blender or spice grinder, pulverize whole cardamom and cinnamon. Add to lamb mixture with paprika, turmeric, coriander, cumin and cayenne. Cover and refrigerate overnight.

2. In a food processor, combine garam masala, tomatoes, garlic, onion and ginger; purée until smooth.

3. In the pressure cooker, heat oil over medium heat. Add tomato mixture and cook for 5 minutes. Stir in lamb and marinade. Stir in water.

4. Lock the lid in place and bring the cooker up to full pressure over medium-high heat. Reduce heat to medium-low, just to maintain even pressure, and cook for 20 minutes. Remove from heat and release pressure quickly. The lamb should be fork-tender. If not, return to full pressure and cook for another 5 minutes. Release pressure quickly.

5. Remove lid and bring to boil. Reduce heat and simmer curry until nicely thickened. Stir in cilantro just before serving.

Orange Pineapple Glazed Ham

This is an old-fashioned way to serve ham, with a citrusy pineapple sauce. Try a mash of white potatoes and orange-fleshed sweet potatoes, flavored with caramelized onions and ginger, on the side. Add a bright green vegetable, such as steamed broccoli, for a colorful, festive plate for Easter or any other family occasion.

• Rack or trivet to fit bottom of pressure cooker

1	boneless smoked ham (about 4 lbs/2 kg)	1
1 cup	crushed pineapple (or pineapple tidbits), with juice	250 mL
½ cup	orange juice	125 mL
¼ cup	packed brown sugar	50 mL
1 tbsp	minced gingerroot	15 mL
2 tbsp	Dijon mustard	25 mL
2 tbsp	orange or lemon marmalade	25 mL
1 tbsp	soy sauce	15 mL
1 tbsp	cornstarch, dissolved in 2 tbsp (25 mL) cold water	15 mL

1. Set rack in the bottom of the pressure cooker. Place ham skin side up on the rack.

2. In a blender or food processor, whirl together pineapple, orange juice, brown sugar, ginger, mustard, marmalade and soy sauce. Pour over ham.

3. Lock the lid in place and bring the cooker up to full pressure over medium-high heat. Reduce heat to medium-low, just to maintain even pressure, and cook for 25 minutes. (If you have a pressure cooker with a low pressure setting, use the lower pressure and increase the cooking time to 45 minutes.) Remove from heat and allow pressure to drop naturally. Remove ham to a platter and let rest for 10 minutes.

4. Meanwhile, whisk the cornstarch solution into the fruit sauce and simmer over medium heat, stirring, for 5 minutes, until sauce is clear and thick. Using a pastry brush, glaze the top of the ham with some of the sauce. Slice the ham and serve with the remaining sauce on the side.

Pork Loin with Calvados and Dried Fruit

The dried and fresh fruit in this recipe cooks down with the stock to create a thick, fruity gravy that's perfect with moist, juicy slices of roast pork. Make a mound of creamy mashed potatoes and some steamed green vegetables to round out this comforting meal.

● **TIP**

For the dried fruit, try 1/3 cup (75 mL) each apricots, pitted prunes and cranberries or currants.

2 tbsp	all-purpose flour	25 mL
1/2 tsp	salt	2 mL
1/4 tsp	freshly ground black pepper	1 mL
3 lb	boneless pork loin roast	1.5 kg
2 tbsp	extra-virgin olive oil	25 mL
1 1/2 cups	chicken stock	375 mL
1/4 cup	Calvados or brandy	50 mL
1	onion, chopped	1
1/2 cup	chopped rhubarb	125 mL
1 cup	chopped dried fruit	250 mL
1/2 tsp	dried thyme	2 mL
1/2 tsp	dried marjoram	2 mL
1 tsp	Worcestershire sauce	5 mL
	Salt and freshly ground black pepper	

1. In a shallow dish, combine flour, salt and pepper. Roll pork in flour to coat all sides. Discard excess flour mixture.

2. In the pressure cooker, heat oil over medium-high heat. Add pork and brown on all sides. Stir in stock, Calvados, onion, rhubarb, dried fruit, thyme, marjoram and Worcestershire sauce.

3. Lock the lid in place and bring the cooker up to full pressure over high heat. Reduce heat to medium-low, just to maintain even pressure, and cook for 40 minutes. Remove from heat and release pressure quickly. Check to make sure there is just a hint of pink remaining in pork. If not, return to full pressure and cook for 3 to 5 minutes longer, depending on doneness. Remove from heat and release pressure quickly.

4. Transfer pork to a warmed platter. Tent with foil and let rest for 10 minutes. Meanwhile, simmer the sauce, uncovered, to reduce slightly, stirring to break up the fruit. Season to taste with salt and pepper. Slice pork and serve drizzled with fruit sauce.

Braised Pork Shoulder Roast with Hoisin Sauce

This is a fast way to tenderize a pork shoulder roast. The resulting meat is tender and juicy, perfect for a casual dinner with friends. Serve with jasmine rice and sautéed bok choy or stir-fried vegetables.

Brine

6 cups	water	1.5 L
½ cup	packed brown sugar	125 mL
¼ cup	kosher salt	50 mL
2 tbsp	minced gingerroot	25 mL
1 tsp	whole black peppercorns	5 mL
1	cinnamon stick (about 2 inches/5 cm)	1
	Grated zest of 1 orange	
1	boneless pork shoulder blade roast (about 3 lbs/1.5 kg)	1
2 tbsp	canola oil	25 mL
1 cup	minced onion	250 mL
1 tbsp	minced garlic	15 mL
1 tsp	five-spice powder	5 mL
¼ cup	sake or sherry	50 mL
¼ cup	freshly squeezed orange juice	50 mL
2 tbsp	packed brown sugar	25 mL
2 tbsp	soy sauce	25 mL
2 tbsp	hoisin sauce	25 mL
1 tbsp	sesame oil	15 mL

1. *Brine:* In a saucepan, combine water, brown sugar, salt, ginger, peppercorns, cinnamon and orange zest; bring to a boil over high heat. Reduce heat and simmer for 2 minutes. Remove from heat and let cool.

2. Place roast in a large non-reactive container and pour brine over top. Cover and refrigerate overnight.

3. Remove roast from brine and pat dry. Discard brine. In the pressure cooker, heat canola oil over medium-high heat and brown roast on all sides. Remove roast and set aside.

4. Add onion to the cooker and sauté for 5 minutes, until starting to brown. Add garlic and five-spice powder; sauté for 1 minute. Stir in sake, orange juice, brown sugar, soy sauce, hoisin sauce and sesame oil. Return roast and any accumulated juices to the pot and spoon some of the liquid over top.

5. Lock the lid in place and bring the cooker up to full pressure over medium-high heat. Reduce heat to medium-low, just to maintain even pressure, and cook for 40 minutes. Release pressure quickly and remove the lid. Skim excess fat from the sauce and continue to simmer for 5 to 10 minutes, spooning sauce over the meat to glaze it.

● **TIP**

Five-spice powder is a classic Chinese spice combination used in a variety of dishes. Look for it at Asian markets or make your own by combining equal amounts of ground cinnamon, star anise, cloves, fennel and Szechwan pepper. Use it sparingly — the flavor of five-spice powder can easily overwhelm a dish.

Kansas City Pulled Pork Butt

Pulled pork is traditionally slow-cooked in a smoker, then shredded and served on a bun with coleslaw. This isn't exactly what you'd find in Kansas (purists would cringe), but it's a reasonable facsimile and makes a delicious, tender shredded pork to pile on a sandwich. The ballpark mustard slather and spices are traditional, though. Don't be tempted to substitute Dijon; it's not sugary enough for this recipe. Try it — you'll like it.

- Rack or trivet to fit bottom of pressure cooker

1	2-lb (1 kg) boneless pork shoulder roast, tied	1
1 tbsp	liquid smoke	15 mL
¼ cup	ballpark-style mustard	50 mL

Dry Rub

2 tbsp	granulated sugar	25 mL
2 tbsp	paprika	25 mL
1 tbsp	packed brown sugar	15 mL
1 tbsp	ground cumin	15 mL
1 tbsp	chili powder	15 mL
1 tbsp	freshly ground black pepper	15 mL
1 tsp	salt	5 mL
1 tsp	cayenne pepper	5 mL
¼ tsp	ground ginger	1 mL
¼ tsp	ground allspice	1 mL
¼ tsp	ground cloves	1 mL
3 tbsp	packed brown sugar	45 mL
½ tsp	salt	2 mL
1 cup	water	250 mL
½ cup	beer	125 mL
¼ cup	tomato paste	50 mL
2 tbsp	vinegar	25 mL
1 tsp	liquid smoke	5 mL
8	crusty whole wheat buns	8
	Coleslaw	

1. Drizzle surface of meat with 1 tbsp (15 mL) liquid smoke and rub to coat well, making sure to get some into the inside surfaces, where the roast is rolled and tied. Let stand for 10 minutes. Spread mustard over pork.

2. *Dry rub:* In a small bowl, combine granulated sugar, paprika, brown sugar, cumin, chili powder, black pepper, salt, cayenne, ginger, allspice and cloves. Sprinkle mixture generously over all surfaces of the pork. Let stand at room temperature until the rub gets nice and tacky, about 10 minutes. (This will form a crust on the meat as it cooks.)

3. In the pressure cooker, whisk together brown sugar, salt, water, beer, tomato paste, vinegar and 1 tsp (5 mL) liquid smoke. Set rack in cooker and place pork on top.

4. Lock the lid in place and bring the cooker up to full pressure over high heat. Reduce heat to medium-low, just to maintain even pressure, and cook for 1½ hours. Remove from heat and allow pressure to drop naturally. The internal temperature should be at least 170°F (75°C) and the pork should be tender enough to shred. If not, return to full pressure and cook for 5 to 10 minutes longer.

5. Transfer pork to a bowl and let cool slightly. Using two forks, shred the meat. Discard any excess fat. Bring braising liquid to a boil; reduce heat and simmer until reduced and slightly thickened. Drizzle some of the sauce over the pork and toss well to combine. Serve pulled pork piled on buns with coleslaw on top and remaining sauce on the side.

● **TIP**

Instead of simmering the braising liquid, thicken with 1 tbsp (15 mL) cornstarch, dissolved in 1 tbsp (15 mL) cold water. Whisk into liquid and simmer for about 3 minutes or until thickened.

Pork Loin Chops with Red Cabbage and Apples

Serves 4

The red cabbage and apples make a colorful and healthful backdrop for tender pork loin chops. The faintly sweet braising liquid makes a wonderful drizzle when you cook it down to a thick syrup.

2 tbsp	extra-virgin olive oil	25 mL
4	lean center-cut pork loin chops, about 1 inch (2.5 cm) thick, trimmed of visible fat	4
3 tbsp	unsalted butter	45 mL
1	red onion, halved and slivered	1
1 lb	red cabbage, shredded	500 g
½ cup	chicken stock	125 mL
½ cup	dry white wine	125 mL
1	bay leaf	1
½ tsp	salt	2 mL
Pinch	freshly ground black pepper	Pinch
2	Granny Smith apples, peeled, cored and cut into wedges	2

1. In the pressure cooker, heat oil over medium-high heat. Add pork chops and cook about 2 minutes per side or until browned. Transfer to a plate. Set aside.

2. Melt butter in cooker and sauté red onion for 5 minutes, until soft and beginning to brown. Stir in cabbage to coat with butter. Add stock, wine, bay leaf, salt, pepper and apples. Place pork chops on top.

3. Lock the lid in place and bring the cooker up to full pressure over medium-high heat. Reduce heat to medium-low, just to maintain even pressure, and cook for 14 minutes. Remove from heat and release pressure quickly. Discard bay leaf.

4. Using a slotted spoon, transfer pork chops and cabbage to a platter with cabbage on the bottom and pork on top and cover loosely with foil to keep warm. Bring braising liquid to boil over high heat; cook until reduced and thickened. Drizzle sauce over pork and cabbage; season to taste with additional pepper.

Mexican Pork Chops

Slightly sweet and spicy, this is a modern version of a traditional dish. You can purée the salsa with the orange juice in a blender or food processor for a smoother sauce, if desired. Serve with refried beans and rice.

1 cup	chunky tomato salsa	250 mL
¼ cup	orange juice	50 mL
2 tsp	dried oregano	10 mL
¼ tsp	ground cinnamon	1 mL
¼ tsp	ground cumin	1 mL
4	thick center-cut pork chops or shoulder steaks, visible fat removed (about 1 lb/500 g)	4
	Salt and freshly ground black pepper	
1 tbsp	extra-virgin olive oil	15 mL
1	onion, sliced and separated into rings	1
1	jalapeño or chipotle pepper, minced	1

1. Combine the salsa and orange juice. Stir in the oregano, cinnamon and cumin and set aside.

2. Season pork on both sides with salt and pepper. Heat the olive oil in the pressure cooker over high heat and sear the pork chops quickly until nicely browned on both sides. Add the salsa sauce and scatter the onion rings and minced chiles over top.

3. Lock the lid in place and bring the cooker up to full pressure over high heat. Reduce heat to medium-low, just to maintain pressure, and cook for 15 minutes. Reduce pressure quickly, remove the lid and continue to simmer for 5 to 10 minutes or until sauce thickens.

Saigon Braised Pork and Eggplant

The eggplant cooks down to form a thick, creamy sauce in this delicious Southeast Asian–style curry. Add another jalapeño pepper (or substitute hotter serrano or Scotch bonnet chiles) if you like your food extra spicy, and serve over lots of fragrant jasmine or basmati rice.

● TIP

If you're pressed for time, instead of simmering the sauce to thicken, whisk together 1 tbsp (15 mL) cornstarch with 1 tsp (5 mL) water; whisk into sauce. Cook, stirring, for about 3 minutes or until thickened.

2 lbs	country-style pork ribs or boneless pork steaks	1 kg
1 tbsp	vegetable oil or peanut oil	15 mL
4	cloves garlic, minced	4
1	onion, chopped	1
1	eggplant, cubed	1
1	jalapeño pepper, seeded and chopped	1
1	large carrot, cubed	1
1 cup	cubed waxy potatoes	250 mL
1 tbsp	granulated sugar	15 mL
1 tbsp	chopped gingerroot	15 mL
1 tsp	curry powder	5 mL
1	whole star anise or ½ tsp (2 mL) anise seed	1
1 cup	water or chicken stock	250 mL
½ cup	chopped tomato (fresh or canned)	125 mL
¼ cup	Thai nuoc nam or Vietnamese nam pla (fish sauce)	50 mL
1	bunch green onions, cut into 2-inch pieces	1
¼ cup	chopped cilantro	50 mL

1. Cut pork ribs into 3-inch pieces. (If using steaks, cut into large chunks.) In the pressure cooker, heat oil over medium-high heat. Add pork in batches and cook for about 10 minutes, until browned. Return pork to cooker. Add garlic and onion; cook, stirring, for 5 minutes. Stir in eggplant, jalapeño pepper, carrot, potatoes, sugar, ginger, curry powder, star anise, water, tomato and fish sauce.

2. Lock the lid in place and bring the cooker up to full pressure over high heat. Reduce heat to medium-low, just to maintain even pressure, and cook for 18 minutes. Remove from heat and release pressure quickly.

3. Simmer, uncovered, for 5 to 10 minutes, until sauce is reduced and thickened. Discard star anise. Stir in green onions and cilantro. Serve immediately over rice.

Bigos (Polish Hunter's Stew)

Serves 6

This traditional "hunter's stew," a savory mix of fermented cabbage, smoky sausages, bacon, beef or pork, game meats and mushrooms, is considered the national dish of Poland. Every Polish family has its own special recipe for *bigos*, a feast dish that's served at winter gatherings. France has a very similar dish, called *choucroute garnie*, served in brasseries across the country. Serve with rye bread and boiled potatoes.

● TIPS

Go to a good Polish butcher to buy the end bits of smoky bacon, ham and sausage to add to the stew.

Bigos is best when reheated and served a day or two after it's made.

2 tbsp	extra-virgin olive oil	25 mL
2	large onions, diced	2
2	cloves garlic, minced	2
1½ lbs	mixed smoked pork (including kielbasa, ham, pork and bacon) cubed	750 g
12 oz	boneless pork shoulder steak, cubed	375 g
½ cup	dry white wine	125 mL
4	prunes, pitted and chopped	4
2	apples, peeled and chopped	2
1	jar (28 oz/796 mL) sauerkraut, rinsed, drained and squeezed dry	1
2 oz	dried porcini mushrooms	60 g
1 cup	tomato juice or tomato vegetable cocktail	250 mL
1 cup	chicken stock	250 mL
1 tsp	dried marjoram	5 mL
½ tsp	crushed allspice berries	2 mL
½ tsp	hot paprika	2 mL
½ tsp	caraway seeds	2 mL
½ tsp	freshly ground black pepper	2 mL
2	bay leaves	2

1. In the pressure cooker, heat oil over medium heat. Add onions and garlic; sauté for 5 minutes, until softened. Stir in mixed smoked pork and pork shoulder. Add wine and stir up any browned bits. Stir in prunes, apples, sauerkraut, mushrooms, tomato juice, chicken stock, marjoram, allspice, paprika, caraway seeds, pepper and bay leaves.

2. Lock the lid in place and bring the cooker up to full pressure over medium-high heat. Reduce heat to medium-low, just to maintain even pressure, and cook for 30 minutes. Release pressure quickly and remove the lid. If necessary, simmer for 10 minutes to thicken the sauce. Discard bay leaves.

Mexican Pulled Pork Tamale Pie

This version of Mexican pork *carnitas* uses the pressure cooker to quickly tenderize the meat, then it's browned until the outside is crisp, shredded and used to fill this tasty tamale pie, also cooked in the pressure cooker.

- 7- or 8-inch (18 or 20 cm) springform pan, buttered (use smaller size if necessary to fit inside pressure cooker)
- Rack or trivet to fit bottom of pressure cooker

Rub

2 tsp	ground cumin	10 mL
2 tsp	chipotle pepper powder	10 mL
1 tsp	sweet Hungarian paprika	5 mL
1 tsp	salt	5 mL
3 lbs	boneless pork shoulder blade roast, cut into 2-inch (5 cm) pieces	1.5 kg
1 cup	water	250 mL
1 cup	minced onions	250 mL
¼ cup	freshly squeezed orange juice	50 mL
2	bay leaves	2

Corn Tamale Dough

2 cups	chicken stock	500 mL
1 cup	water	250 mL
¾ cup	stone-ground cornmeal	175 mL
1 tsp	minced garlic	5 mL
¼ tsp	salt	1 mL
Pinch	freshly ground black pepper	Pinch
1 tbsp	unsalted butter	15 mL
1 tsp	chopped fresh oregano	5 mL
1 cup	shredded Cheddar cheese	250 mL
	Salsa and sour cream	

1. *Rub:* In a small bowl, combine cumin, chipotle powder, paprika and salt.

2. Place pork in a large container and sprinkle with rub, coating on all sides. Cover and refrigerate for at least 4 hours or overnight.

3. In the pressure cooker, combine pork, water, onions, orange juice and bay leaves. Lock the lid in place and bring the cooker up to full pressure over medium-high heat. Reduce heat to medium-low, just to maintain even pressure, and cook for 30 minutes. Release pressure quickly and remove the lid. Simmer, stirring occasionally, until liquid evaporates and pork starts to brown. Remove pork and, using a fork, shred the meat. Set aside. Wipe cooker clean.

4. *Corn Tamale Dough:* Meanwhile, in a saucepan, bring chicken stock and water to a boil over medium heat. Gradually whisk in cornmeal. Reduce heat to medium-low and add garlic, salt and pepper. Cook, stirring often, for 15 to 20 minutes, until dough comes away from the sides of the pan. Stir in butter and oregano.

5. Wrap the base of the springform pan with foil. Spoon half the dough into pan. Layer with half the cheese, a 1-inch (2.5 cm) layer of shredded pork, the remaining cheese, and the remaining dough. Smooth the top with the back of a spoon and cover with foil.

6. Set rack in the bottom of the pressure cooker. Pour in 2 cups (500 mL) water for steaming. Fold a 2-foot (60 cm) long piece of foil several times to make a strip strong enough to lift the pan. Center pan on midpoint of strip and fold the ends together to make a handle. Lower the pan into the cooker.

7. Lock the lid in place and bring the cooker up to full pressure over medium-high heat. Reduce heat to medium-low, just to maintain even pressure, and cook for 10 minutes. Remove from heat and release pressure quickly. Using foil handle, lift pan out of the cooker onto a cooling rack. Remove foil lid and let cool for 15 minutes. Release pie from pan and cut into wedges. Serve topped with salsa and sour cream.

● **TIP**

Leftover pork is perfect as a filling for pulled pork sandwiches, tacos or enchiladas (see page 114). It can be stored in an airtight container in the refrigerator for up to 2 days or frozen for longer storage.

Pork Enchiladas

Serves 4

This recipe incorporates the delicious pork *carnitas* used in the tamale pie on page 112. Enchiladas are a popular family dish that can be made ahead and frozen for up to 1 month.

- Preheat oven to 400°F (200°C)
- Large baking dish, greased with butter or nonstick cooking spray

1	recipe pork *carnitas* (follow steps 1 to 3, page 112)	1
2 cups	shredded mozzarella or Cheddar cheese, divided	500 mL
	Salt	
20	6-inch (15 cm) corn tortillas (or 10 to 12 larger flour tortillas)	20
6	canned tomatoes, chopped	6
2	cloves garlic, minced	2
2	jalapeño peppers, seeded and minced	2
1	mild chile pepper, roasted and minced	1
1 cup	chicken stock	250 mL
½ cup	chopped fresh cilantro	125 mL
2 tbsp	freshly squeezed lime juice	25 mL

1. In a bowl, combine pork and half the cheese. Season to taste with salt and set aside.

2. Wrap tortillas in paper towels and microwave on High for 1 minute, until soft enough to roll without cracking.

3. Fill each tortilla with about ⅓ cup (75 mL) of the pork and roll up. Place rolls seam side down in prepared baking dish, packing tightly in a single layer.

4. In a blender or food processor, combine tomatoes, garlic, jalapeños, chile pepper, chicken stock, cilantro and lime juice; purée until smooth.

5. Pour purée into a saucepan and bring to a boil over medium heat. Reduce heat and simmer for 5 to 10 minutes, until slightly thickened.

6. Pour sauce over tortillas and sprinkle with the remaining cheese. Bake in preheated oven for 10 to 15 minutes, until hot and bubbly.

Creamy Pork Goulash

Serve this goulash with plenty of wide egg noodles to soak up all of the delicious, creamy sauce. For added zip, try it with a black pepper pasta.

● **TIP**

Look for green olives stuffed with garlic.

1 tbsp	extra-virgin olive oil	15 mL
2 lbs	boneless pork shoulder roast or pork steaks, trimmed and cubed	1 kg
1	large onion, sliced	1
2	cloves garlic, minced	2
1	red or yellow bell pepper, sliced	1
1	can (10 oz/284 mL) chicken broth, undiluted	1
¾ cup	dry white wine	175 mL
1 oz	dried porcini mushrooms	30 g
1	tomato, seeded and chopped	1
1 tsp	sweet Spanish paprika	5 mL
6	extra-large green olives, sliced	6
3 tbsp	all-purpose flour	45 mL
¼ cup	sour cream	50 mL
1 lb	wide egg noodles	500 g
	Chopped parsley	

1. In the pressure cooker, heat oil over medium-high heat. Add pork in batches and cook until browned. Transfer to a bowl. Set aside.

2. Reduce heat to medium. Add onion and sauté until it starts to brown. Stir in garlic and red pepper; sauté for 2 minutes. Stir in broth, wine, mushrooms, tomato, paprika and pork, with any accumulated juices.

3. Lock the lid in place and bring the cooker up to full pressure over high heat. Reduce heat to medium-low, just to maintain even pressure, and cook for 12 minutes. Remove from heat and release pressure quickly. Stir in olives.

4. In a small bowl, whisk flour together with sour cream; whisk into the stew. Simmer, stirring, for about 5 minutes, until thickened. Meanwhile, in a large pot of boiling salted water, cook egg noodles until almost tender. Drain and add to stew; cook for about 10 minutes longer or until noodles are tender. Transfer goulash to a deep platter and garnish with parsley.

Pork Wraps with Green Tomatoes and Ancho Chiles

This is a traditional Mexican stew, made with tart, green tomatillos, a vegetable that resembles a small green tomato in a papery husk. You can substitute unripe, green tomatoes in the fall, or even use regular tomatoes with an added 1 tbsp (15 mL) lemon juice for tartness.

2 tbsp	extra-virgin olive oil	25 mL
1½ lbs	pork shoulder, fat removed, cut into chunks	750 g
4	cloves garlic, minced	4
1 tsp	salt	5 mL
1	large onion, chopped	1
1 cup	chopped green tomatoes or tomatillos or one 10-oz (284 mL) can tomatillos	250 mL
1 cup	chopped ripe tomatoes	250 mL
1 cup	dark beer	250 mL
½ cup	orange juice	125 mL
1	jalapeño pepper, seeded and chopped	1
2	dried ancho or pasilla peppers, seeded and crumbled	2
1 tsp	ground cumin	5 mL
2 tbsp	all-purpose flour, whisked with 2 tbsp (25 mL) cold water	25 mL
½ cup	chopped fresh cilantro (about ½ bunch)	125 mL
1½ cups	frozen corn kernels, thawed	375 mL
12	large whole wheat tortillas or hot cooked brown rice	12
	Garnishes: sliced avocado, shredded Cheddar cheese and sour cream	

1. In the pressure cooker, heat oil over medium-high heat. Add pork in batches and cook until browned. Transfer to a bowl. Set aside.

2. Reduce heat to medium. Add garlic and sauté until fragrant. Season to taste with salt. Add onions and sauté for about 10 minutes or until they start to brown. Return pork to cooker; add green tomatoes, ripe tomatoes, beer, orange juice, jalapeño pepper, dried chiles and cumin.

3. Lock the lid in place and bring the cooker up to full pressure over high heat. Reduce heat to medium-low, just to maintain even pressure, and cook for 20 minutes. Remove from heat and release pressure quickly.

4. Whisk in flour mixture and cook, stirring, for 5 minutes or until thickened. Add corn and cook for 2 minutes longer. Stir in cilantro and serve immediately, wrapped in tortillas with garnishes, or over rice.

● **TIP**

Ancho or pasilla chiles are medium-hot dried chiles; fresh banana or Hungarian hot peppers are the closest substitute.

Kung Pao Pork

The pressure cooker simplifies the preparation of this popular pork dish from southern China. This saucy, spicy dish is perfect spooned over a bowl of steamy jasmine rice or Asian noodles.

1 lb	boneless pork loin chops or shoulder, cut into 1-inch (2.5 cm) pieces	500 g
1 tbsp	soy sauce	15 mL
1 tsp	Asian garlic chili paste	5 mL

Sauce

1 cup	chicken stock	250 mL
1 tbsp	packed brown sugar	15 mL
2 tbsp	Chinese black bean sauce	25 mL
1 tbsp	soy sauce	15 mL
2 tsp	Asian chili paste	10 mL
2 tbsp	canola oil	25 mL
2	cloves garlic, minced	2
1	onion, slivered	1
1	red or yellow bell pepper, cut into ½-inch (1 cm) squares	1
1 tbsp	minced gingerroot	15 mL
1½ tbsp	cornstarch, dissolved in 1 tbsp (15 mL) cold water	22 mL
½ cup	frozen baby peas, thawed	125 mL
	Hot cooked jasmine rice or rice noodles	
2	green onions, cut into ½-inch (1 cm) pieces	2
¼ cup	roasted unsalted peanuts, chopped (optional)	50 mL

1. In a bowl, combine pork, soy sauce and garlic chili paste. Cover and refrigerate for 30 minutes.

2. *Sauce:* In a small bowl, combine chicken stock, brown sugar, black bean sauce, soy sauce and chili paste. Set aside.

3. In the pressure cooker, heat oil over high heat until sizzling. Add pork with marinade and sauté for 8 to 10 minutes, until no longer pink on the outside. Stir in garlic, onion, bell pepper and ginger. Pour in the reserved sauce.

4. Lock the lid in place and bring the cooker up to full pressure over high heat. Reduce heat to medium-low, just to maintain even pressure, and cook for 10 minutes. Release pressure quickly and remove the lid. Whisk in the cornstarch solution and bring to a boil over medium heat. Reduce heat and simmer, stirring, for 2 minutes, until thickened. Stir in peas and simmer until heated through.

5. Divide rice among deep bowls and ladle pork mixture over top. Sprinkle with green onions and peanuts, if desired.

● **TIP**

Use regular dry-roasted peanuts or, for authenticity, head to Chinatown for a bag of small unsalted peanuts.

Cabbage Rolls

This old-fashioned combination comes together quickly in the pressure cooker — you can even pressure-steam the head of cabbage to make the leaves easy to roll.

• TIP

If you want to pressure-steam the cabbage, place it in a steamer basket in the pressure cooker and pour in 2 cups (500 mL) water. Pressure cook for 3 to 4 minutes.

1	head cabbage (choose a flat, loose-leaf variety), cored	1
1 lb	lean ground pork	500 g
¾ cup	long-grain white rice	175 mL
2	cloves garlic, minced	2
1 cup	minced onion	250 mL
	Sea salt and freshly ground black pepper	
3 cups	tomato vegetable cocktail or tomato juice	750 mL

1. In a large pot of boiling water, simmer cabbage for about 10 minutes to soften the leaves enough for rolling. Drain well, separate the leaves and cut away any large, thick ribs; reserve ribs. Return inner leaves to the boiling water if necessary to soften them. Remove core and chop the smallest leaves and set aside with the ribs.

2. In a bowl, combine pork, rice, garlic and onion. Season to taste with salt and pepper.

3. Lay cabbage leaves on a work surface. Place 1 to 2 tbsp (15 to 25 mL) of the meat mixture at the base of each leaf and roll up, folding in the sides as you go. (Don't roll them too tight — leave enough room for the rice to expand during cooking.)

4. Place chopped cabbage and ribs in the bottom of the pressure cooker. Arrange the cabbage rolls on top, seam side down, in two layers and fairly tightly packed together (or arrange them vertically in the pot). Pour tomato vegetable cocktail over top.

5. Lock the lid in place and bring the cooker up to full pressure over medium-high heat. Reduce heat to medium-low, just to maintain even pressure, and cook for 25 minutes. Remove from heat and allow pressure to drop naturally.

6. Remove the lid, return cooker to medium-low heat and simmer for about 10 minutes to reduce the sauce slightly. Carefully transfer cabbage rolls to a serving dish and drizzle some of the tomato sauce over top.

Braised Chinese Meatballs

Serves 4

This version of Lion's Head, a famous Shanghai dish, uses the pressure cooker to quickly braise pork meatballs with shredded Chinese cabbage or bok choy. Traditionally, large 4-oz (125 g) meatballs are the center of this one-pot meal, but I prefer to make eight "mini" Lion's Head meatballs.

● **TIP**

If desired, you can thicken the broth before ladling it over the meatballs and cabbage. Dissolve 1 tbsp (15 mL) cornstarch in 1 tbsp (15 mL) cold water and whisk into the broth. Simmer over medium heat until thickened.

1 cup	drained canned water chestnuts	250 mL
2	green onions, chopped	2
1	1-inch (2.5 cm) piece gingerroot	1
1 lb	ground pork	500 g
1	egg, lightly beaten	1
2 tbsp	cornstarch	25 mL
2 tbsp	soy sauce, divided	25 mL
1 tbsp	Chinese rice wine or dry sherry	15 mL
1 tsp	salt	5 mL
1 tsp	granulated sugar	5 mL
2 tsp	sesame oil	10 mL
1 tbsp	canola oil	15 mL
1 lb	Chinese (napa) cabbage or bok choy, coarsely shredded	500 g
1½ cups	chicken stock	375 mL
1 tsp	Asian chili paste	5 mL

1. In a food processor, combine water chestnuts, green onions and ginger; pulse until minced. Transfer to a bowl and add ground pork, egg, cornstarch, half the soy sauce, rice wine, salt, sugar and sesame oil. Mix thoroughly, using your hands, and form into 8 meatballs. Set aside.

2. In the pressure cooker, heat canola oil over medium-high heat. Add meatballs and cook for 5 to 6 minutes, until nicely browned on the bottom. Remove and set aside.

3. Add cabbage to the cooker and sauté for 1 minute, stirring up any browned bits. Arrange meatballs browned side up in a single layer over cabbage. Combine chicken stock, the remaining soy sauce and chili paste; pour over meatballs.

4. Lock the lid in place and bring the cooker up to full pressure over medium-high heat. Reduce heat to medium-low, just to maintain even pressure, and cook for 10 minutes. Remove from heat and release pressure quickly.

5. Serve meatballs in shallow soup bowls, surrounded by cabbage, with some of the broth ladled on top.

Ma Po Tofu

This is a classic Szechwan dish — tofu and lean ground pork in a spicy sauce seasoned with Szechwan peppercorns, a unique spice that will literally make your tongue numb. Look for it in Asian markets.

8 oz	lean ground pork	250 g
2 tbsp	soy sauce, divided	25 mL
2 tbsp	rice wine, divided	25 mL
1 tsp	sesame oil	5 mL
1 tbsp	canola oil	15 mL
1	½-inch (1 cm) piece gingerroot, minced	1
1 tbsp	Asian garlic chili paste	15 mL
1	package (1 lb/500 g) firm tofu, cut into small cubes	1
¾ cup	chicken broth	175 mL
½ tsp	granulated sugar	2 mL
1 tsp	cornstarch, dissolved in 1 tsp (5 mL) cold water	5 mL
2	green onions, minced	2
½ tsp	Szechwan peppercorns, toasted and crushed to a powder	2 mL

1. In a bowl, combine the ground pork with 1 tbsp (15 mL) of the soy sauce, 1 tbsp (15 mL) of the rice wine and the sesame oil. Set aside to marinate for 10 minutes.

2. In the pressure cooker, heat the canola oil over medium-high heat. Add the ground pork and cook, stirring, for 5 minutes, until no longer pink. Add ginger and garlic chili paste. Cook together for 10 seconds. Stir in tofu, broth, sugar and the remaining soy sauce and rice wine.

3. Lock the lid in place and bring to a boil over high heat. Reduce heat to medium-low, just to maintain pressure, and cook for 5 minutes. Release the pressure quickly, remove the lid and stir in the cornstarch solution; simmer, stirring, until the sauce is thickened.

4. Serve sprinkled with green onions and Szechwan peppercorn powder.

Poultry

Grandma's Sunday Chicken

My grandmother used to treat us to her own version of chicken *pot-au-feu* every Sunday after church. Coming into her little house, you were enveloped in the steamy aroma of homemade chicken soup. She served her Sunday lunch in two stages — first, a rich chicken broth filled with hand-cut noodles; then the tender stewed chicken, carrots, parsnips and potatoes, drizzled with creamy dill sauce. My grandma got up very early on Sundays to make this magic — you can make it in the pressure cooker in 20 minutes.

8 to 10	small red potatoes, halved	8 to 10
4	large carrots, cut into large pieces	4
4	stalks celery, cut into large pieces	4
3	whole cloves garlic, peeled	3
2	onions, each cut into 6 pieces	2
2	parsnips, cut into large pieces	2
1	bay leaf	1
1 tbsp	chopped fresh thyme (or 1 tsp/5 mL dried)	15 mL
1 tsp	salt	5 mL
1 tsp	whole peppercorns	5 mL
1	3- to 4-lb (1.5 to 2 kg) chicken or stewing hen	1
6 cups	water or chicken stock	1.5 L
1½ cups	small egg noodles	375 mL

Dill Cream Sauce

2 tbsp	unsalted butter	25 mL
2 tbsp	all-purpose flour	25 mL
¾ cup	cream or milk	175 mL
2 tbsp	minced fresh dill (or 1 tsp/5 mL dried)	25 mL
Pinch	paprika	Pinch
	Salt and freshly ground black pepper	

1. In the pressure cooker, combine potatoes, carrots, celery, garlic, onions, parsnips, bay leaf, thyme, salt and peppercorns. Set the chicken on top and pour water over. Bring to a boil, skimming off any foam that rises to the top.

2. Lock the lid in place and bring the cooker up to full pressure over high heat. Reduce heat to medium-low, just to maintain even pressure, and cook for 20 minutes for a 3-lb (1.5 kg) chicken, 5 to 10 minutes longer for a 3.5- to 4-lb (1.75 to 2 kg) bird. Remove from heat and allow pressure to drop naturally. Check to make sure the chicken is very tender and juices run clear. If not, return to full pressure and cook for 3 to 5 minutes longer, depending on doneness. Allow pressure to drop naturally.

3. Strain the stock through a fine strainer into another pot and skim off any fat that rises to the top. Reserve $1/2$ cup (125 mL) of the stock for the dill cream sauce. Set remaining stock aside. Remove skin from chicken and separate into pieces. Arrange chicken and vegetables on a serving platter and cover loosely with foil. Keep warm in a 200°F (100°C) oven.

4. *Dill Cream Sauce:* In a small saucepan, melt butter over medium heat. Stir in flour and cook for 1 minute. Gradually whisk in the reserved $1/2$ cup (125 mL) of stock and cream. Bring to a boil and cook, stirring, for about 5 minutes or until thickened. Stir in dill and paprika. Season to taste with salt and pepper. Keep warm in a sauceboat.

5. Bring remaining stock to a boil and add egg noodles. Reduce heat and simmer for about 5 minutes or just until noodles are tender.

6. To serve, divide soup between 6 deep soup plates. When the soup course is finished, pass the chicken, vegetables and warm dill sauce.

Whole "Roasted" Chicken with Lemon, Garlic and Herbs

This braised bird comes out meltingly tender and infused with the flavors of lemon, garlic, rosemary and thyme. You can crisp the skin by putting it into a hot (450°F/220°C) preheated oven for 10 to 15 minutes, or simply remove the skin for serving. This chicken is also wonderful cold — the perfect way to create flavorful, moist chicken for your next picnic or salad.

4	cloves garlic, minced	4
1 tbsp	chopped fresh thyme	15 mL
1 tbsp	chopped fresh rosemary	15 mL
1	chicken, about 3 lbs (1.5 kg) or a size that will fit comfortably into your pressure cooker	1
	Grated zest of 1 lemon	
	Juice of 1 lemon	
2 tbsp	extra-virgin olive oil	25 mL
2 cups	chicken stock	500 mL
	Freshly ground black pepper	
2 tbsp	cornstarch, dissolved in 1 tbsp (15 mL) water	25 mL

1. In a small bowl, combine garlic, thyme and rosemary; rub half of the mixture inside chicken. Rub the inside with 1 tbsp (15 mL) of the lemon juice and 1 tsp (5 mL) of the lemon zest.

2. In the pressure cooker, heat oil over high heat. Add chicken and brown on all sides. Pour in stock and remaining lemon juice; sprinkle with remaining garlic mixture.

3. Lock the lid in place and bring the cooker up to full pressure over high heat. Reduce heat to medium-low, just to maintain even pressure, and cook for 25 to 30 minutes. Remove from heat and release pressure quickly. Chicken should be tender, with an internal temperature of 170°F (75°C). If not, return cooker to full pressure and cook for 5 minutes or longer, depending on doneness. Remove from heat and release pressure quickly.

4. Transfer chicken to a carving board and tent with foil to keep warm. Pour cooking juices into a glass measuring cup; skim off any fat. Return liquid to cooker and bring to a boil. Whisk in cornstarch mixture and cook, stirring, for about 3 minutes or until gravy is thickened. Season to taste with pepper and stir in remaining 1 tsp (5 mL) lemon zest. Carve chicken from the bone (remove skin if desired) and serve with gravy.

Speedy Dijon Chicken

This almost-instant chicken dish is ideal for a weekday family meal, but elegant enough to impress dinner guests.

● TIP

Crème fraîche is a thickened heavy cream — easy to make with a little sour cream or yogurt and a container of whipping (35%) cream. Just mix 2 cups (500 mL) whipping cream with ½ cup (125 mL) sour cream and let stand, covered, at room temperature for 12 hours. When the mixture is nicely thickened, you can store it in the refrigerator for up to 2 weeks. Crème fraîche also makes a lovely dessert topping.

1 tbsp	extra-virgin olive oil	15 mL
2 lbs	boneless skinless chicken breasts	1 kg
3 tbsp	Dijon mustard	45 mL
1 tbsp	grainy mustard	15 mL
1 tbsp	liquid honey	15 mL
½ cup	chicken stock	125 mL
¼ cup	dry white wine or apple juice	50 mL
1	small onion, minced	1
½ cup	sour cream or crème fraîche (see note, at left)	125 mL
2 tbsp	all-purpose flour	25 mL
	Chopped fresh herbs	

1. In the pressure cooker, heat oil over medium-high heat. Add chicken in batches and cook for about 5 minutes or until browned.

2. In a small bowl, whisk together Dijon mustard, grainy mustard and honey; gradually whisk in stock and wine. Stir in onion. Pour over the chicken.

3. Lock the lid in place and bring the cooker up to full pressure over high heat. Reduce heat to medium-low, just to maintain even pressure, and cook chicken for 8 minutes. Remove from heat and release pressure quickly.

4. Transfer chicken to a serving platter and tent with foil to keep warm. In a small bowl, whisk sour cream with flour; whisk into cooker. Simmer, stirring, over low heat for 2 to 3 minutes or until thickened. Pour sauce over chicken and garnish with fresh herbs. Serve with steamed broccoli and wild rice or steamed new potatoes.

Chicken in Creamy Mushroom Sauce

Just like that old family favorite — only faster. (And no canned soup!) Serve the chicken and sauce over pasta or mashed potatoes.

2 tbsp	unsalted butter	25 mL
4	boneless skinless chicken breasts	4
2 cups	sliced mushrooms	500 mL
1	onion, chopped	1
1	clove garlic, minced	1
1 cup	chicken stock	250 mL
2 tbsp	sherry	25 mL
1 tsp	Dijon mustard	5 mL
1/3 cup	whipping (35%) cream	75 mL
	Salt and freshly ground black pepper	

1. In the pressure cooker, melt butter over medium-high heat. Add chicken in batches and sauté until lightly browned. Transfer browned chicken to a bowl. Set aside.

2. Add mushrooms, onion and garlic to cooker; sauté until fragrant and beginning to brown. Place browned chicken on top of vegetables. Pour in stock and sherry.

3. Lock the lid in place and bring the cooker up to full pressure over high heat. Reduce heat to medium-low, just to maintain even pressure, and cook for 5 minutes. Remove from heat and release pressure quickly.

4. Transfer chicken to a warm platter. Whisk mustard and cream into cooker; bring to a boil and cook for 3 minutes or until reduced and thickened. Season sauce to taste with salt and pepper; pour over the chicken. Serve with pasta or mashed potatoes.

Moroccan Lemon Chicken Tagine

Serves 4 to 6

A tagine is a Moroccan stew. This version replaces the traditional preserved lemons (lemons cured in salt) with lemon zest and juice.

● **TIP**

Serve this tagine over couscous. To prepare the couscous, in a saucepan, bring 2¼ cups (550 mL) chicken stock to a boil. Stir in 2 cups (500 mL) couscous, cover and remove from heat; let stand for 5 minutes. Fluff couscous with a fork and pile it on a large serving platter, making a well in the center. Arrange chicken pieces in the center, and spoon sauce over and around.

2 tbsp	unsalted butter	25 mL
1 tbsp	extra-virgin olive oil	15 mL
2 lbs	boneless skinless chicken breasts, each halved crosswise	1 kg
2	large onions, finely chopped	2
2	cloves garlic, minced	2
2 tsp	minced gingerroot	10 mL
1 tsp	ground cumin	5 mL
½ tsp	crumbled saffron threads	2 mL
2 cups	chicken stock	500 mL
	Grated zest of 1 lemon	
	Juice of 1 large lemon (about ¼ cup/50 mL)	
2 tbsp	liquid honey	25 mL
12	large green olives, pitted	12
2 tbsp	cornstarch, dissolved in 2 tbsp (25 mL) water	25 mL
2 tbsp	chopped fresh flat-leaf (Italian) parsley	25 mL
	Salt and freshly ground black pepper	

1. In the pressure cooker, heat butter and oil over medium heat. Add chicken in batches and cook until browned, transferring cooked pieces to a bowl. Once all the chicken is browned, return it to the cooker. Add onion, garlic and ginger; sauté for 5 minutes. Stir in cumin, saffron, stock and half of the lemon zest. Add lemon juice and honey.

2. Lock the lid in place and bring the cooker up to full pressure over high heat. Reduce heat to medium-low, just to maintain even pressure, and cook for 8 minutes. Remove from heat and release pressure quickly.

3. Stir in olives and remaining lemon zest. Whisk in cornstarch mixture; simmer, stirring, until sauce is syrupy and smooth. Stir in parsley; season to taste with salt and pepper.

Coq au Vin

This is a classic French country stew, perfect to serve over noodles or boiled potatoes. It's elegant enough for company but easy enough for every day. Don't skip the cognac — it adds authenticity to this hearty bistro fare.

2	sprigs fresh thyme	2
1	sprig fresh parsley	1
1	bay leaf	1
4	slices double-smoked bacon, chopped	4
3½ lbs	boneless skinless chicken pieces (breasts and thighs)	1.75 kg
1 tbsp	extra-virgin olive oil (approx.)	15 mL
10	pearl onions or shallots, peeled (see tip, at right)	10
2	cloves garlic, minced	2
2	stalks celery, sliced	2
1	carrot, grated	1
2 cups	dry red wine	500 mL
¼ cup	cognac	50 mL
8 oz	mushrooms, halved (or quartered, if large)	250 g
2 tbsp	cornstarch, dissolved in 2 tbsp (25 mL) water	25 mL
3 tbsp	chopped fresh parsley	45 mL
	Salt and freshly ground black pepper	

1. Using kitchen string, tie thyme, parsley and bay leaf into a bouquet garni. Set aside.

2. In the pressure cooker over medium-high heat, sauté bacon until starting to crisp. Add chicken pieces in batches and cook until brown, adding more olive oil if necessary to prevent chicken from sticking. Transfer to a bowl and set aside. Reduce heat to medium. Add onions and garlic; sauté until onions start to brown. Stir in celery, carrot, wine, cognac, mushrooms, bouquet garni, chicken, bacon and any accumulated juices.

3. Lock the lid in place and bring the cooker up to full pressure over high heat. Reduce heat to medium-low, just to maintain even pressure, and cook for 10 to 12 minutes. Remove from heat and release pressure quickly.

4. Whisk cornstarch mixture into stew; cook over medium heat, stirring, until juices are thick and glossy. Discard the bouquet garni. Stir in parsley and season to taste with salt and pepper. Serve chicken over wide egg noodles or surrounded by boiled new potatoes, sprinkled with additional chopped parsley.

● **TIP**

To remove skins from pearl onions, submerge them in boiling water for a few minutes, then run under cold water and peel.

Country Captain Curry Chicken

This simple treatment is perfect for a cut-up chicken or for chicken pieces, such as legs with the backs attached. Simply cut the back portions away (save the bones for soup) and separate the legs from the thighs by cutting through at the joint. Serve this curried chicken with lots of fluffy basmati rice.

2½ to 3 lbs	chicken pieces, skin removed	1.25 to 1.5 kg
	Salt, pepper and hot Hungarian paprika	
2 tbsp	unsalted butter	25 mL
2 tbsp	extra-virgin olive oil	25 mL
1	large onion, chopped	1
3	cloves garlic, minced	3
1	red bell pepper, chopped	1
1 tbsp	minced gingerroot	15 mL
4 tsp	curry powder (hot or mild)	20 mL
1	can (19 oz/540 mL) tomatoes, with juice, whirled in a food processor or blender	1
½ cup	chicken stock or water	125 mL
½ cup	whipping (35%) cream	125 mL
	Chopped fresh cilantro	

1. Season chicken well on all sides with salt, pepper and paprika.

2. In the pressure cooker, heat butter and oil over medium heat and, working in batches, brown chicken on both sides. Remove chicken and set aside.

3. Add onion to the cooker, stirring up any browned bits, and sauté for 5 minutes, until softened. Add garlic, red pepper, ginger and curry powder; sauté for 1 minute. Stir in tomatoes and chicken stock. Return chicken and any accumulated juices to the pot.

4. Lock the lid in place and bring the cooker up to full pressure over medium-high heat. Reduce heat to medium-low, just to maintain even pressure, and cook for 15 minutes. Remove from heat and release pressure quickly. Remove chicken to a platter and keep warm.

5. Add cream to the sauce and bring to a simmer over medium heat; simmer for 5 to 10 minutes, until sauce is thickened. Pour over chicken and sprinkle with cilantro.

Chicken and Asian Noodles with Coconut Curry Sauce

Serves 6

When you buy fresh cilantro, look for herbs with the roots attached; you can use them to infuse extra layers of flavor into this creamy curry sauce.

● **TIP**

Thai green curry paste is sold in jars or foil pouches in Asian markets.

6	strips lemon zest	6
3	cilantro roots or stems	3
2	green serrano peppers, halved lengthwise	2
2 lbs	boneless skinless chicken breasts or thighs, cut into strips	1 kg
2 to 3 tbsp	Thai green curry paste	25 to 45 mL
2 cups	light coconut milk	500 mL
1	small Asian eggplant, cut into small cubes	1
1 tbsp	packed brown sugar	15 mL
½ tsp	freshly ground white pepper	2 mL
½ tsp	salt	2 mL
1 tbsp	fish sauce (nam pla)	15 mL
1 tsp	dark soy sauce	5 mL
1 tsp	freshly squeezed lemon juice	5 mL
8 oz	fresh Chinese-style steamed egg noodles, cooked until tender and drained	250 g
3	green onions, cut into thin strips	3
¼ cup	chopped fresh cilantro	50 mL

1. Using kitchen string, tie lemon zest, cilantro roots or stems and serrano peppers into a bundle. Set aside.

2. In the pressure cooker over medium heat, sauté chicken and curry paste for 3 to 5 minutes or until chicken begins to brown. Stir in coconut milk, eggplant, brown sugar, white pepper, salt, fish sauce, soy sauce, lemon juice and lemon zest bundle.

3. Lock the lid in place and bring the cooker up to full pressure over high heat. Reduce heat to medium-low, just to maintain even pressure, and cook for 8 minutes. Remove from heat and release pressure quickly.

4. Discard lemon zest bundle. Simmer curry, uncovered, to thicken if necessary. Serve over noodles in deep bowls, sprinkled with green onions and cilantro.

Chicken Braised in Cider

This dish is reminiscent of the classic cooking of Normandy, where apple orchards and dairy farms dot the landscape. Fresh green peas or asparagus and mashed potatoes round out this rustic meal.

8 oz	smoky bacon, chopped	250 g
2 lbs	bone-in chicken thighs	1 kg
2	carrots, diced	2
2	cloves garlic, minced	2
1	large onion, chopped	1
1 tsp	dried thyme	5 mL
1 cup	hard apple cider	250 mL
2	egg yolks	2
½ cup	whipping (35%) cream	125 mL
1 tbsp	Dijon mustard	15 mL
	Salt and freshly ground black pepper	
1 tbsp	chopped fresh parsley	15 mL

1. In the pressure cooker, sauté bacon over medium heat until starting to brown. Add chicken, skin side down, and cook for 5 to 10 minutes, until starting to brown. Remove chicken and set aside.

2. Add carrots, garlic and onion to the cooker, stirring up any browned bits, and sauté for 5 minutes. Stir in thyme. Arrange chicken skin side up on top of the vegetables. Pour in cider.

3. Lock the lid in place and bring the cooker up to full pressure over medium-high heat. Reduce heat to medium-low, just to maintain even pressure, and cook for 40 minutes. Remove from heat and release pressure quickly. Remove chicken to a deep platter and keep warm.

4. In a bowl, whisk together egg yolks, cream and mustard. Gradually whisk into the braising liquid, return to medium heat and cook, stirring constantly, until thickened. Do not let boil. Season to taste with salt and pepper. Pour sauce over chicken and sprinkle with parsley.

Speedy "Fried" Chicken

A popular fast-food fried chicken franchise uses pressure frying to create a tender product. While it's not safe to fry in home pressure cookers, this recipe uses the pressure cooker to tenderize the meat, then a hot oven to crisp the skin. The results are fast and delicious — complete with 11 herbs and spices — and a lot healthier than the usual takeout. This method removes a lot of the excess fat and leaves you with a flavorful sauce for making gravy, too. Serve with mashed potatoes or biscuits.

● **TIP**

When preheating the oven, use the convection option if you have it.

- Preheat oven to 475°F (240°C)
- Rack or trivet to fit bottom of pressure cooker

2 tsp	each garlic salt and onion salt	10 mL
1 tsp	salt	5 mL
1 tsp	freshly ground black pepper	5 mL
1 tsp	paprika (hot or mild)	5 mL
1 tsp	dry mustard	5 mL
1 tsp	ground ginger	5 mL
1 tsp	dried oregano	5 mL
½ tsp	each dried basil and thyme	2 mL
¼ tsp	ground allspice	1 mL
2½ lbs	bone-in chicken thighs	1.25 kg
1 cup	water or chicken stock	250 mL
½ cup	dry white wine	125 mL
1 tbsp	all-purpose flour or cornstarch	15 mL

1. In a bowl, combine garlic salt, onion salt, salt, pepper, paprika, mustard, ginger, oregano, basil, thyme and allspice. Rub spice mixture all over chicken.

2. Set rack in the bottom of the pressure cooker and pour in water and wine. Arrange chicken skin side up on the rack.

3. Lock the lid in place and bring the cooker up to full pressure over medium-high heat. Reduce heat to medium-low, just to maintain even pressure, and cook for 10 minutes. Remove from heat and release pressure quickly.

4. Transfer chicken skin side up to a nonstick baking sheet. Bake in preheated oven for 12 to 15 minutes, until skin is brown and crisp.

5. Meanwhile, pour the braising liquid into a measuring cup and let cool. As the fat rises to the top, use a spoon to skim off as much as you can; discard the fat. Transfer defatted braising liquid to a small saucepan and reheat over medium heat. Whisk in flour and simmer, stirring, until bubbly and thickened. Serve chicken drizzled with gravy.

Jerk Chicken

This spicy chicken is extremely tender. Try the jerk paste on pork, too.

Jerk Paste

4	green onions, minced	4
1	Scotch bonnet or jalapeño pepper, chopped	1
1 tbsp	minced gingerroot	15 mL
1 tbsp	dried thyme	15 mL
1 tsp	ground allspice	5 mL
1 tsp	ground cinnamon	5 mL
1 tsp	brown sugar	5 mL
1 tsp	salt	5 mL
½ tsp	grated nutmeg	2 mL
1 tbsp	soy sauce	15 mL
1 tbsp	malt vinegar	15 mL
1 tbsp	canola oil	15 mL
2¼ lbs	bone-in chicken thighs	1.125 kg
¼ cup	water	50 mL

1. *Jerk Paste:* In a food processor or blender, whirl together green onions, Scotch bonnet pepper, ginger, thyme, allspice, cinnamon, brown sugar, salt, nutmeg, soy sauce and vinegar until finely chopped.

2. Rub chicken with paste, slathering it on all sides, then place in a bowl or a large sealable plastic bag. Cover or seal and refrigerate overnight.

3. Remove chicken from paste, discarding excess paste. In the pressure cooker, heat oil over medium heat and lightly brown chicken on all sides. Pour in water.

4. Lock the lid in place and bring the cooker up to full pressure over high heat. Reduce heat to medium-low, just to maintain even pressure, and cook for 20 minutes. Remove from heat and allow pressure to drop naturally.

5. Crisp the chicken quickly on a hot barbecue grill or in a hot skillet. Otherwise, remove the skin before serving.

Cajun-Style Smothered Chicken

Serve this tender, creamy Cajun-spiced chicken over lots of fluffy rice at your next Mardi Gras celebration. Or toss it with hot pasta for a sensational supper.

2¼ lbs	boneless skinless chicken thighs	1.125 kg
1 tsp	salt	5 mL
1 tsp	freshly ground black pepper	5 mL
1 tsp	smoked paprika	5 mL
1 tsp	granulated garlic	5 mL
1 tsp	cayenne pepper	5 mL
3 tbsp	extra-virgin olive oil	45 mL
2 tbsp	granulated sugar	25 mL
2	large onions, chopped	2
1	large red bell pepper, chopped	1
3 tbsp	all-purpose flour	45 mL
½ cup	chicken stock or water	125 mL
1 cup	whipping (35%) cream	250 mL
4	green onions, chopped	4
¼ cup	chopped fresh parsley	50 mL

1. Place chicken in a large bowl and season well on all sides with salt, black pepper, paprika, garlic and cayenne. Set aside.

2. In the pressure cooker, heat oil and sugar over medium heat until sugar begins to brown and caramelize. Working in batches, add chicken and brown on all sides. Remove chicken and set aside.

3. Add onions and red pepper to the cooker, stirring up any browned bits, and sauté for 2 minutes. Stir in flour, then gradually stir in chicken stock. Return chicken and any accumulated juices to the pot and stir to combine.

4. Lock the lid in place and bring the cooker up to full pressure over medium-high heat. Reduce heat to medium-low, just to maintain even pressure, and cook for 15 minutes. Release pressure quickly and remove the lid. Stir in cream and simmer for 5 minutes, until sauce is thickened. Stir in green onions and parsley.

Jamaican Chicken Fricassee

Start the chicken marinating the night before you plan to serve this savory, island-inspired dish, or at least get it going in the morning before you head off to work.

Marinade

	Juice of 1 lime	
2	cloves garlic	2
2 tsp	fresh thyme	10 mL
1	Scotch bonnet pepper	1
1 tbsp	Worcestershire sauce	15 mL
1 tsp	whole or ground allspice	5 mL
	Salt and freshly ground black pepper	
3 lbs	boneless skinless chicken thighs or 4 lbs (2 kg) chicken pieces, skin removed	1.5 kg
1 tbsp	vegetable oil	15 mL
1 tbsp	packed dark brown sugar	15 mL
1	onion, minced	1
3	tomatoes, peeled and chopped	3
1 cup	chicken stock	250 mL
1	bay leaf	1
1 tsp	hot pepper sauce	5 mL
5	green onions, minced	5
	Chopped fresh parsley	

1. *Marinade:* In a food processor or mini-chopper, purée lime juice, garlic, thyme, Scotch bonnet, Worcestershire sauce and allspice. In a large shallow glass dish, pour marinade over chicken pieces and turn to coat well. Cover and refrigerate for at least 2 hours or overnight. Drain, reserving marinade.

2. In the pressure cooker, heat oil and brown sugar over medium-high heat; cook, stirring, until sugar is melted. Add chicken pieces in batches and cook, turning frequently, for about 10 minutes or until browned. Transfer to a bowl and set aside.

3. Reduce heat to medium. Add onion and sauté for 5 minutes. Stir in reserved marinade, tomatoes, stock, bay leaf and hot pepper sauce. Return chicken to the cooker with any accumulated juices.

4. Lock the lid in place and bring the cooker up to full pressure over high heat. Reduce heat to medium-low, just to maintain even pressure, and cook for 10 minutes. Remove from heat and release pressure quickly. Discard bay leaf.

5. Transfer chicken to a warmed deep serving platter. Bring braising liquid to a boil and reduce until thickened to desired consistency. Pour sauce over chicken and garnish with green onions and parsley.

• VARIATION

Scotch bonnet chiles are the hottest type you can buy. Substitute jalapeño or serrano chiles, but up the amount to give this dish the right amount of spicy flavor. Or pass one of those searing Jamaican hot pepper sauces now available for those who like their chicken really smokin'.

Chicken Niçoise

Start with chicken thighs, on or off the bone, for this tasty Mediterranean chicken stew studded with black olives and artichoke hearts. It's even better the second day. Serve it with a French baguette, or over fresh pasta or soft polenta.

TIPS

Instead of the bacon, you could use 1/3 cup (75 mL) slivered ham.

Try using flat-leaf (Italian) parsley instead of the basil.

2¼ lbs	boneless skinless chicken thighs, quartered	1.125 kg
	Salt and freshly ground black pepper	
2 tbsp	extra-virgin olive oil, divided	25 mL
3	thick slices smoky bacon, chopped	3
4	cloves garlic, minced	4
1	large onion, chopped	1
1	large red bell pepper, chopped	1
½ cup	dry white or red wine	125 mL
2 cups	chopped canned tomatoes	500 mL
1 tsp	each dried oregano and thyme	5 mL
1	bay leaf	1
1	can (14 oz/398 mL) artichoke hearts, drained and chopped	1
½ cup	pitted black niçoise or kalamata olives	125 mL
1 tsp	grated lemon zest	5 mL
½ tsp	Asian chili paste (or hot pepper sauce)	2 mL
1 tbsp	chopped fresh basil	15 mL

1. Season chicken with salt and pepper. Set aside.

2. In the pressure cooker, heat half the oil over medium heat. Sauté bacon for 3 minutes. Add chicken and sauté until nicely browned. Remove chicken and bacon and set aside.

3. Add the remaining oil to the cooker. Sauté garlic, onion and red pepper until softened. Stir in wine and simmer for 1 minute, stirring up any browned bits. Add tomatoes, oregano, thyme and bay leaf. Season to taste with salt and pepper. Return chicken, bacon and any accumulated juices to the pot.

4. Lock the lid in place and bring the cooker up to full pressure over medium-high heat. Reduce heat to medium-low, just to maintain even pressure, and cook for 20 minutes. Release pressure quickly and remove the lid. Simmer for 10 minutes, until sauce is thickened. Stir in artichoke hearts, olives, lemon zest and chili paste; simmer until heated through. Serve sprinkled with basil.

Chicken with Chorizo Sausage and Rice

This is a South American–style rice dish, reminiscent of Spanish paella or jambalaya. The timing is critical here — after 10 minutes under pressure, and another 5 minutes of steaming, all of the liquid should be absorbed and the rice should be fluffy.

3 cups	chicken stock	750 mL
6	threads saffron, crushed	6
2 tbsp	extra-virgin olive oil	25 mL
2 lbs	boneless skinless chicken thighs, cut into 2-inch (5 cm) chunks	1 kg
2	cloves garlic, minced	2
1	onion, chopped	1
1	green bell pepper, chopped	1
1	red bell pepper, chopped	1
4 to 8 oz	chorizo or other spicy sausage, chopped (or crumbled if fresh)	125 to 250 g
1¾ cups	long-grain rice	425 mL
2	plum (Roma) tomatoes, seeded and chopped	2
1 cup	frozen peas, thawed	250 mL
2 tbsp	chopped parsley	25 mL

1. In a bowl, stir together stock and saffron; set aside to infuse.

2. In the pressure cooker, heat oil over medium-high heat. Add chicken in batches and cook until browned. Remove chicken to a bowl and set aside.

3. Reduce heat to medium. Add garlic, onion and green and red peppers; sauté for 5 minutes or until onion is softened. Stir in sausage, rice and tomatoes; sauté for another 3 minutes. Arrange browned chicken on top of rice and pour stock mixture over top.

4. Lock the lid in place and bring the cooker up to full pressure over high heat. Reduce heat to medium-low, just to maintain even pressure, and cook for 10 minutes. Remove from heat and allow pressure to drop naturally for 5 minutes. Release any remaining pressure quickly. Stir in peas and sprinkle with parsley.

Cajun Chicken and Beer Stew

Serves 8 to 10

This boneless chicken stew takes its inspiration from the spicy cuisine of Cajun country. You'll need a large 7-quart (7 L) pressure cooker to accommodate this stew — halve the recipe if necessary.

1 tbsp	salt	15 mL
1 tbsp	garlic powder	15 mL
1 tbsp	cayenne pepper	15 mL
4 lbs	boneless skinless chicken thighs, cut into large chunks	2 kg
¼ cup	all-purpose flour	50 mL
¼ cup	extra-virgin olive oil, divided	50 mL
3	cloves garlic, chopped	3
2	stalks celery, chopped	2
1	large onion, chopped	1
1	green bell pepper, chopped	1
1	red bell pepper, chopped	1
1	green chile pepper, seeded and chopped	1
2	bay leaves	2
2 tsp	dried marjoram	10 mL
1	can (14 oz/398 mL) tomatoes, puréed	1
1	bottle (12 oz/341 mL) dark beer (try Big Rock Traditional or Alley Kat ale if you can find it)	1
½ cup	chicken stock	125 mL
1 tbsp	Worcestershire sauce	15 mL
	Salt and freshly ground black pepper	

1. In a small bowl, combine salt, garlic powder and cayenne. Rub chicken all over with 1 tbsp (15 mL) of the spice mixture and let stand at room temperature for 10 minutes.

2. In a plastic bag, combine flour with another 1 tbsp (15 mL) of the spice mixture. Add chicken pieces and shake in spiced flour to coat. Set aside any excess spiced flour.

3. In the pressure cooker, heat 2 tbsp (25 mL) of the oil over medium-high heat. Add chicken in batches and cook until browned. Transfer chicken to bowl and set aside.

4. Reduce heat to medium. Add garlic, celery, onions, green and red bell peppers and chile pepper; sauté for 5 minutes or until onions are tender. Stir in bay leaves, marjoram, tomatoes, beer, stock, Worcestershire sauce and remaining 1 tbsp (15 mL) of spice mixture. Stir in chicken.

5. Lock the lid in place and bring the cooker up to full pressure over high heat. Reduce heat to medium-low, just to maintain even pressure, and cook for 15 to 20 minutes. Remove from heat and release pressure quickly. Discard bay leaves.

6. Meanwhile, in a skillet, heat remaining 2 tbsp (25 mL) oil over medium heat. Sprinkle in 2 tbsp (25 mL) of the reserved spiced flour, adding extra oil if necessary to create a smooth paste; cook, stirring constantly, until the roux turns the color of peanut butter, about 10 minutes. (Be careful — this gets very hot and burns easily.) Whisk a little of the braising liquid from the pressure cooker into skillet. Add this mixture back into the stew and simmer, uncovered, until thick. Season to taste with salt and pepper.

• **TIP**

Mashed potatoes, brown rice or cornbread make perfect accompaniments to this dish.

Spicy Ethiopian Chicken Stew (Doro Wat)

This spicy chicken stew is traditionally served atop large round pieces of injera — a spongy African flatbread made with teff flour. The stew is served communally. The idea is to tear off a bit of bread and use it to scoop up the stew and ferry it to your mouth. You can also serve the chicken over rice, or with fresh flour tortillas.

Berbere Spice Mixture

1 tbsp	hot paprika	15 mL
2 tsp	ground ginger	10 mL
1 tsp	fenugreek seeds	5 mL
1 tsp	salt	5 mL
1/4 tsp	onion powder	1 mL
1/4 tsp	garlic powder	1 mL
1/4 tsp	ground cardamom	1 mL
1/4 tsp	ground coriander	1 mL
1/4 tsp	grated nutmeg	1 mL
1/4 tsp	ground cinnamon	1 mL
1/4 tsp	ground allspice	1 mL
1/4 tsp	cayenne pepper	1 mL
3 lbs	boneless skinless chicken thighs, cut into 2 to 3 pieces	1.5 kg
1/4 cup	unsalted butter	50 mL
2	large onions, chopped	2
3	large cloves garlic, minced	3
1	can (5 1/2 oz/156 mL) tomato paste	1
1 cup	chicken stock	250 mL
1/4 cup	smooth peanut butter	50 mL

1. *Berbere Spice Mixture:* In a spice grinder or blender, grind paprika, ginger, fenugreek, salt, onion powder, garlic powder, cardamom, coriander, nutmeg, cinnamon, allspice and cayenne until powdered.

2. Place chicken in a large bowl and add 1 tbsp (15 mL) of the spice mixture, rubbing the spices over the meat to coat well. Set aside.

3. In the pressure cooker, heat butter over medium heat. Add onions and sauté for 10 minutes, until starting to brown. Stir in garlic and 1 tbsp (15 mL) of the spice mixture; sauté for 1 minute. Stir in tomato paste, chicken stock and peanut butter. Stir in chicken, coating it in sauce.

4. Lock the lid in place and bring the cooker up to full pressure over medium-high heat. Reduce heat to medium-low, just to maintain even pressure, and cook for 15 minutes. Release pressure quickly and remove the lid. Simmer for 5 to 10 minutes, until sauce is thickened.

● **TIP**

Traditionally, this stew includes one hard-boiled egg per diner, so garnish each serving with sliced or chopped hard-boiled eggs, if desired.

Chicken Stew with New Potatoes and Baby Carrots

The dark meat of boneless chicken thighs is perfect in the pressure cooker and makes a classic, homestyle stew.

● **TIP**

Instead of the fresh thyme and sage, you could use ½ tsp (2 mL) each dried thyme and sage.

1 tbsp	vegetable oil	15 mL
3 lbs	boneless skinless chicken thighs, cut into 2-inch (5 cm) chunks	1.5 kg
1	large onion, minced	1
2	cloves garlic, minced	2
1 tbsp	all-purpose flour	15 mL
8 to 10	red new potatoes, halved (or quartered, if large)	8 to 10
3	stalks celery, diced	3
2 cups	baby carrots	500 mL
1	parsnip, peeled and diced	1
1	small turnip, peeled and diced	1
1 cup	chicken stock	250 mL
½ cup	dry white wine or sherry	125 mL
1	bay leaf	1
2 tbsp	chopped fresh parsley	25 mL
1 tsp	chopped fresh thyme	5 mL
1 tsp	chopped fresh sage	5 mL
	Salt and freshly ground black pepper	

1. In the pressure cooker, heat oil over medium heat. Add chicken in batches and cook until browned. Set aside.

2. Drain off all but 1 tbsp (15 mL) of fat. Add onion and garlic; sauté for 2 minutes. Stir in flour, potatoes, celery, carrots, parsnip and turnip. Gradually stir in stock and wine. Add bay leaf. Bring to a boil and return chicken and any accumulated juices to cooker.

3. Lock the lid in place and bring the cooker up to full pressure over high heat. Reduce heat to medium-low, just to maintain even pressure, and cook for 12 minutes. Remove from heat and release pressure quickly.

4. Discard bay leaf. Stir in parsley, thyme and sage. Season to taste with salt and pepper.

Curried Chicken Thighs with Couscous

Garam masala is an Indian spice mixture that you can find in the Asian section of most large supermarkets.

● **TIP**

If you're pressed for time, use 2 tbsp (25 mL) curry paste to replace the minced garlic, chili powder, cayenne, coriander, cumin and turmeric.

2 tbsp	unsalted butter	25 mL
2	cloves garlic, minced	2
1	large onion, finely chopped	1
1 tsp	chili powder	5 mL
½ tsp	cayenne pepper	2 mL
2 tsp	ground coriander	10 mL
1 tsp	each ground cumin and tumeric	5 mL
1 cup	chopped plum (Roma) tomatoes	250 mL
2 lbs	boneless skinless chicken thighs, cut into 1-inch (2.5 cm) cubes	1 kg
	Juice of 1 lemon	
½ tsp	salt	2 mL
½ cup	chicken stock	125 mL
2 tsp	garam masala	10 mL
1	small red bell pepper, cut into slivers	1
1	small zucchini, cut into matchstick strips	1
1 cup	couscous	250 mL
¼ cup	chopped fresh cilantro	50 mL
	Salt	

1. In the pressure cooker, melt butter over medium heat. Add garlic and onion; cook until softened. Add chili powder, cayenne, coriander, cumin, turmeric and tomatoes; sauté until tomatoes are soft. Add chicken and sprinkle with lemon juice and salt. Pour in stock.

2. Lock the lid in place and bring the cooker up to full pressure over high heat. Reduce heat to medium-low, just to maintain even pressure, and cook for 12 minutes. Remove from heat and release pressure quickly.

3. Stir in garam masala, red pepper, zucchini strips and couscous. Return lid to cooker (do not lock into place) or cover with another pot lid and let stand for 5 minutes. Fluff couscous with a fork. Stir in cilantro and season to taste with salt. Serve immediately.

Butter Chicken

Traditionally, butter chicken is made with chicken that has been cooked in a tandoori oven, but you can grill the marinated chicken thighs on the barbecue for this creamy pressure cooker version. Serve with rice or naan.

2	cloves garlic, minced	2
½ cup	plain yogurt	125 mL
2 to 3 tbsp	tandoori paste	25 to 45 mL
1 tbsp	freshly squeezed lemon juice	15 mL
2¼ lbs	boneless skinless chicken thighs	1.125 kg

Sauce

3	cloves garlic, minced or puréed	3
1	2-inch (5 cm) piece gingerroot, minced	1
1	onion, chopped	1
1	can (28 oz/796 mL) tomatoes, with juice	1
½ tsp	salt	2 mL
½ tsp	cayenne pepper	2 mL
3 tbsp	unsalted butter	45 mL
1 tbsp	canola oil	15 mL
1 tbsp	garam masala	15 mL
1 tsp	ground cumin	5 mL
1 tsp	crushed dried fenugreek leaves (kasoori methi)	5 mL
1	jalapeño pepper, seeded and minced	1
¾ cup	whipping (35%) cream	175 mL
¼ cup	ground raw cashews or almonds	50 mL
2 tbsp	granulated sugar	25 mL
2 tbsp	chopped fresh cilantro	25 mL

1. In a large bowl or sealable plastic bag, combine garlic, yogurt, tandoori paste and lemon juice. Add chicken and toss to coat. Cover or seal and refrigerate for at least 4 hours or overnight.

2. Heat the barbecue over high heat. Remove chicken from marinade, discarding excess marinade, and grill for about 5 minutes per side, until well browned on both sides. Let cool slightly, then cut into 2-inch (5 cm) chunks. Set aside.

3. *Sauce:* In a food processor, purée garlic, ginger, onion, tomatoes with juice, salt and cayenne. Set aside.

4. In the pressure cooker, heat butter and oil over medium-high heat until sizzling. Stir in garam masala, cumin and fenugreek; cook, stirring, for 1 minute, until fragrant. Add jalapeño and sauté for 1 minute. Add the reserved purée and stir until starting to boil. Stir in chicken.

5. Lock the lid in place and bring the cooker up to full pressure over medium-high heat. Reduce heat to medium-low, just to maintain even pressure, and cook for 15 minutes. Release pressure quickly and remove the lid. Stir in cream, cashews and sugar; simmer for 5 to 10 minutes, until sauce is thickened. Pour into a serving dish and sprinkle with cilantro.

● **TIPS**

Look for tandoori paste in a jar in the ethnic food section of your supermarket.

For the best results, start marinating the chicken the night before you plan to serve this popular Indian dish.

Turkey with Prunes and Armagnac

This dish is inspired by the classic combination of rabbit, Agen prunes and brandy, which is popular in the southwestern part of France. Turkey makes a great substitute, but by all means try this recipe with rabbit if it is available. The rich, dark sauce in this dish also works well with chicken or duck. Serve it over spaetzle (fresh dumplings), noodles or rice.

● TIP

If you decide to use duck in this recipe, precook it in the pressure cooker to remove the fat before adding it to the sauce. This eliminates the browning step used for turkey. Just place a trivet or steamer basket in the cooker and add 3 cups (750 mL) water. Place 3 lbs (1.5 kg) duck legs in the cooker and steam under full pressure for 10 minutes. Drain, remove trivet, then add remaining ingredients; cook for 10 minutes longer.

¼ cup	all-purpose flour	50 mL
½ tsp	salt	2 mL
¼ tsp	freshly ground black pepper	1 mL
3 lbs	boneless skinless turkey thighs or breast, cut into 8 to 10 pieces	1.5 kg
3 tbsp	extra-virgin olive oil	45 mL
2 oz	finely diced bacon	60 g
4	carrots, sliced	4
2	cloves garlic, minced	2
2 tsp	chopped fresh thyme	10 mL
1	onion, slivered	1
1	stalk celery, minced	1
1 cup	chopped pitted prunes	250 mL
1 cup	dry red wine	250 mL
2 tbsp	liquid honey	25 mL
⅓ cup	Armagnac or other brandy	75 mL
½ cup	water or chicken stock	125 mL

1. In a plastic bag, combine flour with salt and pepper. Add turkey pieces and toss to coat.

2. In the pressure cooker, heat oil over medium heat. Add bacon and cook, stirring, until bacon begins to render its fat. Add turkey in batches and cook until browned. Transfer turkey to a bowl and set aside.

3. Add carrots, garlic, thyme, onion and celery to cooker; sauté for 2 minutes. Add cooked turkey and top with prunes. In a bowl, combine wine, honey, brandy and water; pour over turkey.

4. Lock the lid in place and bring the cooker up to full pressure over high heat. Reduce heat to medium-low, just to maintain even pressure, and cook for 10 minutes. Remove from heat and release pressure quickly.

5. Transfer turkey to a warmed deep platter. If desired, simmer sauce to reduce and thicken; spoon over turkey and serve.

Fish and Seafood

Steamed Rock Cod with Fermented Black Beans and Miso

This is a light and flavorful way to serve fish. Make some fragrant Thai rice and stir-fried bok choy with sesame seeds to serve alongside.

- 7- or 8-inch (18 or 20 cm) glass pie plate (use smaller size if necessary to fit inside pressure cooker)
- Rack or trivet to fit bottom of pressure cooker

2 lbs	rock cod or red snapper fillets	1 kg
1 tsp	salt	5 mL
1 tbsp	red miso paste	15 mL
1 tbsp	rice wine	15 mL
2 tsp	fermented black beans	10 mL
2 tsp	sesame oil	10 mL
1 tsp	dark soy sauce	5 mL
½ tsp	Asian chili paste	2 mL
1	2-inch (5 cm) piece gingerroot, cut into matchsticks	1
2	cloves garlic, minced	2
4	green onions, halved lengthwise and cut into 2-inch (5 cm) pieces	4

1. In a shallow glass dish, rub fish on all sides with salt. In a bowl, combine miso, rice wine, black beans, sesame oil, soy sauce and chili paste. Rub mixture over both sides of fillets. Let stand for 10 minutes.

2. Sprinkle bottom of pie plate with half of the ginger, half of the garlic and half of the green onions; arrange fish fillets over top. Drizzle with any remaining sauce and sprinkle with remaining ginger, garlic and green onions. Set rack in bottom of cooker. Pour in enough water to fill just below top of rack. Place pie plate on rack.

3. Lock the lid in place and bring the cooker up to full pressure over high heat. Reduce heat to medium-low, just to maintain even pressure, and cook for 3 minutes. Remove from heat and release pressure quickly. Serve immediately.

Halibut Steaks with Peppers

Try making this colorful dish in the late summer, when there are lots of pretty peppers in the market. Add a couple of banana peppers for extra spice.

● **TIP**

If halibut is unavailable, use another firm-fleshed fish, such as salmon.

¼ cup	extra-virgin olive oil	50 mL
1	red bell pepper, sliced	1
1	yellow bell pepper, sliced	1
1 cup	zucchini, cut into matchsticks	250 mL
1 tsp	minced garlic	5 mL
½ cup	sliced shallots or leeks	125 mL
1 tbsp	minced fresh thyme	15 mL
1 tbsp	minced fresh rosemary	15 mL
4	halibut steaks, ¾ inch (2 cm) thick, about 1½ lbs (750 g) total	4
1 cup	white wine	250 mL
½ tsp	salt	2 mL
¼ tsp	freshly ground black pepper	1 mL
	Sprigs of thyme or rosemary	

1. In the pressure cooker, heat oil over high heat. Add red and yellow peppers, zucchini, garlic and shallots; sauté for about 10 minutes or until vegetables start to brown. Stir in thyme and rosemary.

2. Place fish in a single layer on the vegetables and pour in wine. Sprinkle with salt and pepper.

3. Lock the lid in place and bring the cooker up to full pressure over high heat. Reduce heat to medium-low, just to maintain even pressure, and cook for 3 to 4 minutes. Remove from heat and release pressure quickly. The fish should flake easily with a fork. If not, return to full pressure and cook for 1 to 2 minutes longer. Remove from heat and release pressure quickly.

4. Serve fish in shallow bowls with rice, topped with the mixed vegetables and a drizzle of the braising liquid. Garnish with sprigs of thyme or rosemary.

Braised Halibut Provençal

The browning of both the fish and the vegetables adds an extra layer of flavor to the final dish.

4	pieces halibut fillet, 1½ inches (4 cm) thick, about 1½ lbs (750 g) total	4
1 tbsp	all-purpose flour	15 mL
3 tbsp	extra-virgin olive oil	45 mL
2	leeks, white and pale green parts only, halved and sliced	2
3	cloves garlic, coarsely chopped	3
2	carrots, thinly sliced	2
1	bulb fennel, white part only, trimmed and slivered	1
1 cup	small mushrooms, halved	250 mL
½	red or yellow bell pepper, diced	½
1	large plum (Roma) tomato, seeded and chopped	1
½ tsp	dried thyme	2 mL
½ tsp	dried oregano	2 mL
½ tsp	salt	2 mL
½ tsp	freshly ground black pepper	2 mL
¼ cup	chicken stock	50 mL
¼ cup	white wine	50 mL
2 tbsp	chopped fresh flat-leaf (Italian) parsley	25 mL
1 to 2 tsp	cornstarch, dissolved in 1 tsp (5 mL) water (optional)	5 to 10 mL

1. Remove skin from halibut, if desired. Dust each fillet on one side with flour. In the pressure cooker, heat oil over high heat until almost smoking. In batches, cook fish, floured side down, for 1 minute or just until golden brown. Transfer to a plate. Set aside.

2. Reduce heat to medium. Add leeks, garlic, carrots, fennel and mushrooms; cook, stirring, for 5 minutes or until beginning to brown and caramelize. Add red pepper and sauté 1 minute longer. Stir in tomato, thyme, oregano, salt and pepper; cook for 30 seconds. Place fish browned side up on top of vegetables; pour in chicken stock and wine.

3. Lock the lid in place and bring the cooker up to full pressure over high heat. Reduce heat to medium-low, just to maintain even pressure, and cook for 3 to 4 minutes, depending on thickness of fish. Remove from heat and release pressure quickly. The fish should flake easily with a fork. If not, return to full pressure and cook for 1 to 2 minutes longer. Remove from heat and release pressure quickly.

4. Transfer fish to a platter and tent with foil to keep warm. If desired, whisk cornstarch mixture into sauce. Bring to a boil; reduce heat and simmer, stirring, until slightly thickened. Spoon sauce over each serving of fish and vegetables. Sprinkle with chopped parsley.

● **TIP**

Leeks are an extremely sweet and flavorful member of the onion family. Trim away all of the dark green tops, then cut the white and pale green bases in half lengthwise and rinse well under running water to remove any grit. Farmers pile soil around leeks as they grow (to keep the bases tender and white), so they can be sandy inside and need to be washed well.

Stuffed Sole

Steamed broccoli and new potatoes rolled in melted butter are perfect alongside this simple fish dish. Steaming the rolls quickly in the pressure cooker keeps delicate white fish very moist and tender.

- Rack or trivet to fit bottom of pressure cooker
- Small bamboo or perforated metal steamer

4 tbsp	unsalted butter, divided	60 mL
1	clove garlic, minced	1
2	green onions, chopped	2
¼ cup	chopped fresh parsley	50 mL
¼ cup	dry bread crumbs	50 mL
1	can (6 oz/170 g) baby shrimp, drained, or crabmeat, drained and shells picked out	1
	Salt and freshly ground black pepper	
6	skinless sole fillets	6
1	lemon, thinly sliced	1

1. In a small skillet, heat 3 tbsp (45 mL) of the butter over medium heat. Add garlic and sauté for 1 minute. Add green onions and sauté for 1 minute. Remove from heat and stir in parsley, bread crumbs and shrimp. Mash slightly, leaving shrimp chunky. Season to taste with salt and pepper.

2. Lay sole on a work surface and spread evenly with stuffing. Starting with one narrow end, roll up jellyroll-style and secure each roll with a toothpick.

3. Set rack in the bottom of the pressure cooker. Pour in 1½ cups (375 mL) water for steaming. Arrange sliced lemons in the bottom of the steamer. Place fish rolls upright, on their spiral ends, on top of the lemons. Dot each roll with some of the remaining butter. Set steamer on the rack.

4. Lock the lid in place and bring the cooker up to full pressure over high heat. Reduce heat to medium-low, just to maintain even pressure, and cook for 4 minutes. Remove from heat and release pressure quickly. Remove sole from the steamer and discard lemon slices.

Steamed Salmon with Red Wine Glaze

While there's not much time to save when cooking fish, the pressure cooker is nevertheless extremely fast and keeps the fish deliciously moist. Careful timing is critical for fish, however, to avoid overcooking. If you have a shallow sauté pan base for your cooker, use it when cooking fish to help cut down on the time it takes for the unit to reach full pressure.

1	small onion, sliced	1
½ cup	dry white wine	125 mL
½ cup	fish stock or clam juice or water	125 mL
2	sprigs thyme	2
2	sprigs parsley	2
4	pieces salmon fillet, skin on, or 4 salmon steaks, about 2 lbs (1 kg) total	4

Glaze

1 tbsp	packed brown sugar	15 mL
½ cup	freshly squeezed orange juice	125 mL
½ cup	dry red wine	125 mL
1 tbsp	tomato paste	15 mL
1 tbsp	unsalted butter	15 mL
	Salt	

1. In the pressure cooker, combine onion, wine, stock, thyme and parsley; bring to a boil. Arrange fish in a single layer in cooker.

2. Lock the lid in place and bring the cooker up to full pressure over high heat. Reduce heat to medium-low, just to maintain even pressure, and cook for 3 minutes. Remove from heat and release pressure quickly. The fish should flake easily with a fork. If not, return to full pressure and cook for 1 to 2 minutes longer. Remove from heat and release pressure quickly.

3. *Glaze:* Meanwhile, in a small saucepan, combine brown sugar, orange juice, wine and tomato paste. Bring to a boil over high heat; cook until reduced to ⅓ cup (75 mL). Whisk in butter and keep warm.

4. Transfer salmon to individual serving plates. Season to taste with salt. Spoon some of the red wine glaze over each serving.

Spicy Salmon Steamed in Greens

Steamed fish is popular in Southeast Asia, and in this recipe, it's salmon that gets an elegant Asian twist. Top salmon fillets with a spicy herbed pesto, then steam in leafy packets — try using large sorrel leaves, Swiss chard, tender napa cabbage or even green corn husks to enclose the fish.

- 1 or 2 small stackable bamboo steamers
- Rack or trivet to fit bottom of pressure cooker

	Large Swiss chard, sorrel or napa cabbage leaves	
4	cloves garlic	4
2	green onions, chopped	2
1	1-inch (2.5 cm) piece gingerroot, chopped	1
¼ cup	chopped fresh cilantro	50 mL
¼ cup	chopped fresh Thai basil	50 mL
2 tbsp	freshly squeezed lime juice	25 mL
1 tbsp	canola oil	15 mL
2 tsp	Asian chili paste	10 mL
½ tsp	cumin seeds	2 mL
½ tsp	fennel seeds	2 mL
½ tsp	salt	2 mL
1½ lb	skinless salmon fillet, cut into 3- by 2-inch (7.5 by 5 cm) pieces	750 g
	Leek or green onion tops (optional)	

1. Remove tough stems from chard leaves and, if too stiff to roll, place on a microwave-safe plate and microwave on High for 30 seconds.

2. In a blender or food processor, combine garlic, green onions, ginger, cilantro, basil, lime juice, oil, chili paste, cumin seeds, fennel seeds and salt; blend to form a smooth paste.

3. Rub fish pieces on both sides with paste. Wrap each piece of fish in a leaf, folding in the sides to enclose completely (you may need to use two leaves, overlapping them slightly). If desired, use leek or green onion tops to tie the packages. Place fish packets seam side down in the steamer (use two stacked steamers, if necessary).

4. Set rack in the bottom of the pressure cooker. Pour in 2 cups (500 mL) water for steaming and bring to a boil. Set or stack steamer(s) on the rack. Lock the lid in place and bring the cooker up to full pressure over high heat. Reduce heat to medium-low, just to maintain even pressure, and steam fish for 3 to 4 minutes, depending on the thickness of the fish. Remove from heat and release pressure quickly. Serve fish in the packets and let diners unwrap at the table.

● TIP

The super-heated steam inside the pressure cooker is perfect for cooking a variety of foods in packages, or "en papillote," as they do in France. Use parchment paper to make packages to steam fish, seafood, chicken breasts and aromatic vegetables and herbs in the pressure cooker. Just fold the paper to seal all of the flavorful juices inside and make sure to leave room between the packages to allow the steam to circulate. Traditionally, parchment is cut into large circles or heart shapes, with the paper folded over the food to form a semicircle that's sealed with several small overlapping folds along the edge. Or try wrapping fish or chicken (even quenelle or tamale mixtures) in banana leaves, as they do in Southeast Asian countries, or corn husks as they do in Mexico. Discard the cooking package before eating.

Steamed Snapper with Baby Bok Choy

Line small bamboo steamers with bok choy, stack them in the pressure cooker, and you'll have an almost instant, healthy meal. Feel free to substitute other white fish in this recipe — pickerel, flounder or sole are also lovely steamed Chinese-style. Serve the fish and bok choy over rice.

- 2 small stackable bamboo steamers
- Rack or trivet to fit bottom of pressure cooker

1 lb	skinless snapper fillets	500 g
1 tbsp	sodium-reduced soy sauce	15 mL
1 tbsp	rice vinegar	15 mL
6	baby bok choy	6
3	green onions, cut into slivers	3
2 tbsp	minced gingerroot	25 mL
2 tbsp	Chinese black bean sauce	25 mL
1 tsp	sesame oil	5 mL

1. Cut fish into 4 single-serving pieces and place in a bowl. Combine soy sauce and rice vinegar and drizzle over fish. Let stand for 15 minutes.

2. Cut bok choy in half lengthwise and rinse well. Line steamers with bok choy and set fish on top. Drizzle fish with any remaining marinade and top with green onions, ginger, black bean sauce and sesame oil.

3. Set rack in the bottom of the pressure cooker. Pour in 2 cups (500 mL) water for steaming. Stack steamers on the rack. Lock the lid in place and bring the cooker up to full pressure over medium-high heat. Reduce heat to medium-low, just to maintain even pressure, and cook for 3 minutes. Remove from heat and release pressure quickly. Transfer steamed vegetables and fish to a warm platter.

Spanish Cod and Mussel Stew with Tomatoes and Green Olives

The pressure cooker instantly infuses and mingles the flavors of this Mediterranean-inspired fish stew. The mixture is hot enough to perfectly steam the mussels at the end without any additional cooking. Serve the stew over polenta or with plenty of French bread.

● TIP

Before cooking, inspect mussels and discard any that do not fully close when tapped. After cooking, discard any mussels that have not opened.

¼ cup	extra-virgin olive oil	50 mL
1	onion, finely chopped	1
2	cloves garlic, minced	2
1 tsp	sweet Spanish paprika	5 mL
¼ tsp	cayenne pepper	1 mL
¼ tsp	crushed saffron threads	1 mL
½ cup	dry white wine	125 mL
1	can (14 oz/398 mL) plum tomatoes, chopped	1
2 oz	prosciutto, cut into slivers	50 g
½ cup	sliced green olives	125 mL
2 lbs	firm white cod (or monkfish or halibut), cut into 2-inch (5 cm) chunks	1 kg
2 lbs	mussels, scrubbed and debearded	1 kg
¼ tsp	salt	1 mL
¼ tsp	freshly ground black pepper	1 mL

1. In the pressure cooker, heat oil over medium heat. Add onion and sauté until soft. Stir in garlic, paprika and cayenne; sauté for 1 minute. Add saffron, wine, tomatoes, prosciutto and green olives. Stir in the fish.

2. Lock the lid in place and bring the cooker up to full pressure over high heat. Reduce heat to low, just to maintain even pressure, and cook for 3 minutes. Remove from heat and release pressure quickly.

3. Add mussels to cooker; cover, but don't lock the lid in place. Bring to a boil, then set aside, covered, for 5 minutes until mussels open. Stir in salt and black pepper.

4. Serve stew in deep soup bowls over polenta, or with lots of crusty bread for sopping up the juices.

East-West Curried Seafood Stew

This is a bouillabaisse with Southeast Asian overtones. It's rich and creamy — the perfect dish for those times when you feel like something a little exotic. Try serving it in shallow bowls over mounds of fragrant basmati or jasmine rice.

2	cloves garlic, minced	2
1	apple, peeled and chopped	1
1	banana, peeled and sliced	1
½ cup	raisins	125 mL
¼ cup	curry powder	50 mL
2 tbsp	packed brown sugar	25 mL
¼ tsp	ground cumin	1 mL
¼ tsp	crushed saffron threads	1 mL
2 cups	unsweetened coconut milk	500 mL
2 cups	chicken stock	500 mL
2 tbsp	freshly squeezed lemon or lime juice	25 mL
1 tsp	Worcestershire sauce	5 mL
¾ cup	whipping (35%) cream	175 mL
12	large mussels, scrubbed and debearded	12
16	large shrimp, peeled and deveined	16
16	sea scallops	16
12 oz	snapper (or halibut or other firm white fish), cubed	375 g
½ cup	cooked chickpeas (see table, page 16)	125 mL
½ cup	diced red bell pepper	125 mL
¼ cup	chopped cilantro	50 mL

1. In the pressure cooker, combine garlic, apple, banana, raisins, curry powder, brown sugar, cumin, saffron, coconut milk, stock, lemon juice and Worcestershire sauce.

2. Lock the lid in place and bring the cooker up to full pressure over high heat. Reduce heat to medium-low, just to maintain even pressure, and cook for 10 minutes. Remove from heat and release pressure quickly.

3. Using an immersion blender or food processor, purée the soup. (If using a food processor, allow soup to cool slightly, then process in batches.) Stir in cream. Add mussels, shrimp, scallops, fish, chickpeas and red peppers.

4. Lock the lid in place and bring the cooker up to full pressure over medium-high heat. Reduce heat to medium-low, just to maintain even pressure, and cook for 2 minutes. Remove from heat and release pressure quickly.

5. Divide fish and seafood between 4 deep soup bowls. Ladle soup over top and sprinkle each serving with cilantro.

TIP

Unsweetened coconut milk comes in a can and is easy to find in Asian markets. It adds an exotic flavor to soups and curries but is high in saturated fat and calories. For most recipes, you can substitute "light" coconut milk, which has half the fat of regular coconut milk. Shake canned coconut milk before opening, as the thick coconut cream sometimes separates and rises to the top.

Cajun Seafood Gumbo

This is truly a meal in a bowl. Boil some rice to serve in the middle of deep serving bowls, and ladle the soup/stew over top. If you don't live in an area where fresh crab is available, substitute frozen or canned crabmeat.

½ cup	vegetable oil, divided	125 mL
1 cup	chopped onions	250 mL
1 cup	chopped red bell pepper	250 mL
¾ cup	chopped celery	175 mL
2 tbsp	minced garlic	25 mL
8 oz	smoked andouille sausages, sliced (or substitute any spicy smoked sausage)	250 g
2 tbsp	dried thyme	25 mL
½ tsp	freshly ground black pepper	2 mL
6 cups	fish stock (see recipe, page 284)	1.5 L
½ cup	all-purpose flour	125 mL
1 lb	large shrimp, peeled and deveined	500 g
1 lb	crabmeat or crawfish meat	500 g
24	oysters, shucked	24
	Salt and cayenne pepper	
½ cup	chopped green onions	125 mL
¼ cup	chopped fresh parsley	50 mL
6 to 8 cups	hot cooked rice	1.5 to 2 L

1. In the pressure cooker, heat 2 tbsp (25 mL) of the oil over medium heat. Stir in onions, red pepper, celery and garlic; sauté for 5 minutes, until vegetables are beginning to brown. Stir in sausages, thyme, black pepper and fish stock.

2. Lock the lid in place and bring the cooker up to full pressure over high heat. Reduce heat to medium-low, just to maintain even pressure, and cook for 10 minutes. Remove from heat and release pressure quickly.

3. In a saucepan, heat remaining oil over medium-low heat. Sprinkle in flour and cook, stirring constantly, until the roux turns the color of peanut butter, about 12 minutes. (Be careful — this gets very hot and burns easily.) Remove from heat and let cool slightly.

4. Whisk some of the broth into the roux and pour mixture into cooker; cook, stirring, until nicely thickened. Add shrimp, crabmeat and oysters.

5. Lock the lid in place and bring the cooker up to full pressure over medium-high heat. Cook for 1 minute. Remove from heat and release pressure quickly.

6. Season to taste with salt and cayenne pepper. Stir in green onions and parsley. Heat through before serving over rice.

● **TIP**

If your oysters arrive shucked in a jar, add the oyster liquor to the stew.

Bouillabaisse

The pressure cooker makes this classic seafood stew super-speedy. You can make the savory broth in advance and reheat it to cook the seafood. Buy your seafood from a good market — fish and seafood should be stored in the cooler or on ice, not wrapped in plastic. Test mussels to ensure they're still alive when you use them. Tap the mussels on the counter; if they don't snap shut, they're dead and you should toss them. When cooked, mussels and clams should pop open; discard any that don't.

Broth

2 tbsp	extra-virgin olive oil	25 mL
3	cloves garlic, minced	3
2	onions, finely chopped (about 2 cups/500 mL)	2
1 cup	slivered fresh fennel (see tip, at left)	250 mL
1	can (14 oz/398 mL) tomatoes, with juice, whirled in a blender until smooth	1
6 cups	fish stock or clam broth	1.5 L
1½ cups	dry white wine	375 mL
3 tbsp	tomato paste	45 mL
1 tsp	saffron threads, crumbled	5 mL
2	bay leaves	2
1	sprig fresh thyme (or ½ tsp/2 mL dried)	1
1	dried red chile pepper, crumbled	1
	Grated zest of 1 orange	
	Salt and freshly ground black pepper	
2 lbs	boneless white fish (such as bass, halibut, sablefish or sole), cut into 1-inch (2.5 cm) pieces	1 kg
2 lbs	mussels or clams, scrubbed and debearded	1 kg
1 lb	large shrimp, peeled and deveined	500 g
	Chopped fresh parsley	
	Sliced baguette	
	Rouille (see recipe, opposite)	

1. *Broth:* In the pressure cooker, heat oil over medium heat. Add garlic, onions and fennel; sauté for 10 minutes. Stir in tomatoes, fish stock, wine, tomato paste, saffron, bay leaves, thyme, chile pepper and orange zest.

2. Lock the lid in place and bring the cooker up to full pressure over high heat. Reduce heat to medium-low, just to maintain even pressure, and cook for 10 minutes. Remove from heat and release pressure quickly. Discard bay leaves and thyme. Season to taste with salt and pepper.

3. Increase heat to high and bring soup to a boil. Add fish, mussels and shrimp. Lock the lid in place and bring back to full pressure over medium-high heat. As soon as the pot reaches full pressure, remove from heat and release pressure quickly. Discard any mussels that are not open.

4. Divide fish and seafood among shallow soup bowls and ladle broth over top. Sprinkle each serving with parsley. Serve with sliced baguette and pass the rouille at the table so diners can add a dollop to their fish stew.

Rouille

Here's a simple version of rouille, a spicy red sauce that's traditionally served with bouillabaisse. In a blender or food processor, combine ¹/₂ cup (125 mL) mayonnaise and 2 to 3 cloves garlic, chopped; blend until smooth. Add ¹/₂ tsp (2 mL) Dijon mustard. With the motor running, through the feed tube, drizzle in ¹/₃ cup (75 mL) extra-virgin olive oil. Add ¹/₂ to 1 tsp (2 to 5 mL) cayenne pepper or hot Hungarian paprika to make it red and spicy. Transfer to a bowl, cover and refrigerate for up to 2 days.

● TIPS

Instead of the fresh fennel, you could use 1 cup (250 mL) slivered celery and 1 tsp (5 mL) fennel seeds or a splash of Pernod.

After step 2, you can cool the broth, refrigerate overnight or for several hours and reheat just before serving.

Portuguese-Style Mussel Stew

In Portugal, the classic combination is pork and clams, but by using fat cultured mussels you can avoid any issues with sand in your stew. The result is a spicy combination to serve over pasta, or with a loaf of fresh Portuguese cornbread on the side.

1 lb	lean boneless pork shoulder, cut into 1-inch (2.5 cm) cubes	500 g
3	cloves garlic, minced	3
1 tbsp	sweet paprika	15 mL
1 tsp	hot paprika	5 mL
½ cup	dry white wine	125 mL
2 tbsp	extra-virgin olive oil	25 mL
1	large onion, chopped	1
8 oz	spicy pork sausage (such as chorizo or Italian sausage), sliced	250 g
1	can (14 oz/398 mL) tomatoes, chopped, with juice	1
1	red bell pepper, chopped	1
1	bay leaf	1
8 oz	spaghetti or linguine	250 g
1 lb	mussels (18 to 24), scrubbed and debearded	500 g
2 tbsp	chopped fresh cilantro	25 mL
2 tbsp	chopped fresh flat-leaf (Italian) parsley	25 mL
1	lemon, cut into wedges	1

1. In a bowl, combine pork, garlic and sweet and hot paprika; stir to coat the meat well. Stir in wine and let stand at room temperature for 30 minutes (or cover and refrigerate for up to 3 hours).

2. In the pressure cooker, heat oil over medium heat. Add onion and sauté until starting to brown. Add pork mixture and sausage; sauté for 5 minutes, until pork is browned on all sides and sausage is no longer pink. Stir in tomatoes with juice, red pepper and bay leaf.

3. Lock the lid in place and bring the cooker up to full pressure over high heat. Reduce heat to medium-low, just to maintain even pressure, and cook for 15 minutes.

4. Meanwhile, in a pot of boiling water, cook spaghetti until tender to the bite.

5. Remove pressure cooker from heat and release pressure quickly. Add mussels. Lock the lid in place and bring back to full pressure over high heat. As soon as the pot reaches full pressure, remove from heat and allow pressure to drop naturally. Discard any mussels that are not open. Stir in cilantro and parsley.

6. Divide spaghetti among deep soup bowls and ladle stew over top. Serve lemon wedges on the side.

TIP

Mussels often have a "beard" protruding from the shell — really just the fibers that help the mollusks attach themselves to rocky outcrops in the ocean. To remove the beard, grab it with your fingers, or a towel, and yank sharply down toward the base, or hinge end, of the mussel. Tear the beard away and discard. Make sure the mussels you buy are alive — the shells should be tightly closed, or should snap closed when you tap the mussel lightly on the counter. Any that aren't closed should be discarded. Store mussels for up to 5 days in the refrigerator, wrapped in wet newspaper or covered with a moist cloth. Don't seal them up — they need to breathe to stay alive.

Braised Baby Squid (or Calamari)

Squid must be cooked either quickly or for a long time to make it tender. This recipe is inspired by the braised squid dishes you find throughout the Mediterranean. Serve it as a hot appetizer with bread for sopping up the sauce, or over short pasta or rice as a main dish. Find precleaned squid tubes at your local fish market.

2 lbs	cleaned baby squid or medium-sized squid tubes, about 4 to 5 inches (10 to 12 cm) long	1 kg
3 tbsp	extra-virgin olive oil	45 mL
2	onions, minced	2
2	cloves garlic, minced	2
1 cup	canned tomatoes with juice, puréed	250 mL
½ cup	white wine	125 mL
Pinch	cayenne pepper	Pinch
	Salt	
¼ cup	minced fresh parsley, divided	50 mL

1. Cut the squid tubes into rings or small squares. Leave the tentacles of baby squid whole.

2. In the pressure cooker, heat the olive oil and sauté the minced onions and garlic until they are beginning to brown. Add the tomato purée, white wine and cayenne, and bring to a boil. Stir in the squid.

3. Lock the lid in place and bring the cooker up to full pressure over medium-high heat. Reduce the heat to medium-low, just to maintain even pressure, and cook for 30 minutes. Remove from heat and release the pressure quickly. Season to taste with salt and stir in 2 tbsp (25 mL) of the parsley.

4. Serve in soup plates and sprinkle with the remaining parsley.

Vegetarian Dishes

Braised Greens

Use Swiss chard, beet greens, turnip greens or spinach in this healthy combination, inspired by the wild *horta* served in the mountains of Greece. Make sure to include some bitter greens like dandelion or endive. A nice side dish to any grilled meat or fish.

1½ lbs	mixed greens (chard, spinach, beet greens, dandelion greens, endive, etc.)	750 g
3	cloves garlic, minced	3
1 tsp	salt	5 mL
1 tsp	vinegar	5 mL
¼ cup	good-quality peppery extra-virgin olive oil	50 mL
1	lemon, cut into wedges	1

1. Wash greens well to remove any grit. Remove woody stems and discard. Roll leafy greens into cigar-like tubes and slice into strips.

2. In the pressure cooker, combine the greens, garlic, 2 cups (500 mL) water, salt and vinegar. Lock the lid in place and bring the cooker up to full pressure over high heat. Reduce heat to medium, just to maintain even pressure, and steam for 10 minutes. Release pressure quickly and remove the lid.

3. Drain excess liquid from greens, if desired, or serve in deep bowls with the juices. Drizzle with olive oil and squeeze fresh lemon juice over each serving.

Chestnuts with Red Cabbage and Apples

This dish makes a nice accompaniment to grilled sausages, baked ham or roast goose, and is a nice holiday alternative to the usual Brussels sprouts. Despite their rich flavor, chestnuts are actually low in fat.

• TIPS

The pressure cooker makes peeling chestnuts fast and easy. Cut an X in the base of each nut and place in the cooker; cover nuts with plenty of water, lock the lid in place, and cook at full pressure for 6 minutes. You'll find it's easy to peel off the shells and the brown, papery skin (which is bitter).

You can also use your pressure cooker to speed-soak the smoky-flavored dried chestnuts sold in Italian and Asian markets throughout the year. Allow 2 minutes of cooking under pressure and 10 minutes of natural pressure release to rehydrate the dried chestnuts.

2 tbsp	unsalted butter	25 mL
1	onion, chopped	1
1 lb	shredded red cabbage	500 g
2	green apples, peeled and cut into wedges	2
1 cup	peeled fresh chestnuts or rehydrated dried chestnuts (see tip, at left)	250 mL
1 tsp	salt	5 mL
½ cup	dry white wine	125 mL
½ cup	water or chicken stock	125 mL
¼ tsp	freshly ground black pepper	1 mL

1. In the pressure cooker, melt butter over medium heat. Add onions and sauté for 5 minutes or until softened. Add cabbage, stirring to coat with butter. Add apples, chestnuts, salt, wine and water.

2. Lock the lid in place and bring the cooker up to full pressure over high heat. Reduce heat to medium-low, just to maintain even pressure, and cook for 10 minutes. Remove from heat and release pressure quickly.

3. Simmer, uncovered, until liquid is reduced. Stir in pepper and serve immediately.

Sweet Pepper and Mushroom Goulash

Portobello mushrooms stand in for meat in this creamy, paprika-laced vegetarian sauce to serve over fat egg noodles.

1 tbsp	unsalted butter	15 mL
1 tbsp	extra-virgin olive oil	15 mL
1	large onion, slivered	1
6	cloves garlic, minced	6
2	large portobello mushrooms, sliced	2
1	red bell pepper, slivered	1
1	yellow bell pepper, slivered	1
½ cup	chopped tomato (fresh or canned) or tomato sauce	125 mL
1 tbsp	sweet Hungarian paprika	15 mL
½ tsp	hot Hungarian paprika	2 mL
½ cup	dry white wine	125 mL
½ cup	water or vegetable stock	125 mL
1 tbsp	Worcestershire sauce	15 mL
½ cup	sour cream	125 mL
2 tbsp	all-purpose flour	25 mL
1 tbsp	chopped fresh dill	15 mL
	Salt and freshly ground black pepper	
12 oz	wide egg noodles, cooked, drained and tossed with butter	375 g

1. In the pressure cooker, heat butter and oil over medium-high heat. Add onion and sauté until starting to soften. Add garlic, mushrooms, red pepper, yellow pepper, tomato, sweet paprika and hot paprika; sauté for about 5 minutes, until vegetables start to soften and give up their juices. Stir in wine, stock and Worcestershire sauce.

2. Lock the lid in place and bring the cooker up to full pressure over medium-high heat. Reduce heat to medium-low, just to maintain even pressure, and cook for 8 minutes. Remove from heat and release pressure quickly.

3. In a bowl, combine sour cream and flour, mixing until smooth. Stir into the stew, return to medium heat and simmer, stirring, for about 5 minutes, until thickened. Stir in dill and season to taste with salt and pepper. Serve over egg noodles.

Thai Vegetable Curry

Serves 4 to 6

The sweet potato in this spicy curry breaks down to thicken the sauce and give it a deep orange color. If seasoned pressed tofu is not available, substitute extra-firm tofu.

1	can (14 oz/398 mL) coconut milk, divided	1
2 tbsp	Thai red curry paste	25 mL
1	orange-fleshed sweet potato, peeled and cubed	1
1	Japanese eggplant, cubed	1
1	small onion, chopped	1
1 tbsp	packed brown sugar	15 mL
2 tbsp	soy sauce	25 mL
1 tbsp	fish sauce (nam pla)	15 mL
	Grated zest and juice of 1 lime	
6	baby bok choy, coarsely chopped	6
1	package (12 oz/375 g) seasoned pressed tofu, cubed	1
¼ cup	fresh cilantro leaves, chopped	50 mL
¼ cup	fresh basil leaves, chopped	50 mL
	Hot cooked basmati rice	

1. In the pressure cooker, combine 2 tbsp (25 mL) of the coconut milk and the curry paste; cook, stirring, over medium heat until fragrant, about 5 minutes. Add sweet potato, eggplant and onion; sauté for 5 minutes. Stir in the remaining coconut milk, brown sugar, soy sauce, fish sauce, lime zest and lime juice.

2. Lock the lid in place and bring the cooker up to full pressure over medium-high heat. Reduce heat to medium-low, just to maintain consistent pressure, and cook for 8 minutes. Remove from heat and release pressure quickly.

3. Stir in bok choy and tofu, return to medium heat and simmer for 5 minutes, until bok choy is wilted. Stir in cilantro and basil. Serve over basmati rice.

Summer Stew

Serves 4

This comforting combination of fresh green or yellow beans with tomatoes, new potatoes and zucchini is perfect in July or August, when the first summer vegetables arrive on the scene.

¼ cup	extra-virgin olive oil	50 mL
1	large onion, chopped	1
3	cloves garlic, chopped	3
2	large tomatoes, seeded and chopped (about 1½ cups/375 mL)	2
2	small (6-inch/15 cm) zucchini or yellow summer squash, cut into rounds or 1-inch (2.5 cm) cubes	2
1	yellow or red bell pepper, chopped	1
6 cups	green and/or yellow (wax) beans, trimmed and cut into 2-inch (5 cm) lengths	1.5 L
2 cups	new potatoes, quartered	500 mL
	Salt and freshly ground black pepper	
1 tbsp	chopped fresh dill or parsley	15 mL

1. In the pressure cooker, heat oil over medium heat. Add onion and sauté for 5 to 10 minutes, until softened but not browned. Add garlic and sauté for 1 minute. Stir in tomatoes, zucchini, yellow pepper, beans and potatoes. Season to taste with salt and pepper.

2. Lock the lid in place and bring the cooker up to full pressure over medium-high heat. Reduce heat to medium-low, just to maintain pressure, and cook for 8 minutes. Remove from heat and release pressure quickly. If the stew seems too watery, return to medium heat and simmer for about 10 minutes to reduce the liquid. Stir in dill. Taste and adjust the seasoning with salt and pepper, if desired.

Green Bean and Potato Curry

Serves 4

This is a simple way to serve your beans in a vegetarian dish. Roti (Indian flatbread) is nice on the side, or serve over rice.

● **TIP**

Ghee is clarified butter. Buy prepared ghee in jars at Indian or South Asian groceries, or make it at home. Simply heat unsalted butter in a saucepan over medium heat until the butter melts and begins to boil, then reduce heat to low and simmer until the water has boiled off and the milk solids drop to the bottom. The ghee is done when the butter turns a clear golden color and the solids in the bottom of the pan are browned. Spoon the ghee into a jar, leaving the milk solids behind. Ghee can be stored in a jar at room temperature for up to 1 month.

2 tbsp	unsalted butter or ghee (see tip, at left)	25 mL
1 tsp	cumin seeds	5 mL
1	onion, chopped (about 1 cup/250 mL)	1
1 tbsp	minced gingerroot	15 mL
2 to 3	plum (Roma) tomatoes, seeded and chopped (about 1½ cups/375 mL)	2 to 3
4 cups	green or yellow (wax) beans (about 1 lb/500 g), trimmed	1 L
2 cups	chopped peeled potatoes (2-inch/5 cm chunks)	500 mL
½ cup	water	125 mL
1 tsp	ground turmeric	5 mL
1 tsp	methi (dried fenugreek leaves), crushed (optional)	5 mL
1 tbsp	chopped fresh cilantro	15 mL
1 tsp	garam masala	5 mL
½ tsp	Asian chili paste	2 mL

1. In the pressure cooker, melt butter over medium-high heat. Add cumin seeds and stir until starting to sizzle and pop. Add onion and ginger; sauté for 5 minutes, until onion is softened and starting to brown. Stir in tomatoes, beans, potatoes, water, turmeric and methi (if using).

2. Lock the lid in place and bring the cooker up to full pressure over medium-high heat. Reduce heat to medium-low, just to maintain even pressure, and cook for 8 minutes. Remove from heat and release pressure quickly. Stir in cilantro, garam masala and chili paste.

Curried Potatoes with Carrots and Peas

You can add any vegetable to this savory vegetarian dish. Add some chopped zucchini or red pepper for extra color and crunch, or try using a combination of potatoes and cauliflower. Serve with roti (Indian flatbread) or rice.

2 tbsp	unsalted butter or ghee (see tip, page 177)	25 mL
1 tsp	cumin seeds	5 mL
1	onion, chopped (about 1 cup/250 mL)	1
2	cloves garlic, minced	2
1 tbsp	minced gingerroot	15 mL
2 to 3	plum (Roma) tomatoes, seeded and chopped (about 1 1/2 cups/375 mL)	2 to 3
2 cups	chopped peeled potatoes (2-inch/5 cm chunks)	500 mL
2 cups	sliced carrots (about 5)	500 mL
1 cup	baby peas and/or chopped zucchini	250 mL
1/2 cup	water	125 mL
1 tsp	ground turmeric	5 mL
1 tsp	methi (dried fenugreek leaves), crushed (optional)	5 mL
1/2 tsp	salt	2 mL
1/4 cup	chopped fresh cilantro	50 mL
1 tsp	garam masala	5 mL
1/2 tsp	Asian chili paste	2 mL

1. In the pressure cooker, melt butter over medium-high heat. Add cumin seeds and stir until starting to sizzle and pop. Add onion and sauté for 5 minutes, until softened and starting to brown. Stir in garlic and ginger; sauté for 1 minute. Stir in tomatoes, potatoes, carrots, peas, water, turmeric, methi and salt.

2. Lock the lid in place and bring the cooker up to full pressure over medium-high heat. Reduce heat to medium-low, just to maintain even pressure, and cook for 6 minutes. Remove from heat and release pressure quickly. Stir in cilantro, garam masala and chili paste.

Spanish Potatoes and Chickpeas

With its rich, garlicky saffron sauce, this dish is the ultimate vegetarian comfort food. Serve it in little bowls with crusty bread for a hot tapas starter, as an everyday main course, or as an exotic side dish with fried fish. For a more substantial (non-vegetarian) version, fry ½ cup (125 mL) chopped chorizo sausage or prosciutto ham with the onions and potatoes.

1 cup	dried chickpeas	250 mL
¼ cup	extra-virgin olive oil	50 mL
4	Yukon gold potatoes (or other yellow-fleshed variety), peeled and cut into 1-inch (2.5 cm) cubes	4
2	onions, chopped	2
5	large cloves garlic, minced	5
½ tsp	saffron threads	2 mL
3	bay leaves	3
3 cups	vegetable stock or water	750 mL
1 tbsp	sweet Spanish paprika	15 mL
1½ cups	quartered artichoke hearts (1 can, 14 oz/398 mL)	375 mL
	Salt and freshly ground black pepper	
3 tbsp	chopped fresh parsley	45 mL
	Shaved Parmesan (optional)	
	Lemon wedges (optional)	

1. Soak chickpeas overnight in water to cover or use the quick pressure-soak method (page 208). Drain.

2. In the pressure cooker, heat oil over medium heat. Add potatoes and onions; sauté until onions are tender. Add garlic and saffron; sauté for 1 minute. Stir in chickpeas, bay leaves and stock.

3. Lock the lid in place and bring the cooker up to full pressure over high heat. Reduce heat to medium-low, just to maintain even pressure, and cook for 18 minutes. Remove from heat and release pressure quickly.

4. Discard bay leaves. Stir in paprika and artichoke hearts. Simmer, uncovered, over medium heat, breaking up some of the potatoes, until the stew is nicely thickened. Season to taste with salt and pepper. Stir in parsley. If desired, serve with shaved Parmesan and lemon wedges to squeeze over top.

Mediterranean Chickpea Stew

Serve this vegetarian stew over cooked brown rice or barley, and crumble a little feta cheese on top for extra flavor. The eggplant breaks down to form a silky sauce.

1½ cups	dried chickpeas	375 mL
1	large purple eggplant, unpeeled	1
1 tsp	salt	5 mL
½ cup	extra-virgin olive oil, divided	125 mL
1	onion, slivered	1
3	cloves garlic, minced	3
1	can (14 oz/398 mL) diced tomatoes, with juice	1
1 tsp	granulated sugar	5 mL
1 tsp	freshly ground black pepper	5 mL
½ tsp	paprika	2 mL
¼ tsp	ground cumin	1 mL
¼ cup	chopped fresh flat-leaf (Italian) parsley	50 mL
	Hot cooked brown rice or barley	
	Crumbled feta cheese (optional)	

1. Soak chickpeas overnight in water to cover or using the quick pressure-soak method (page 208). Drain and set aside.

2. Cut eggplant into cubes and toss with salt. Set in a colander in the sink to drain for 30 minutes, then rinse with cold water and squeeze dry.

3. Meanwhile, in the pressure cooker, combine chickpeas and 4 cups (1 L) cold water. Lock the lid in place and bring the cooker up to full pressure over high heat. Reduce heat to medium-low, just to maintain even pressure, and cook for 10 minutes. Remove from heat and allow pressure to drop naturally. Drain chickpeas and set aside. Wipe cooker clean.

4. In the pressure cooker, heat 2 tbsp (25 mL) of the oil over medium heat. Add onion and sauté for 10 minutes, until starting to brown. Add garlic and sauté for 2 minutes. Add eggplant and the remaining oil; sauté for 5 minutes. Stir in chickpeas, tomatoes with juice, sugar, pepper, paprika and cumin.

5. Lock the lid in place and bring the cooker up to full pressure over medium-high heat. Reduce heat to medium-low, just to maintain even pressure, and cook for 10 minutes. Remove from heat and allow pressure to drop naturally. Stir in parsley. Serve over brown rice and, if desired, garnish with crumbled feta.

● **TIP**

Brown rice is only partially milled and, because its brown husk is intact, it has significantly more vitamins, fiber and flavor than more highly processed white rice. Because it retains its healthy oils and endosperm, brown rice has a shorter shelf life — about 6 months — and takes a little longer to cook, but it is well worth the effort when it comes to nutrition. Brown rice has a lovely, nutty flavor and slightly chewy texture that's perfect for risotto and pilafs with chicken, nuts and vegetables.

Chickpea Salad with Roasted Onions and Bell Pepper

This flavorful and healthy salad is ideal for taking to a picnic or to carry on a hike. The salad is delicious on the day you make it, but just as good the next day. You'll be amazed how toothsome and delicious chickpeas can be when cooked from scratch in the pressure cooker.

1 cup	dried chickpeas	250 mL
1	red bell pepper	1
1	large onion	1
1	head garlic	1
2 tsp	extra-virgin olive oil	10 mL
2	plum (Roma) tomatoes, seeded and chopped	2
1 tbsp	chopped fresh thyme (or 1 tsp/5 mL dried)	15 mL
1 tbsp	chopped fresh sage leaves (or 1 tsp/5 mL dried)	15 mL
1 tsp	sea salt	5 mL
½ tsp	freshly ground black pepper	2 mL
½ tsp	cayenne pepper	2 mL
¼ cup	extra-virgin olive oil	50 mL
3 tbsp	freshly squeezed lemon juice	45 mL
¼ cup	minced Italian parsley	50 mL

1. Soak chickpeas overnight in water to cover or use the quick pressure-soak method (page 208). Drain.

2. In the pressure cooker, combine chickpeas and 4 cups (1 L) cold water. Lock the lid in place and bring the cooker up to full pressure over high heat. Reduce heat to medium-low, just to maintain even pressure, and cook for 15 minutes. Remove from heat and allow pressure to drop naturally. Drain. Transfer to a large bowl.

3. Meanwhile, on the barbecue or under the broiler, char the red pepper. Place in a bag to cool. Peel off skin, remove seeds and chop. Add to chickpeas in bowl. Wrap onion and garlic, unpeeled, in a piece of foil and drizzle with the 2 tsp (10 mL) olive oil. Roast in a preheated 400°F (200°C) oven for 45 minutes or until very soft. Peel onion and cut into slivers; add to chickpeas in bowl. Squeeze garlic out of skins into the bowl.

4. Add tomatoes, thyme, sage, salt, black pepper, cayenne, $1/4$ cup (50 mL) olive oil and lemon juice; toss to coat. Cool to room temperature and let stand for 1 hour to allow flavors to meld. Just before serving, stir in parsley.

● **TIP**

Roasting vegetables concentrates their sugars and flavors. It's a great way to prepare vegetables as a side dish or to add to pasta, sauces and salads. Many vegetables are perfect for roasting. Just peel and cut into even pieces, toss with a little olive oil and roast in a 400°F (200°C) oven until tender and starting to brown, from 30 to 45 minutes depending on the vegetable. Onions and garlic should be wrapped loosely in foil, but other vegetables — tomatoes, carrots, winter squash, peppers, cauliflower, potatoes, sweet potatoes — need only to be tossed with 1 to 2 tbsp (15 to 25 mL) oil and spread out on a rimmed baking sheet. For extra flavor, add some chopped fresh herbs, such as thyme or rosemary, and some sea salt and pepper.

Eggplant and Chickpea Curry

Eggplant is used a lot in classic Indian cuisine. In this delicious dish, it forms a rich, silky sauce to balance the toothsome chickpeas. Serve the curry over lots of hot, aromatic basmati rice or with toasted naan.

⅔ cup	dried chickpeas	150 mL
2	large purple eggplants, unpeeled (about 1½ lbs/750 g total)	2
1 tbsp	sea salt	15 mL
3 tbsp	extra-virgin olive oil	45 mL
1	large onion, chopped	1
4	cloves garlic, minced	4
1	red bell pepper, cut into ½-inch (1 cm) squares	1
1 tbsp	minced gingerroot	15 mL
1 tsp	ground coriander	5 mL
1 tsp	ground cumin	5 mL
1 tsp	ground turmeric	5 mL
1 tsp	garam masala	5 mL
	Seeds from 2 cardamom pods	
1	can (19 oz/540 mL) tomatoes, chopped, with juice	1
1 cup	water	250 mL
1 tsp	granulated sugar	5 mL
2 tsp	Asian chili paste	10 mL
2	potatoes, peeled and cubed	2
3 tbsp	chopped fresh cilantro	45 mL
	Salt	
	Hot cooked basmati rice or toasted naan	

1. Soak chickpeas overnight in water to cover or using the quick pressure-soak method (page 208). Drain and set aside.

2. Cut eggplants into cubes and place in a bowl. Add salt and fill bowl with cold water. Let stand for 30 minutes, then drain well and squeeze eggplant dry. Set aside.

3. Meanwhile, in the pressure cooker, combine chickpeas and 4 cups (1 L) cold water. Lock the lid in place and bring the cooker up to full pressure over high heat. Reduce heat to medium-low, just to maintain even pressure, and cook for 15 minutes. Remove from heat and allow pressure to drop naturally. Drain chickpeas and set aside. Wipe cooker clean.

4. In the pressure cooker, heat oil over medium heat. Add onion and sauté for 10 minutes, until starting to brown. Add garlic and eggplant; sauté for 5 minutes. Add red pepper, ginger, coriander, cumin, turmeric, garam masala and cardamom seeds; sauté for 1 minute. Stir in tomatoes with juice, water, sugar and chili paste. Stir in potatoes and chickpeas.

5. Lock the lid in place and bring the cooker up to full pressure over high heat. Reduce heat to medium-low, just to maintain even pressure, and cook for 20 minutes. Remove from heat and allow pressure to drop naturally. Remove the lid, return to medium heat and simmer for about 10 minutes, until thickened. Stir in cilantro and season to taste with salt. Serve over basmati rice or with naan.

TIP

There are many different kinds of eggplant, but the most common are the large, deep purple Mediterranean eggplant and the lighter, long and slender Asian varieties. The former can be bitter and should be sliced and salted, then rinsed to remove any of the dark juices; Asian eggplants tend to be sweeter and don't require salting.

Boston "Baked" Beans

Serves 6

While this pressure cooker version of classic baked beans is vegetarian, feel free to add about 8 oz (125 mL) sautéed chopped bacon or salt pork for a richer, more traditional flavor.

3 cups	dried white navy beans or Great Northern beans	500 mL
2	cloves garlic, minced	2
1 cup	chopped onions	250 mL
1 cup	tomato sauce	250 mL
¼ cup	packed brown sugar	50 mL
¼ cup	light (fancy) molasses	50 mL
2 tbsp	extra-virgin olive oil	25 mL
2 tbsp	Dijon mustard	25 mL
¼ tsp	freshly ground black pepper	1 mL
1 to 2 tsp	salt	5 to 10 mL

1. Soak beans overnight in water to cover or use the quick pressure-soak method (page 208). Drain.

2. In the pressure cooker, combine beans with 6 cups (1.5 L) cold water. Lock the lid in place and bring the cooker up to full pressure over high heat. Reduce heat to medium-low, just to maintain even pressure, and cook 6 minutes for navy beans or 10 minutes for Great Northern. Remove from heat and allow pressure to drop naturally. Drain.

3. Whisk ½ cup (125 mL) water into cooker, along with the garlic, onions, tomato sauce, brown sugar, molasses, oil, mustard and pepper. Stir in beans.

4. Lock the lid in place and bring the cooker up to full pressure over high heat. Reduce heat to medium-low, just to maintain even pressure, and cook for 2 minutes. Remove from heat and allow pressure to drop naturally. The beans should be tender. If not, add a little water (if necessary) and lock the lid in place. Return to full pressure and cook for 2 to 3 minutes longer. Remove from heat and allow pressure to drop naturally.

5. Drain off any excess liquid or let beans sit, covered, for 30 minutes, until more of the liquid is absorbed. Season to taste with salt.

Beans and Greens

This classic Italian combination makes a lovely winter side dish or, when served with rice, a simple vegetarian meal.

● **TIP**

Purée any leftovers in a food processor and combine with some crumbled goat cheese for a hearty dip to scoop up with pita chips.

1 cup	dried white beans	250 mL
6 tbsp	extra-virgin olive oil, divided	90 mL
4	cloves garlic, minced (2 to 3 tbsp/25 to 45 mL)	4
8 cups	chopped greens (such as mustard greens, kale or broccoli rabe)	2 L
1½ cups	vegetable stock	375 mL
2 tsp	Asian chili paste (or 1 tsp/5 mL hot pepper flakes)	10 mL
1 tsp	balsamic vinegar	5 mL
	Salt and freshly ground black pepper	

1. Soak beans overnight in water to cover or using the quick pressure-soak method (page 208). Drain.

2. In the pressure cooker, combine beans, 1 tbsp (15 mL) of the oil and 4 cups (1 L) cold water. Lock the lid in place and bring the cooker up to full pressure over high heat. Reduce heat to medium-low, just to maintain even pressure, and cook for 5 minutes. Remove from heat and allow pressure to drop naturally. Drain beans and set aside. Wipe cooker clean.

3. In the pressure cooker, heat 4 tbsp (60 mL) of the oil over medium heat. Add garlic and sauté for 2 minutes. Stir in beans, greens, vegetable stock and chili paste.

4. Lock the lid in place and bring the cooker up to full pressure over medium-high heat. Immediately remove from heat and let the pressure drop naturally. Remove the lid, return to medium heat and simmer for about 10 minutes, until most of the liquid is absorbed. Season to taste with vinegar and salt and pepper. Serve with the remaining oil drizzled over top.

Caribbean Red Beans and Barley

Here's a flavorful combination of Canadian beans and barley, with a burst of Island heat. It's the perfect side dish for Jamaican Chicken Fricassee (see recipe, page 138).

● **TIP**

Use pearl or hulled barley; in the pressure cooker, pearl barley needs about 7 minutes to cook, while hulled barley takes twice as long, about 15 minutes.

1 cup	dried red kidney beans	250 mL
2	cloves garlic, minced	2
2	stalks celery, chopped	2
1	small onion, chopped	1
1½ cups	pearl or hulled barley (see tip, at left)	375 mL
1	whole Scotch bonnet pepper or 2 whole jalapeño peppers	1
2 tsp	dried thyme	10 mL
2 cups	unsweetened coconut milk	500 mL
3	green onions, minced	3
1 tbsp	unsalted butter	15 mL
	Salt and freshly ground white pepper	

1. Soak beans overnight in water to cover or use the quick pressure-soak method (page 208). Drain.

2. In the pressure cooker, combine beans, garlic, celery, onion and 4 cups (1 L) water. Lock the lid in place and bring the cooker up to full pressure over high heat. Reduce heat to medium-low, just to maintain even pressure, and cook for 10 minutes. Remove from heat and allow pressure to drop naturally.

3. Stir in barley, Scotch bonnet pepper, thyme and coconut milk. Lock the lid in place and bring the cooker up to full pressure over high heat. Reduce heat to medium-low, just to maintain even pressure, and cook 7 minutes for pearl barley, 15 minutes for hulled barley. Remove from heat and allow pressure to drop naturally.

4. Discard Scotch bonnet pepper. Stir in green onions and butter. Season to taste with salt and white pepper. Serve immediately.

Warm Gigandes Bean Salad

I discovered these giant white beans while on a trip to Greece. Use any large white bean, but try to find an heirloom variety like these meaty white beans, which are as big as your thumb and are usually available at Greek or Mediterranean groceries. Serve as a side dish alongside grilled meats, or as a starter salad over sturdy mixed greens, such as romaine, curly chicory and arugula.

1 cup	dry gigandes beans	250 mL
2	plum (Roma) tomatoes, seeded and finely chopped	2
⅓ cup	air-cured black olives, seeded and chopped	75 mL
¼ cup	extra-virgin olive oil (preferably Greek)	50 mL
	Grated zest and juice of ½ lemon (about 1 tsp/5 mL minced zest and 2 tbsp/25 mL juice)	
2 tbsp	basil pesto (homemade or commercial)	25 mL
	Salt and freshly ground black pepper	

1. Soak beans overnight in water to cover or use the quick pressure-soak method (page 208).

2. Drain the beans and place th[...]sure cooker. Add enough cold water to cover t[...]ches. Lock the lid in place and bring the coo[...] [pr]essure over high heat. Cook for 12 minut[...] [t]he pressure to drop naturally (this helps to ke[...]tact). Drain beans well.

3. While the beans are cooking, c[...] [cho]pped tomatoes, olives, olive oil, lemo[...] in a bowl. Stir in the warm beans and pest[...]e with salt and pepper.

Curried Lentils with Spinach

With a pressure cooker, this classic Indian dish is ready in a fraction of the time normally required to prepare it. Serve as a side dish with an Indian meal, as a healthy accompaniment to lamb or pork, or simply over a pile of basmati rice.

2 tbsp	vegetable oil	25 mL
2	dried hot chile peppers, crushed	2
½ tsp	cumin seeds	2 mL
½ tsp	yellow mustard seeds or dried mustard	2 mL
½ tsp	ground coriander	2 mL
2	cloves garlic, minced	2
1	onion, minced	1
1	large tomato, seeded and chopped	1
1 tbsp	minced gingerroot	15 mL
1 cup	brown or green lentils	250 mL
½ tsp	salt	2 mL
3½ cups	water	875 mL
2 tbsp	freshly squeezed lemon juice	25 mL
2 cups	fresh spinach, washed thoroughly and finely chopped (or 1 package frozen chopped spinach, thawed and squeezed dry)	500 mL
	Coriander chutney or mango chutney as a condiment	

1. In the pressure cooker, heat oil over medium heat. Add hot peppers, cumin seeds, mustard seeds and coriander; sauté for about 20 seconds or until fragrant. Add garlic, onion, tomato and ginger; sauté for 3 minutes or until vegetables are soft and tomato begins to break down. Stir in lentils, salt, water, lemon juice and spinach.

2. Lock the lid in place and bring the cooker up to full pressure over high heat. Reduce heat to medium-low, just to maintain even pressure, and cook for 12 minutes. Remove from heat and allow pressure to drop naturally.

3. Simmer, uncovered, to reduce liquid if necessary. Serve over basmati rice with a dollop of coriander or mango chutney on the side.

Green Lentil and Spinach Gratin

Start this simple vegetarian combination of toothsome lentils and silky spinach in the pressure cooker, then finish it quickly under the broiler. Brown rice is the perfect accompaniment.

- Preheat broiler
- Shallow 8-cup (2 L) casserole dish

1	onion, quartered	1
1	large carrot, quartered	1
1	stalk celery, cut into chunks	1
3 tbsp	extra-virgin olive oil	45 mL
1	bay leaf	1
1½ cups	green lentils, rinsed and drained	375 mL
2½ cups	vegetable stock	625 mL
4 cups	chopped baby spinach	1 L
2 tbsp	unsalted butter	25 mL
2	cloves garlic, slivered	2
¼ cup	whipping (35%) cream	50 mL
Pinch	grated nutmeg	Pinch
½ cup	shredded Gruyère or freshly grated Parmesan cheese	125 mL
	Salt and freshly ground black pepper	

1. In a food processor, pulse onion, carrot and celery until finely chopped.

2. In the pressure cooker, heat oil over medium heat. Add chopped vegetables and sauté for 5 minutes, until softened and fragrant. Stir in bay leaf and lentils, then vegetable stock.

3. Lock the lid in place and bring the cooker up to full pressure over high heat. Reduce heat to medium-low, just to maintain even pressure, and cook for 10 minutes. Remove from heat and allow pressure to drop naturally. Transfer lentil mixture to the casserole dish and stir in spinach. Set aside.

4. In a skillet, melt butter over medium heat. Add garlic and sauté for about 1 minute, until just beginning to color and brown (be careful not to burn it). Stir in cream and nutmeg; simmer for 1 minute. Add cheese, stirring to create a smooth, creamy sauce. Season to taste with salt and pepper.

5. Drizzle cheese sauce over lentil mixture. Broil for 5 to 10 minutes, until brown and bubbly.

Creamy Lentils and Cheddar

This vegetarian dish is simple and homey — your high-fiber alternative to mac and cheese. Try it as a side dish with sliced grilled bratwurst, European frankfurters or ham.

2	cloves garlic, minced	2
1 cup	brown or green lentils	250 mL
1 cup	chopped onions	250 mL
1	carrot, grated	1
1	yellow or red bell pepper, minced	1
1	bay leaf	1
½ tsp	dried thyme	2 mL
1	can (14 oz/398 mL) tomatoes, puréed	1
1 cup	water	250 mL
½ cup	whipping (35%) cream	125 mL
1 cup	shredded old Cheddar cheese	250 mL

1. In the pressure cooker, combine garlic, lentils, onions, carrot, red pepper, bay leaf, thyme, tomatoes and water. Make sure cooker is no more than half full.

2. Lock the lid in place and bring the cooker up to full pressure over high heat. Reduce heat to medium-low, just to maintain even pressure, and cook for 10 minutes. Remove from heat and allow pressure to drop naturally. The lentils should be tender. If not, return to full pressure and cook for 2 to 4 minutes longer. Remove from heat and allow pressure to drop naturally.

3. Discard bay leaf. Stir in cream and bring to a boil. Reduce heat and simmer until the sauce is thickened. Remove from heat and add cheese; stir gently until cheese is melted and combined.

Curried Chicken Thighs with Couscous (page 147)

Braised Halibut Provençal (page 154)

East-West Curried Seafood Stew (page 162)

Green Bean and Potato Curry (page 177)

Chunky Tex-Mex Chili over Crispy Rice Cake (page 198)

Paella (page 228)

Italian Sausage Risotto with Peas (page 234)

Barley with Mint and Root Vegetables (page 238)

Lemon-Lime Cheesecake (page 252)

Sticky Toffee Pudding (page 264)

Apricot Bread-and-Butter Pudding with Brandy Cream Sauce (page 274)

Mixed Berry and Red Fruit Jam (page 295)

Mixed Dhal

In India, almost any kind of curried bean or lentil dish is called dhal, as are the various legumes that go into this daily fare. Feel free to alter the dhal according to what you have in your pantry — any type of bean or lentil will work. This combination of toor dhal (yellow split peas), moong dhal (mung beans) and masoor dhal (tiny red lentils) is a favorite, and the coconut milk adds a little southern Indian flair. Serve over basmati rice.

● TIPS

Leftovers can be thinned with water or broth for a tasty lentil soup.

Instead of the cilantro, you can stir in 1 tbsp (15 mL) coriander chutney.

½ cup	dried yellow split peas	125 mL
½ cup	red lentils	125 mL
½ cup	dried mung beans	125 mL
2 tbsp	unsalted butter or ghee (see tip, page 177)	25 mL
1 tbsp	black mustard seeds or kalonji seeds	15 mL
2 tsp	cumin seeds	10 mL
4	cloves garlic, minced	4
1	large onion, chopped	1
1	1-inch (2.5 cm) piece gingerroot, grated	1
1 tbsp	ground coriander	15 mL
1 tsp	ground turmeric	5 mL
1 to 2 tsp	Asian chili paste	5 to 10 mL
2	cans (each 19 oz/540 mL) diced tomatoes, with juice	2
2 cups	vegetable stock or water	500 mL
⅔ cup	unsweetened coconut milk or half-and-half (10%) cream	150 mL
	Salt and freshly ground black pepper	
¼ cup	chopped fresh cilantro	50 mL

1. Rinse peas, lentils and mung beans separately. Combine in a bowl, cover with cold water and soak for 15 minutes. Drain.

2. In the pressure cooker, melt butter over medium-high heat. Add black mustard and cumin seeds; stir until starting to sizzle and pop. Add garlic, onion and ginger; sauté for 10 minutes, until onion is light brown. Stir in coriander, turmeric and chili paste to taste; sauté for 1 minute. Stir in tomatoes with juice, vegetable stock and dhal mixture.

3. Lock the lid in place and bring the cooker up to full pressure over medium-high heat. Reduce heat to medium-low, just to maintain even pressure, and cook for 10 minutes. Remove from heat and allow pressure to drop naturally.

4. Stir in coconut milk, return to low heat and simmer until heated through. Season to taste with salt and pepper. Stir in cilantro.

Warm Lemon Lentil Salad

Use the regular brown or green lentils in this dish or the smaller French green (Puy) lentils if you can find them. Lentil salad is a traditional French first course, but also makes a nice base for grilled fish or lamb chops.

1	sprig thyme	1
1	sprig rosemary	1
1	bay leaf	1
1 cup	brown or green lentils	250 mL
2	cloves garlic, peeled	2
1	carrot, quartered	1
3 cups	water	750 mL
1 tbsp	vegetable oil	15 mL

Dressing

	Grated zest of 1 lemon, minced	
	Juice of 1 lemon (about 3 tbsp/45 mL juice)	
2 tsp	chopped fresh thyme (or 1 tsp/5 mL dried)	10 mL
1	clove garlic, minced	1
1 tsp	salt	5 mL
1 tbsp	Dijon mustard	15 mL
¼ cup	extra-virgin olive oil	50 mL
	Freshly ground black pepper	
4	plum (Roma) tomatoes, seeded and chopped	4
3	green onions, chopped	3
¼ cup	chopped fresh parsley	50 mL
	Mixed greens	

1. Using kitchen string, tie thyme, rosemary and bay leaf into a bundle. In the pressure cooker, combine herb bundle, lentils, garlic, carrot, water and oil.

2. Lock the lid in place and bring the cooker up to full pressure over high heat. Reduce heat to medium-low, just to maintain even pressure, and cook for 8 minutes. Remove from heat and allow pressure to drop naturally. Drain well. Discard herb bundle, carrot and garlic. Transfer lentils to a bowl.

3. *Dressing:* In a bowl, whisk together lemon zest, lemon juice, thyme, garlic, salt and mustard. Slowly whisk in olive oil to emulsify. Season to taste with pepper.

4. Pour dressing over the lentils and toss to coat. Stir in tomatoes, green onions and parsley. Serve salad warm over mixed greens or as a base for grilled meat or fish.

● TIP

In place of the fresh herb bundle, use a tea ball containing 1 tsp (5 mL) dried thyme, 1 tsp (5 mL) dried rosemary and a bay leaf. Remove from cooker at the end of step 2.

Chickpea and Mixed Vegetable Stew

Serves 8

This substantial stew provides a gardenful of healthy vegetables in one pot. Here's proof positive that vegetarian food can be hearty enough for the coldest winter day.

1 cup	dried chickpeas	250 mL
2 tbsp	extra-virgin olive oil	25 mL
3	cloves garlic, minced	3
2	stalks celery, chopped	2
1	onion, chopped	1
2	large potatoes, peeled and chopped	2
1	red bell pepper, chopped	1
1	large carrot, chopped	1
½ cup	red lentils	125 mL
2 cups	vegetable stock	500 mL
½ cup	dry white wine	125 mL
3 tbsp	chopped fresh basil or basil pesto	45 mL
1 tbsp	chopped fresh rosemary	15 mL
	Salt and freshly ground black pepper	
2 cups	polenta, cooked (see recipe, opposite)	500 mL
	Extra-virgin olive oil for drizzling	
½ cup	freshly grated Parmesan cheese	125 mL

1. Soak chickpeas overnight in water to cover or use the quick pressure-soak method (page 208). Drain.

2. In the pressure cooker, combine chickpeas and 4 cups (1 L) cold water. Lock the lid in place and bring the cooker up to full pressure over high heat. Reduce heat to medium-low, just to maintain even pressure, and cook for 14 minutes. Remove from heat and allow pressure drop naturally. Drain. Set aside.

3. Wipe cooker clean. Add oil and heat over medium heat. Add garlic, celery and onion; sauté until onion is soft. Add potatoes, red pepper and carrot; toss to coat with oil. Add chickpeas, lentils, stock and wine.

4. Lock the lid in place and bring the cooker up to full pressure over high heat. Reduce heat to medium-low, just to maintain even pressure, and cook for 5 minutes. Remove from heat and allow pressure to drop naturally.

5. Stir in basil and rosemary. Heat, uncovered, over low heat for 5 minutes; season to taste with salt and pepper. Serve stew in deep bowls over a mound of soft polenta, drizzled with extra-virgin olive oil and sprinkled with Parmesan.

Polenta

8 cups	water	2 L
2 cups	coarsely ground cornmeal	500 mL
½ cup	finely grated Parmesan cheese	125 mL
¼ cup	butter	50 mL

1. In a large heavy saucepan, bring water to a boil. Reduce heat to low and add cornmeal in a slow, thin stream, whisking constantly. With a wooden spoon, stir every minute or so until the mixture pulls away from the side of the pan in one mass. Depending on the coarseness of the cornmeal, this will take from 5 to 20 minutes. Stir in cheese and butter.

● **TIP**

This is the kind of vegetable stew that morphs easily into a hearty soup. Just whirl any leftover soup in the food processor until smooth (or leave it slightly chunky), thin with vegetable or chicken stock, then heat through.

Chunky Tex-Mex Chili over Crispy Rice Cake

This is a vegetarian family favorite, created and endorsed by my friend Deb Cummings. You can use leftover rice and save time by using the pressure cooker to precook enough beans for a week.

● **TIP**

Tex-Mex cheese mix usually consists of shredded Cheddar, mozzarella and jalapeño Jack cheese.

1½ cups	dried black beans	375 mL
1½ cups	short-grain white rice	375 mL
2 cups	shredded Tex-Mex cheese mix or spiced Monterey Jack cheese	500 mL
1 tbsp	minced seeded jalapeño pepper	15 mL
8	green onions, white and green parts chopped separately	8
1	can (14 oz/398 mL) diced tomatoes, with juice	1
1 tbsp	chili powder	15 mL
¾ cup	frozen corn kernels, thawed (or canned corn kernels)	175 mL
4 tbsp	chopped fresh cilantro, divided	60 mL
	Salt and freshly ground black pepper	
1	egg, lightly beaten	1
1 tbsp	canola oil	15 mL
	Additional shredded cheese	

1. Soak beans overnight in water to cover or using the quick pressure-soak method (page 208). Drain and set aside.

2. In a heavy saucepan, combine rice and 3 cups (750 mL) water; bring to a boil. Reduce heat to low, cover and cook for about 20 minutes, until water is absorbed and rice is tender. Remove from heat and stir in cheese and jalapeño. Let cool.

3. Meanwhile, place beans in the pressure cooker and add 6 cups (1.5 L) cold water. Lock the lid in place and bring the cooker up to full pressure over high heat. Reduce heat to medium-low, just to maintain even pressure, and cook for 8 minutes. Remove from heat and allow pressure to drop naturally.

4. Drain beans and return to the cooker. Stir in white parts of green onions, tomatoes with juice and chili powder. Lock the lid in place and bring the cooker up to full pressure over medium-high heat. Reduce heat to medium-low, just to maintain even pressure, and cook for 4 minutes. Release pressure quickly and remove the lid. Simmer for 1 minute to thicken. Stir in green parts of green onions, corn and half the cilantro. Season to taste with salt and pepper. Keep warm.

5. Mix egg into rice mixture. In a large nonstick skillet, heat oil over high heat. Add rice mixture and, using a spatula, press into even layer, covering the bottom of the skillet completely. Reduce heat to medium, cover and cook for about 10 minutes, until bottom of pancake is brown and crisp. Turn pancake out onto a cutting board, brown side up, and cut into quarters.

6. Place a piece of rice pancake in each shallow soup bowl and spoon chili over top. Garnish with the remaining cilantro and shredded cheese.

● **TIP**

The rice can be made a day ahead and stored in the refrigerator. Mix in the beaten egg just before cooking.

Vegetarian Barley, Lentil and Black Bean Chili

Here's a great alternative to traditional meat-based chili. The beans, lentils and grains combine to form a complete protein — plus a chewy, meaty texture that will satisfy any carnivore.

● TIP

Choose a jalapeño pepper for a modest amount of heat. For extra fire, use a Scotch bonnet pepper.

2 tbsp	vegetable oil	25 mL
3	cloves garlic, minced	3
1	large Spanish onion, chopped	1
1	jalapeño, Scotch bonnet or serrano pepper, seeded and minced	1
1 cup	brown or green lentils	250 mL
1 cup	cooked black beans (see page 16 for cooking times)	250 mL
1 cup	pearl barley	250 mL
3 tbsp	chili powder	45 mL
1 tbsp	sweet Hungarian paprika	15 mL
1 tsp	dried oregano	5 mL
1 tsp	ground cumin	5 mL
6 cups	vegetable stock	1.5 L
1	chipotle pepper in adobo sauce, chopped	1
1	can (28 oz/796 mL) plum (Roma) tomatoes, crushed	1
	Salt and freshly ground black pepper	

1. In the pressure cooker, heat oil over medium heat. Add garlic and onion; sauté until tender. Add jalapeño and sauté for 1 minute. Stir in lentils, black beans, barley, chili powder, paprika, oregano, cumin, stock, chipotle pepper and tomatoes.

2. Lock the lid in place and bring the cooker up to full pressure over high heat. Reduce heat to medium-low, just to maintain even pressure, and cook for 10 minutes. Remove from heat and allow pressure to drop naturally for 10 minutes. Release any remaining pressure quickly. The barley and lentils should be tender. If not, return to full pressure for 2 to 3 minutes longer. Remove from heat and allow pressure to drop naturally.

3. Simmer, uncovered, until thickened. Season to taste with salt and pepper.

Barley Risotto Primavera

This dish is just like the famous Italian specialty, but made with whole barley for a unique prairie twist.

● **TIP**

To save preparation time, mince onion, garlic, zucchini, carrot and celery in a food processor.

2 tbsp	extra-virgin olive oil	25 mL
1 cup	pearl or pot barley	250 mL
1	small onion, minced	1
1	clove garlic, minced	1
½ cup	finely chopped zucchini	125 mL
¼ cup	minced carrot	50 mL
¼ cup	minced celery	50 mL
2½ cups	vegetable stock or water	625 mL
1 tsp	tamari soy sauce	5 mL
¼ cup	freshly grated Parmesan cheese	50 mL
Pinch	freshly ground black pepper	Pinch

1. In the pressure cooker, heat oil over medium heat. Add barley and sauté for 1 minute or until toasted. Add onion, garlic, zucchini, carrot and celery; sauté for 1 minute longer or until vegetables begin to soften. Stir in the stock and soy sauce.

2. Lock the lid in place and bring the cooker up to full pressure over high heat. Reduce heat to medium-low, just to maintain even pressure, and cook for 18 minutes. Remove from heat and allow pressure to drop naturally.

3. Fluff risotto with a spoon. Stir in Parmesan cheese and pepper. Serve immediately.

Biryani

You can add almost any vegetable or meat to this wonderful Indian rice dish. It makes the perfect accompaniment to tandoori chicken or grilled lamb. And while this version is vegetarian, feel free to experiment by adding cooked meats to make it into a non-vegetarian main dish. Stir in cooked leftover chicken, beef or lamb after releasing pressure, then heat through before serving.

● TIP

Garam masala is an Indian spice mixture that you can find in the Asian section of most large supermarkets.

2 tbsp	vegetable oil	25 mL
2 tsp	salt	10 mL
2 tsp	sweet Spanish or Hungarian paprika	10 mL
2 tsp	ground turmeric	10 mL
2 tsp	garam masala	10 mL
½ tsp	cayenne pepper	2 mL
1	onion, halved and sliced	1
½ cup	small mushrooms, halved	125 mL
½	green bell pepper, diced	½
1 cup	basmati rice	250 mL
½ cup	small florets cauliflower	125 mL
½ cup	diced carrots	125 mL
¼ cup	chopped dried apricots or raisins	50 mL
2 cups	water or vegetable stock	500 mL
½ cup	frozen peas, thawed	125 mL

1. In the pressure cooker, heat oil over low heat. Add salt, paprika, turmeric, garam masala and cayenne; cook, stirring, for 1 minute.

2. Increase heat to medium. Add onion, mushrooms and green pepper; sauté for 2 to 3 minutes or until the mushrooms begin to give up their liquid. Stir in rice, cauliflower, carrots and apricots. Pour in water.

3. Lock the lid in place and bring the cooker up to full pressure over high heat. Reduce heat to medium-low, just to maintain even pressure, and cook for 7 minutes. Remove from heat and allow pressure to drop naturally for 2 minutes; release remaining pressure quickly.

4. Stir in the peas. Replace cover on cooker (but do not lock) and let steam for 5 minutes. Fluff with a fork.

Japanese Brown Rice with Shiitakes

This is a rich, hearty rice dish — sort of an Asian risotto. For a vegetarian feast, top with a medley of stir-fried vegetables. If you're not a vegetarian, it's perfect alongside grilled salmon or tuna that has been brushed with soy sauce and ginger, or with slices of grilled flank steak.

1 cup	dried shiitake mushrooms	250 mL
3 cups	hot water	750 mL
¼ cup	soy sauce	50 mL
1 tbsp	canola oil	15 mL
1	small onion (or 2 shallots), finely chopped	1
2 cups	short-grain brown rice	500 mL
2	green onions, slivered	2
½	sheet nori (seaweed), shredded (or 2 tbsp/25 mL chopped wakame)	½
1 tsp	sesame oil	5 mL
2 tbsp	toasted sesame seeds	25 mL

1. Soak mushrooms in hot water for 30 minutes, until softened. Drain, reserving soaking liquid. Squeeze mushrooms to remove any excess liquid. Chop mushrooms, discarding any tough stems, and set aside. Strain soaking liquid through a fine-mesh sieve or coffee filter to remove any grit. Measure soaking liquid and add enough water to make $3\frac{1}{2}$ cups (875 mL). Stir in soy sauce and set broth aside.

2. In the pressure cooker, heat oil over medium heat. Add onion and sauté for 10 minutes, until starting to brown. Add rice and sauté for 2 minutes, until toasted. Stir in mushrooms and broth.

3. Lock the lid in place and bring the cooker up to full pressure over high heat. Reduce heat to medium-low, just to maintain even pressure, and cook for 15 minutes. Remove from heat and allow pressure to drop naturally. Stir in green onions, nori and sesame oil. Serve sprinkled with sesame seeds.

Vegetable Couscous

Couscous is one of those wonderful accompaniments that add interest to everyday meals without a lot of fuss. This is an almost instant vegetarian meal in a pot, featuring plenty of healthy vegetables and exotic Moroccan flavors.

1 cup	dried chickpeas	250 mL
2 tbsp	extra-virgin olive oil	25 mL
1	onion, chopped	1
1	clove garlic, minced	1
1	red or yellow bell pepper, chopped	1
2 tsp	ground cumin	10 mL
1 tsp	Hungarian paprika	5 mL
½ tsp	salt	2 mL
¼ tsp	freshly ground black pepper	1 mL
¼ tsp	ground cinnamon	1 mL
Pinch	cayenne pepper	Pinch
¼ cup	currants or raisins	50 mL
2 cups	vegetable stock	500 mL
1½ cups	couscous	325 mL
1	small zucchini, diced	1
1 cup	frozen green peas, thawed	250 mL
3 tbsp	chopped fresh cilantro	45 mL

1. Soak chickpeas overnight in water to cover or use the quick pressure-soak method (page 208). Drain.

2. In the pressure cooker, combine chickpeas and 4 cups (1 L) cold water. Lock the lid in place and bring the cooker up to full pressure over high heat. Reduce heat to medium-low, just to maintain even pressure, and cook for 14 minutes. Remove from heat and allow pressure to drop naturally. Drain if necessary.

3. Wipe cooker clean. Add oil and heat over medium heat. Add onion, garlic and red pepper; sauté until softened. Stir in cumin, paprika, salt, pepper, cinnamon and cayenne; cook for 2 minutes. Stir in chickpeas and currants. Pour in stock.

4. Lock the lid in place and bring the cooker up to full pressure over high heat. Reduce heat to medium-low, just to maintain even pressure, and cook for 4 minutes. Remove from heat and release pressure quickly. Stir in couscous, zucchini and peas. Let stand, covered, for 10 minutes. Fluff with a fork and stir in cilantro.

Savory Bread Pudding

Serves 4

This is the perfect way to use up that stale baguette. It makes a tasty vegetarian meal or an easy make-ahead brunch dish — just assemble the night before for quick cooking in the morning. Classic comfort food!

• TIPS

For the bread cubes, a day-old baguette with lots of crusty bits is best.

For the shredded cheese, try Gruyère, Gouda or fontina.

- 8-inch (20 cm) soufflé dish, buttered
- Rack or trivet to fit bottom of pressure cooker

2 tbsp	extra-virgin olive oil	25 mL
1	onion, thinly sliced	1
3	cloves garlic, minced	3
1	red bell pepper, chopped	1
4 cups	whole-grain bread cubes	1 L
3 cups	chopped spinach	750 mL
3 tbsp	chopped fresh dill	45 mL
2 cups	shredded cheese	500 mL
4	eggs, lightly beaten	4
1 cup	milk	250 mL
½ tsp	salt	2 mL
½ tsp	freshly ground black pepper	2 mL

1. In a nonstick skillet, heat oil over medium-low heat. Add onion and sauté for 20 to 30 minutes, until caramelized. Add garlic and red pepper; sauté until tender.

2. In a large bowl, toss onion mixture with bread cubes, spinach and dill. Mix in cheese. In another bowl, whisk eggs, milk, salt and pepper. Pour over bread mixture and stir to make sure the custard soaks into the bread. Pour into prepared soufflé dish and cover with buttered foil, sealing well.

3. Set rack in the bottom of the pressure cooker. Pour in 2 cups (500 mL) water for steaming. Fold a 2-foot (60 cm) long piece of foil several times to make a strip strong enough to lift the dish. Center dish on midpoint of strip and fold the ends together to make a handle. Lower the dish into the cooker.

4. Lock the lid in place and bring the cooker up to full pressure over high heat. Reduce heat to medium-low, just to maintain even pressure, and cook for 40 minutes. Remove from heat and release pressure quickly. Using foil handle, lift dish out of the cooker onto a cooling rack and let cool for 10 minutes. Remove foil lid and serve hot from the dish.

Chinese Braised Tofu Puffs with Mushrooms

Serves 4 to 6

This is a sweet and spicy vegetarian stew — add more chili paste or some hot pepper sauce if you like it fiery. You can also substitute frozen tofu for the tofu puffs to create something closer to a meat sauce to spoon over rice or pan-fried Chinese noodles. Freeze the tofu first, and it will crumble naturally.

1½ cups	vegetable stock	375 mL
2 tbsp	brown sugar	25 mL
2 tbsp	dark soy sauce	25 mL
2 tbsp	hoisin sauce	25 mL
2 tsp	Asian chili paste	10 mL
2 tbsp	canola oil	25 mL
4	cloves garlic, minced	4
1 tbsp	minced or grated gingerroot	15 mL
12	fresh shiitake mushrooms (or reconstituted dried shiitakes), sliced (about 2 cups/500 mL)	12
1	package (4 oz/114 g) deep-fried tofu puffs, cut into ½-inch (1 cm) thick slices	1
1 tsp	cornstarch, dissolved in 2 tsp (10 mL) cold water	5 mL
3	green onions, chopped	3
1 tbsp	toasted sesame seeds	15 mL

1. In a bowl, combine vegetable stock, brown sugar, soy sauce, hoisin sauce and chili paste. Set aside.

2. In the pressure cooker, heat oil over medium-high heat. Add garlic and ginger; sauté for 1 minute. Add mushrooms and sauté for about 5 minutes, until starting to brown. Stir in stock mixture and tofu puffs.

3. Lock the lid in place and bring the cooker up to full pressure over medium-high heat. Reduce heat to medium-low, just to maintain even pressure, and cook for 5 minutes. Remove from heat and release pressure quickly.

4. Whisk the cornstarch solution into the sauce and simmer, stirring, over medium heat until sauce is thickened and clear and tofu is nicely glazed. Stir in green onions. Serve sprinkled with sesame seeds.

Beans and Grains

Tips for Preparing Beans

Soaking Methods

All beans need to be soaked before cooking. Soaking rehydrates the beans and helps to remove some of the complex sugars (or oligosaccharides) that give beans a bad name in polite company. There are several procedures for soaking beans, which are described below.

Traditional soaking. If you have time, just put your beans in a pot with 3 or 4 times their volume in water and let them sit for 4 to 8 hours at room temperature.

Quick soaking. To speed up the soaking process, you can place the beans and water in a pot and bring them to a full, rolling boil. Simmer the beans for 2 minutes, then remove the pot from the heat, cover it, and let the beans soak for 1 hour. Drain away those gaseous complex carbs and proceed with your recipe.

Pressure soaking. You can speed up the soaking process even further by using the pressure cooker. Place beans and water in the pressure cooker (3 cups/750 mL water for every 1 cup/250 mL beans, plus 1 tbsp/15 mL vegetable oil if you have a jiggle-top cooker). Lock the lid in place and bring up to full pressure over high heat. What you do next depends on the size and type of beans you are preparing.

- For small beans, remove the cooker from the heat immediately and let the pressure come down naturally for 10 minutes before releasing remaining steam using the quick-release valve.

- For larger beans, cook under pressure for 1 minute, then allow the pressure to come down naturally for 10 minutes.

- For chickpeas and very large beans, cook for 2 to 3 minutes on high pressure before allowing the pressure to come down naturally for 10 minutes, then releasing any pressure with the quick-release valve.

Checking whether beans are fully soaked

The goal of soaking is to have water penetrate to the center of the bean. You can check this by cutting one open to make sure the color is even. An opaque spot in the center indicates the bean needs further soaking, or that you will have to add a few minutes of cooking time while pressure cooking the beans.

Special Precautions for Pressure Cooking Beans and Lentils

If you like legumes or cook a lot of vegetarian dishes, the pressure cooker is a miracle. It allows you to cook inexpensive and healthy dried beans in minutes. Still, there are some precautions to take when you're cooking beans and lentils under pressure.

Leave room for the beans to cook. Make sure you never overload the pressure cooker when cooking beans. Because beans and lentils froth up and expand substantially (up to 4 times their dry size and weight) while cooking, never fill the pressure cooker more than one-third full.

Use enough water. Always use at least 2 cups (500 mL) water or other liquid for every 1 cup (250 mL) dry beans in a recipe. If you have an old-fashioned jiggle-top pressure cooker, always watch it carefully while cooking beans, since the vent can easily become clogged. If it does, you will hear a loud hissing noise. Immediately remove the cooker from the heat and release the pressure. As noted above in the section on soaking beans, jiggle-top pressure cooker users should add 1 tbsp (15 mL) oil to the beans and water before cooking to help reduce foaming and potential clogging.

Watch your cooking time. Cooking times for beans can vary substantially, depending on a variety of factors, such as the age and dryness of the beans. Even local humidity can affect cooking times. Where a recipe offers a range of cooking times, it's always best to start with the shorter one. You can always finish the beans conventionally or add another minute or two of pressure cooking if they're not quite done. To check for doneness, cut a bean in half with a sharp knife and look at the center. If the beans are done, they will be one color throughout, and tender.

Let pressure drop naturally. When cooking time is complete, remove the cooker from the heat and allow it to stand until the pressure indicator drops. This helps to avoid clogging the center pipe and safety valve with pulpy cooking liquid. It also prevents the beans from splitting.

Keep your cooker clean. Always clean the pressure regulator and lid carefully after cooking beans to make sure there are no obstructions.

No salt. Never add salt to a bean recipe before cooking. If you do, the beans can become tough and never really soften properly.

Basic Heirloom Beans

Heirloom beans are older, unusual varieties, often found in specialty health food stores and ethnic markets or through mail-order sources. It's a revelation to cook varieties such as Vallarta, Rio Zape or Yellow Indian Woman beans — their flavor and texture are far beyond those of the white and red varieties we all know, and every variety tastes completely different, even when prepared the same way. This is a good basic recipe to serve as a side dish or for a speedy vegetarian meal when you want the unique flavors of heirloom beans to shine.

● **TIP**

To season the beans after they're cooked, try adding a chopped chipotle pepper in adobo sauce with chopped cilantro for a Latin meal, or stir chopped rosemary and thyme, with a little minced garlic and butter or cream, into a pot of tiny French flageolets.

1 cup	dried heirloom beans (see tip, at left)	250 mL
2	cloves garlic	2
1	carrot, coarsely chopped	1
1	small onion, coarsely chopped	1
1	stalk celery, coarsely chopped	1
1 tbsp	extra-virgin olive oil	15 mL
	Salt and freshly ground black pepper	

1. Soak beans for 4 hours in water to cover or using the quick pressure-soak method (page 208). Drain, reserving 2 cups (500 mL) of the soaking liquid, and set aside.

2. In a food processor, pulse garlic, carrot, onion and celery until minced.

3. In the pressure cooker, heat oil over medium-high heat. Add minced vegetables and sauté for 10 minutes, until fragrant. Stir in beans and reserved soaking liquid.

4. Lock the lid in place and bring the cooker up to full pressure over high heat. Reduce heat to medium-low, just to maintain even pressure, and cook for 10 to 14 minutes (depending on the size and age of the beans). Remove from heat and allow pressure to drop naturally. Remove the lid, return to medium heat and simmer until slightly thickened. Season to taste with salt and pepper.

Braised Lima Beans and Bacon

Look for a good butcher where the bacon is double-smoked in-house. The stronger, extra-smoky flavor means that you can use only a small amount of bacon — and therefore add less fat to the dish — without compromising taste.

1 tbsp	extra-virgin olive oil	15 mL
2	slices double-smoked bacon, chopped	2
1	small onion, chopped	1
1	clove garlic, minced	1
1	package (1 lb/450 g) frozen baby lima beans	1
½ tsp	freshly ground black pepper	2 mL
1	small plum (Roma) tomato, chopped	1
¼ cup	water	50 mL
2 tbsp	chopped parsley	25 mL

1. In the pressure cooker, heat oil over medium-high heat. Add bacon, onion and garlic; sauté until bacon is partly crisp and onion is softened. Stir in lima beans, pepper, tomato and water.

2. Lock the lid in place and bring the cooker up to full pressure over high heat. Reduce heat to medium-low, just to maintain even pressure, and cook for 10 minutes. Remove from heat and release pressure quickly. Stir in parsley. Serve immediately.

Warm White Beans with Fresh Tomatoes and Pasta

Toss this combination of warm white beans, fresh tomato sauce and cheese with short pasta for a simple vegetarian supper, or skip the pasta and serve the bean mixture alongside grilled fish.

1 cup	dried small white beans	250 mL
3	cloves garlic, minced	3
¼ cup	packed fresh basil leaves	50 mL
¼ cup	packed fresh flat-leaf (Italian) parsley leaves	50 mL
1 tsp	sea salt	5 mL
½ tsp	freshly ground black pepper	2 mL
½ cup	extra-virgin olive oil	125 mL
1 tsp	Asian chili paste	5 mL
3 cups	chopped tomatoes (or diced canned tomatoes)	750 mL
1 tsp	extra-virgin olive oil	5 mL
2 cups	short pasta (such as rotini, orechiette or fusilli)	500 mL
8 oz	aged fontina cheese, finely diced	250 g

1. Soak beans overnight in water to cover or using the quick pressure-soak method (page 208). Drain and set aside.

2. In a food processor, purée garlic, basil, parsley, salt, pepper, ½ cup (125 mL) oil and chili paste. Transfer to a bowl and stir in tomatoes. Set aside.

3. In the pressure cooker, combine beans, 4 cups (1 L) cold water and 1 tsp (5 mL) oil. Lock the lid in place and bring the cooker up to full pressure over high heat. Reduce heat to medium-low, just to maintain even pressure, and cook for 8 minutes. Remove from heat and allow pressure to drop naturally.

4. Meanwhile, cook pasta according to package directions until al dente (tender to the bite). Drain and keep warm.

5. Drain the beans, reserving a little of the cooking liquid. Add beans and tomato mixture to pasta. Stir in enough of the reserved cooking liquid to make the mixture a bit saucy. Stir in cheese. Serve warm or at room temperature.

White Beans with Orzo and Feta

This is a quintessential Mediterranean combination — simple vegetarian fare that's both healthy and hearty. It's perfect for a potluck buffet or a simple summer supper. The oil-cured black olives add a real punch of flavor.

1 cup	dried small white beans	250 mL
1¼ cups	orzo or other small pasta	300 mL
2	cloves garlic, chopped	2
1 lb	baby spinach or Swiss chard, finely shredded or chopped	500 g
2	roasted red bell peppers (from a jar), drained and chopped	2
½ cup	oil-cured black olives, pitted and chopped	125 mL
½ cup	extra-virgin olive oil	125 mL
¼ cup	freshly squeezed lemon juice	50 mL
¾ cup	crumbled sheep feta cheese	175 mL
¼ cup	chopped fresh basil or dill	50 mL
	Sea salt and freshly ground black pepper	

1. Soak beans overnight in water to cover or using the quick pressure-soak method (page 208). Drain and set aside.

2. Cook the orzo in plenty of salted water, according to the package directions, until tender. Drain and set aside.

3. In the pressure cooker, combine beans, garlic and 4 cups (1 L) cold water. Lock the lid in place and bring the cooker up to full pressure over high heat. Reduce heat to medium-low, just to maintain even pressure, and cook for 8 minutes. Remove from heat and allow pressure to drop naturally.

4. Quickly drain beans and return to the cooker. Add spinach, stirring until bright green and wilted. Stir in roasted peppers, olives, oil and lemon juice. Stir in orzo, feta and basil. Season to taste with salt and pepper. Serve warm or at room temperature.

Great Northern Beans Navarre-Style

This recipe draws its inspiration from Spain, where cooks traditionally use that country's famous *jamón ibérico* to flavor the beans. Here we use ham or prosciutto with good results. Serve this savory side dish as an accompaniment to grilled or roasted lamb.

1½ cups	dried Great Northern beans	375 mL
1 tbsp	extra-virgin olive oil	15 mL
3 tbsp	minced smoky ham or prosciutto	45 mL
3	cloves garlic, minced	3
1	large onion, peeled and chopped	1
1	carrot, finely chopped or grated	1
1	bay leaf	1
1	large plum (Roma) tomato, seeded and chopped	1
¼ tsp	freshly ground black pepper	1 mL
	Salt	
2 tbsp	chopped fresh parsley	25 mL

1. Soak beans overnight in water to cover or use the quick pressure-soak method (page 208). Drain.

2. In the pressure cooker, heat oil over medium heat. Add ham, garlic, onion, carrot, bay leaf, tomato and pepper; sauté until vegetables are softened. Stir in beans and 4 cups (1 L) water.

3. Lock the lid in place and bring the cooker up to full pressure over high heat. Reduce heat to medium-low, just to maintain even pressure, and cook for 10 minutes. Remove from heat and allow pressure to drop naturally. Drain, if necessary.

4. Discard bay leaf. Season to taste with salt and stir in the parsley.

Campfire Beans with Cheese

This fast and easy dish makes a healthy alternative to mac and cheese that kids love. For adult tastes, you can torque up the spice with more hot pepper sauce at the table.

2 cups	dried pinto beans	500 mL
1	ham hock or ham bone	1
1	onion, peeled, whole	1
3 tbsp	unsalted butter	45 mL
8 oz	old Cheddar cheese, shredded	250 g
1 cup	finely chopped onions	250 mL
2	cloves garlic, minced	2
1 to 2 tsp	hot pepper sauce (Prairie Fire, Tabasco, Durkee's or other hot sauce)	5 to 10 mL
	Salt and freshly ground black pepper	

1. Soak beans overnight in water to cover or use the quick pressure-soak method (page 208). Drain.

2. In the pressure cooker, combine beans, ham hock, whole onion and 4 cups (1 L) water. Lock the lid in place and bring the cooker up to full pressure over high heat. Reduce heat to medium-low, just to maintain even pressure, and cook for 10 minutes. Remove from heat and allow pressure to drop naturally.

3. Drain, reserving liquid. Discard onion. Remove hock; cut away any meat from bone, chop and set aside. Discard bone and scraps. Return meat and beans to cooker; stir in butter, cheese, minced onions, garlic and hot pepper sauce to taste. Stir to combine well, adding enough of the reserved cooking liquid to make a creamy sauce. Warm gently over low heat until cheese melts; simmer, stirring, just until everything is tender. Season to taste with salt and pepper. Serve with hot pepper sauce.

White Beans with Rosemary and Italian Sausage

Sausage forms the flavor backbone of this speedy bean dish; feel free to use your favorite fresh sausage. Serve boiled or mashed potatoes on the side for a hearty weekday meal.

¾ cup	dried small white beans	175 mL
2 tbsp	extra-virgin olive oil	25 mL
2	mild or hot Italian sausages (about 12 oz/375 g), sliced	2
1	large onion, chopped	1
2	cloves garlic, chopped	2
1 cup	chopped canned tomatoes, with juice	250 mL
1 cup	water	250 mL
1	sprig fresh rosemary	1
	Salt and freshly ground black pepper	
2 tbsp	chopped fresh flat-leaf (Italian) parsley	25 mL

1. In the pressure cooker, combine beans and $2\frac{1}{2}$ cups (625 mL) cold water. Lock the lid in place and bring the cooker up to full pressure over high heat. Reduce heat to medium-low, just to maintain even pressure, and cook for 3 minutes. Remove from heat and allow pressure to drop naturally. Drain beans and set aside. Wipe cooker clean.

2. In the pressure cooker, heat oil over medium heat. Add sausage and sauté for 5 minutes, until starting to brown. Add onion and sauté for 3 to 4 minutes, until starting to color. Add garlic, tomatoes with juice, water and rosemary. Stir in beans.

3. Lock the lid in place and bring the cooker up to full pressure over medium-high heat. Reduce heat to medium-low, just to maintain even pressure, and cook for 6 minutes. Remove from heat and release pressure quickly. Season to taste with salt and pepper. Stir in parsley.

Beans with Short Ribs Chuckwagon-Style

This classic combination was first prepared for me by Alberta rancher Leo Maynard, who won a cooking contest with his tender beef and beans, prepared the old-fashioned way on a wood-fired cook stove. I've speeded up the process considerably using a pressure cooker. Enjoy this excellent dish as Leo does — with homemade biscuits.

2 cups	dried pinto beans	500 mL
1 tbsp	vegetable oil	15 mL
2 lbs	boneless beef short ribs	1 kg
2	onions, chopped	2
¼ cup	packed brown sugar	50 mL
1 tbsp	chili powder	15 mL
4 cups	water	1 L
½ cup	tomato sauce	125 mL
1 tbsp	prepared mustard	15 mL
2 tsp	cider vinegar	10 mL
1 tsp	Worcestershire sauce	5 mL
1 tsp	liquid smoke	5 mL
1 tsp	salt	5 mL

1. Soak beans overnight in water to cover or use the quick pressure-soak method (page 208). Drain.

2. In the pressure cooker, heat oil over medium-high heat. Add ribs in batches and cook until browned. Transfer to a plate. Set aside.

3. Reduce heat to medium. Add onions and sauté for 10 minutes, until tender. Stir in beans, brown sugar, chili powder, water, tomato sauce, mustard, vinegar, Worcestershire sauce and liquid smoke. Place ribs on top.

4. Lock the lid in place and bring the cooker up to full pressure over high heat. Reduce heat to medium-low, just to maintain even pressure, and cook for 30 minutes. Remove from heat and release pressure quickly. Stir in salt before serving.

Black Bean Chili

With earthy black beans, smoky chipotle chiles and a good shot of prairie rye whisky, this is truly an outstanding vegetarian bean dish. Serve it over rice or rolled up in flour tortillas with chopped tomatoes and grated cheese.

2 cups	dried black turtle beans	500 mL
3 tbsp	vegetable oil	45 mL
1	large onion, chopped	1
2 tbsp	paprika	25 mL
1 tbsp	dried oregano	15 mL
2 tsp	cumin seeds	10 mL
¼ tsp	cayenne pepper	1 mL
2	cloves garlic, minced	2
1	chipotle pepper in adobo sauce, chopped, or 1 rehydrated dried chipotle, chopped	1
1	green bell pepper, chopped	1
1	can (28 oz/796 mL) plum tomatoes, chopped	1
1	bay leaf	1
1 cup	water	250 mL
½ cup	rye whisky	125 mL
2 tsp	salt	10 mL
½ cup	chopped fresh cilantro	125 mL
1 cup	shredded Cheddar cheese	250 mL
1 cup	sour cream (preferably a low-fat variety)	250 mL

1. Soak beans overnight in water to cover or use the quick pressure-soak method (page 208). Drain.

2. In the pressure cooker, heat oil over medium heat. Add onion and sauté for 5 minutes or until just starting to brown. Add paprika, oregano, cumin seeds and cayenne; cook, stirring constantly, for 2 minutes or just until spices are fragrant. Add garlic, chipotle, green pepper and tomatoes. Stir in beans, bay leaf, water and rye whisky.

3. Lock the lid in place and bring the cooker up to full pressure. Reduce heat to medium-low, just to maintain even pressure, and cook for 20 minutes. Remove from heat and allow pressure to drop naturally. The beans should be tender. If not, return to full pressure and cook for 2 to 3 minutes longer. Remove from heat and allow pressure to drop naturally.

4. If beans are too soupy, simmer, uncovered, until reduced and thickened. (Alternatively, transfer ½ cup/125 mL of the beans to a bowl or food processor and mash or purée; stir into the pot.) Discard bay leaf. Season to taste with salt and stir in cilantro. Serve over a mound of fluffy rice, topped with a sprinkling of cheese and a dollop of sour cream.

● **TIP**

Chipotle chiles are jalapeño chiles that have been smoked over a wood fire, giving them a dark color and distinctive flavor. You can buy them dried or canned in adobo sauce at Latin groceries or well-stocked supermarkets.

Pork and Beef Chili with Ancho Sauce

This is a chunky, main-dish chili, packed with tender cubes of meat and earthy black beans. Ancho chiles are deep-red, medium-hot dried chiles with a rich, sweet flavor that's reminiscent of dried fruit. Chipotle chiles are actually smoked jalapeño chiles. They come dried in packages or packed in adobo sauce in small cans. Both of these special chiles give this dish a complex, smoky flavor that you can't get from fresh chiles alone. Look for them in the produce section of your supermarket or in specialty grocery stores.

½ cup	dried black turtle beans	125 mL
2	whole ancho chile peppers	2
¼ cup	extra-virgin olive oil	50 mL
1 lb	pork shoulder stew meat, cut into small cubes	500 g
1 lb	beef chuck steak, cut into small cubes	500 g
5	cloves garlic, minced	5
1	large onion, chopped	1
8 oz	spicy Italian sausages, casings removed, meat crumbled	250 g
1 tbsp	hot pepper flakes	15 mL
1 tbsp	ground cumin	15 mL
1 tbsp	dried oregano	15 mL
2	cans (each 19 oz/540 mL) tomatoes, chopped	2
1½ cups	water	375 mL
¼ cup	rye whisky	50 mL
¼ cup	tomato paste	50 mL
	Salt and freshly ground black pepper	

1. Soak beans overnight in water to cover or use the quick pressure-soak method (page 208). Drain. Set aside.

2. In a bowl of hot tap water, soak ancho chiles until softened. Drain and chop, discarding stems and seeds. Set aside.

3. In the pressure cooker, heat oil over medium-high heat. Add pork and beef in batches and cook until browned. Using a slotted spoon, transfer meat to a bowl as it is cooked. Set aside.

4. Add garlic, onion and sausage to cooker; sauté until the onion is softened and sausage is no longer pink. Add hot pepper flakes and cumin; sauté for 3 minutes longer. Stir in beans, reserved ancho chiles, pork and beef (with any accumulated juices), oregano, tomatoes, water, rye whisky and tomato paste.

5. Lock the lid in place and bring the cooker up to full pressure over high heat. Reduce heat to medium-low, just to maintain even pressure, and cook for 25 minutes. Remove from heat and allow pressure to drop naturally.

6. Season to taste with salt and pepper before serving.

● **TIP**

If you can't find chipotles, an appropriate substitute is a couple of fresh poblano chiles and a hot jalapeño or serrano chili. You can approximate the chipotle's smokiness by adding a drop of liquid smoke.

Mushroom, Italian Sausage and Braised Lentil Stew

Serve this savory lentil stew over rice (or short pasta such as orecchiette or rotini) for a fast, healthy supper.

● **TIP**

Beans and lentils tend to froth up in the pressure cooker, so make sure the cooker is no more than one-third full. If there's too much of this stew for your pot, cook it in two batches, cleaning the pressure release valve carefully after cooking each batch.

1 to 2 tbsp	extra-virgin olive oil	15 to 25 mL
1 lb	mild or spicy fresh Italian sausage, casings removed, meat crumbled	500 g
2	stalks celery, chopped	2
2	cloves garlic, minced	2
1	large onion, chopped	1
1 cup	chopped mushrooms	250 mL
1	carrot, minced	1
2 cups	small French green (Puy) lentils	500 mL
3	plum (Roma) tomatoes, chopped	3
½ tsp	dried thyme	2 mL
½ tsp	dried sage	2 mL
3 cups	chicken stock	750 mL
1 cup	dry red wine	250 mL
	Salt and freshly ground black pepper	
2 tbsp	chopped fresh basil or basil pesto	25 mL
	Cooked brown rice or short pasta (orecchiette, rotini, penne)	

1. In the pressure cooker, heat 1 tbsp (15 mL) of the oil over medium-high heat. Add sausage and cook until browned. Transfer to a bowl. Set aside.

2. Reduce heat to medium; add more oil if necessary to prevent burning. Add celery, garlic, onion, mushrooms and carrot; sauté for 5 minutes or until vegetables are soft and beginning to color. Add lentils, tomatoes, thyme, sage, ¼ tsp (1 mL) salt, ¼ tsp (1 mL) pepper, stock and wine. Stir in cooked sausage.

3. Lock the lid in place and bring the cooker up to full pressure over high heat. Reduce heat to medium-low, just to maintain even pressure, and cook for 8 minutes. Remove from heat and allow pressure to drop naturally.

4. Simmer, uncovered, to reduce any excess liquid in the pot. Stir in basil and season to taste with salt and pepper. Serve over rice or pasta.

Red Beans and Rice

In this classic from Cajun country and points south, beans and rice with smoky sausage make a simple one-dish dinner.

● **TIP**

For the sausage, try andouille, smoked garlic ham sausage or chorizo.

2 cups	dried small red beans	500 mL
1 tbsp	extra-virgin olive oil	15 mL
8 oz	spicy smoked pork sausage, chopped	250 g
3	cloves garlic, minced	3
1	onion, finely chopped	1
1	red bell pepper, finely chopped	1
1	large jalapeño pepper, seeded and chopped	1
⅔ cup	coconut milk	150 mL
1 cup	short-grain white rice	250 mL
1 tbsp	Worcestershire sauce	15 mL
1 tsp	dried thyme	5 mL
1	bay leaf	1
	Salt and freshly ground black pepper	
	Hot pepper sauce	

1. Soak beans overnight in water to cover or using the quick pressure-soak method (page 208). Drain.

2. In the pressure cooker, combine beans and 4 cups (1 L) cold water. Lock the lid in place and bring the cooker up to full pressure over high heat. Reduce heat to medium-low, just to maintain even pressure, and cook for 6 minutes. Remove from heat and allow pressure to drop naturally. Drain beans, reserving 2 cups (500 mL) of the cooking liquid, and set aside. Wipe cooker clean.

3. In the pressure cooker, heat oil over medium heat. Add sausage, garlic, onion, red pepper and jalapeño; sauté for 5 minutes, until sausage is starting to brown. Stir in beans, reserved cooking liquid, coconut milk, rice, Worcestershire sauce, thyme and bay leaf.

4. Lock the lid in place and bring the cooker up to full pressure over medium-high heat. Reduce heat to medium-low, just to maintain even pressure, and cook for 10 minutes. Remove from heat and allow pressure to drop naturally. Discard bay leaf. Season to taste with salt, black pepper and hot pepper sauce.

Chinese Sticky Rice

This dim sum specialty is traditionally wrapped in banana leaves for steaming, but you can prepare it quickly in the pressure cooker. It makes a simple lunch or part of a traditional Chinese meal.

3 cups	Chinese or Japanese short-grain sticky rice	750 mL
½ cup	dried shiitake mushrooms	125 mL
2 cups	hot water	500 mL
1 tbsp	canola oil	15 mL
1	clove garlic, minced	1
2 tsp	minced gingerroot	10 mL
3 to 4	Chinese sausages (about 6 oz/175 g total), cut into ¼-inch (0.5 cm) dice	3 to 4
1	can (10 oz/284 mL) water chestnuts, drained and finely chopped	1
2 cups	chicken stock or water	500 mL
3 tbsp	oyster sauce	45 mL
3 tbsp	soy sauce	45 mL
3 tbsp	Chinese cooking wine	45 mL
1 tbsp	sesame oil	15 mL
½ tsp	salt	2 mL
1 cup	frozen green peas, thawed	250 mL
4	green onions, chopped	4

1. Place rice in a bowl and add enough cold water to cover by at least 1 inch (2.5 cm). Let soak for 1 hour, then drain and set aside.

2. Meanwhile, soak mushrooms in hot water for 15 minutes, until softened. Drain, squeezing mushrooms to remove any excess liquid. Chop mushrooms, discarding any tough stems, and set aside.

3. In the pressure cooker, heat canola oil over medium-high heat. Add garlic and ginger; sauté for 1 minute. Add sausages and mushrooms; sauté for 1 minute. Stir in water chestnuts, chicken stock, oyster sauce, soy sauce, wine, sesame oil, salt and rice.

4. Lock the lid in place and bring the cooker up to full pressure over medium-high heat. Reduce heat to medium-low, just to maintain even pressure, and cook for 15 minutes. Remove from heat and allow pressure to drop naturally. Stir in peas and half the green onions.

5. Spoon rice into a serving dish (including the crusty layer that has formed on the bottom of the pot) and sprinkle with the remaining green onions.

● **TIPS**

Sticky rice is sometimes labeled "sweet" or "glutinous" rice.

Look for small dried Chinese sweet sausages and Chinese cooking wine at Asian markets.

Indian Rice Pilau

Here's the perfect rice dish to accompany Lamb Rogan Josh (see recipe, page 101) or, for vegetarians, Curried Lentils with Spinach (see recipe, page 190). The brown basmati gives extra flavor and fiber, but takes a little longer to cook than regular rice. For extra color and crunch, finish this dish by adding your choice of raisins, currants, chopped red bell pepper or green onions.

¼ cup	unsalted butter	50 mL
1	small onion, minced	1
4	whole green cardamom pods	4
1	cinnamon stick (about 3 inches/7.5 cm)	1
1	bay leaf	1
½ tsp	ground turmeric	2 mL
½ tsp	ground cumin	2 mL
1½ cups	brown basmati rice	375 mL
½ tsp	salt	2 mL
2 cups	water or vegetable stock	500 mL
½ cup	raisins or currants and/or finely chopped red bell pepper and green onions to finish (optional)	125 mL

1. In the pressure cooker, heat butter over medium heat. Add onion, cardamom, cinnamon, bay leaf, turmeric and cumin; sauté until onion is soft and spices are fragrant. Add rice, stirring to coat. Add salt and water; bring to a boil.

2. Lock the lid in place and bring the cooker up to full pressure over high heat. Reduce heat to medium-low, just to maintain even pressure, and cook for 9 minutes. Remove from heat and allow pressure to drop naturally for 7 to 10 minutes. Release any remaining pressure quickly.

3. Fluff rice with a fork; discard cinnamon stick and bay leaf. If desired, stir in raisins, currants, red pepper or green onions.

Indian Rice with Lamb

This is the classic rice dish served in central India. Serve it with cucumber and yogurt raita.

½ cup	dried chickpeas	125 mL
2 tbsp	unsalted butter	25 mL
1 lb	boneless lamb shoulder or shoulder chops, cut into 1-inch (2.5 cm) cubes	500 g
1	onion, chopped	1
6	whole cardamom pods	6
1	cinnamon stick (about 3 inches/7.5 cm)	1
1 tsp	each ground turmeric and cumin	5 mL
½ tsp	each cayenne pepper, salt and freshly ground black pepper	2 mL
2 cups	beef stock	500 mL
2 cups	basmati rice	500 mL
2 tbsp	chopped fresh cilantro	25 mL
½	lemon, cut into wedges	½
	Chopped fresh parsley	

1. Soak chickpeas overnight in water to cover or using the quick pressure-soak method (page 208). Drain and set aside.

2. In the pressure cooker, melt butter over medium heat. Add lamb and sauté for about 10 minutes, until starting to brown. Add onion and sauté for 5 minutes, then stir in cardamom, cinnamon, turmeric, cumin, cayenne, salt, black pepper, chickpeas, stock and enough water to cover.

3. Lock the lid in place and bring the cooker up to full pressure over high heat. Reduce heat to medium-low, just to maintain even pressure, and cook for 25 minutes. Remove from heat and release pressure quickly.

4. Stir in rice and 2 cups (500 mL) water. Lock the lid in place and bring the cooker up to full pressure over medium-high heat. Reduce heat to medium-low, just to maintain even pressure, and cook for 7 minutes. Remove from heat and allow pressure to drop naturally for 2 minutes, then release remaining pressure quickly. Stir in cilantro. Serve garnished with lemon wedges and parsley.

Paella

This classic Spanish paella combines spicy chorizo sausage and chicken with seafood. Feel free to add or substitute other seafood, such as squid, clams or cod, or include rabbit or portobello mushrooms in the mix, as they do in the interior of Spain.

¼ cup	extra-virgin olive oil	50 mL
6 oz	chorizo sausage, cubed	175 g
6	boneless skinless chicken thighs (about 1 lb/500 g total), cut into chunks	6
1	large Spanish onion, finely chopped	1
3	cloves garlic, minced	3
2	large tomatoes, seeded and chopped	2
2 cups	Valencia or short-grain white rice	500 mL
½ cup	dry white wine	125 mL
1	large red bell pepper, chopped	1
4 cups	water or chicken stock	1 L
1 tsp	salt	5 mL
½ tsp	saffron threads, crushed	2 mL
18	medium shrimp, peeled, deveined and butterflied	18
¾ cup	frozen peas	175 mL
18	large mussels, scrubbed and debearded (optional)	18
	Chopped fresh flat-leaf (Italian) parsley	
	Lemon wedges	

1. In the pressure cooker, heat oil over medium-high heat. Add chorizo and chicken; sauté for 5 minutes, until starting to brown on all sides. Add onion and sauté for 5 minutes, until softened and starting to brown. Stir in garlic, tomatoes, rice and wine; cook until most of the wine is absorbed. Stir in red pepper, water, salt and saffron.

2. Lock the lid in place and bring the cooker up to full pressure over medium-high heat. Reduce heat to medium-low, just to maintain even pressure, and cook for 10 minutes. Remove from heat and allow pressure to drop naturally for 5 minutes, then release remaining pressure quickly.

3. Quickly stir in shrimp and peas. Lock the lid in place and steam for 5 minutes, until shrimp are pink and opaque. (Alternatively, if using mussels, set them on top of the rice and bring the cooker up to full pressure over medium-high heat. Remove from heat and let stand for 3 minutes. Release the pressure and discard any mussels that are not open.)

4. Spoon paella onto a large platter and garnish with parsley and lemon wedges.

● TIP

Butterflying the shrimp helps them cook quickly in the hot mixture.

Rice with Chicken and Lentils

Serves 4 to 6

This Greek-inspired dish uses lean ground chicken or turkey to reduce fat, but you can also make it the traditional way with ground lamb, or leave out the meat and use vegetable stock for a vegetarian option.

3 tbsp	extra-virgin olive oil	45 mL
2	cloves garlic, minced	2
1	onion, chopped	1
1 lb	lean ground chicken or turkey	500 g
1 cup	green lentils	250 mL
1 tbsp	dried mint	15 mL
1/2 tsp	ground cinnamon	2 mL
3/4 cup	long-grain white rice	175 mL
3 cups	chicken stock	750 mL
1 cup	tomato sauce	250 mL
2	plum (Roma) tomatoes, seeded and chopped	2
2/3 cup	crumbled feta cheese	150 mL
1 tbsp	chopped fresh mint	15 mL
	Freshly ground black pepper	

1. In the pressure cooker, heat oil over medium heat. Add garlic and onion; sauté for 10 minutes, until starting to brown. Add ground chicken and sauté for about 5 minutes, until no longer pink. Stir in lentils, mint and cinnamon; sauté for 1 minute to release the aromas in the spices. Stir in rice, chicken stock and tomato sauce.

2. Lock the lid in place and bring the cooker up to full pressure over medium-high heat. Reduce heat to medium-low, just to maintain even pressure, and cook for 9 minutes. Remove from heat and allow pressure to drop naturally. Stir in tomatoes, feta and mint. Season to taste with pepper.

Basic Risotto

Serves 4 as a side dish

The pressure cooker makes cooking creamy risotto so easy, you'll be serving it instead of regular rice all the time. The saffron is optional, but it gives the risotto a wonderful earthy flavor and golden color. Try using a Microplane grater to grate the Parmesan.

● **TIP**

Use homemade chicken stock (see recipe, page 283) for the best flavor. Otherwise, use a good-quality commercially prepared stock.

1 tbsp	unsalted butter	15 mL
1 tbsp	extra-virgin olive oil	15 mL
1	small onion, minced	1
1 cup	Arborio or other short-grain white rice	250 mL
¼ cup	dry white wine	50 mL
2 cups	chicken stock or vegetable stock	500 mL
½ tsp	crushed saffron threads (optional)	2 mL
½ cup	freshly grated Parmesan cheese	125 mL
	Freshly ground black pepper	

1. In the pressure cooker, heat butter and oil over medium heat. Add onion and sauté for 5 minutes, until soft (but not brown). Stir in rice, coating well with oil. Add wine. If using, crumble saffron into stock. Pour stock over rice.

2. Lock the lid in place and bring the cooker up to full pressure over high heat. Reduce heat to medium-low, just to maintain even pressure, and cook for 7 minutes. Remove from heat and release pressure quickly. Stir in Parmesan cheese and season to taste with pepper. Serve immediately.

Risotto with Grilled Vegetables and Beet Greens

Loaded with grilled vegetables and healthy greens, this risotto may be served as a vegetarian main course.

● **TIP**

Use homemade chicken stock (see recipe, page 283) for the best flavor. Otherwise, use a good-quality commercially prepared stock.

¼ cup	extra-virgin olive oil	50 mL
1	clove garlic, minced	1
1	small Japanese eggplant, sliced	1
1	small zucchini, sliced	1
1	portobello mushroom, stem removed	1
1	red or yellow bell pepper, seeded and halved	1
1	onion, thickly sliced	1
	Salt and freshly ground black pepper	
¼ cup	unsalted butter, divided	50 mL
1 cup	Arborio or other short-grain white rice	250 mL
½ cup	dry white wine	125 mL
2 cups	chicken stock	500 mL
2 cups	slivered young beet greens	500 mL
¼ cup	slivered basil leaves	50 mL
½ cup	freshly grated Parmesan cheese	125 mL

1. In a small bowl, combine oil and garlic; let stand at room temperature for 10 minutes. Brush over eggplant, zucchini, mushroom, bell pepper and onion. Season with salt and pepper. Grill over medium heat, turning once, until softened. Let cool. Chop coarsely and set aside.

2. In the pressure cooker, heat 3 tbsp (45 mL) of the butter with any of the remaining oil and garlic over medium heat. Add rice, stirring to coat. Stir in wine and stock.

3. Lock the lid in place and bring the cooker up to full pressure over high heat. Reduce heat to medium-low, just to maintain even pressure, and cook for 7 minutes. Remove from heat and release pressure quickly.

4. Stir in grilled vegetables, beet greens and basil. Cover (but do not lock) and let stand just until the greens are wilted, about 5 minutes. Stir in Parmesan cheese and remaining butter; season to taste with pepper.

Roasted Garlic Risotto with Asiago

Roasting tames the natural harshness of garlic and gives it a buttery, nutty flavor that works perfectly with the strong cheese in this dish. The lemon zest adds sparkle; the green onion, a touch of color. There's nothing complicated about this risotto, and it demonstrates once again just how easy it is to make a spectacular side dish in 7 short minutes.

• Preheat oven to 350°F (180°C)

1	head garlic	1
1 tsp	extra-virgin olive oil	5 mL
3 tbsp	unsalted butter	45 mL
1	large onion, finely chopped	1
2 cups	Arborio or other short-grain white rice	500 mL
½ cup	dry white wine	50 mL
4 cups	chicken stock	500 mL
1 cup	freshly grated Asiago cheese	250 mL
¼ cup	minced green onions	50 mL
1 tsp	grated zest of 1 lemon	5 mL
	Freshly ground black pepper	

1. To roast garlic, cut top ¼ inch (0.5 cm) from whole head to expose cloves; drizzle with oil and wrap loosely in foil. Roast in preheated oven for 30 to 40 minutes, until garlic is very soft. Press roasted garlic out of skins and mash with the flat side of a knife. Set aside.

2. In the pressure cooker, heat butter over medium heat. Add onion and sauté for 5 minutes, until soft (but not brown). Add rice, stirring to coat. Stir in the wine and cook until it has been absorbed. Stir in reserved garlic and chicken stock.

3. Lock the lid in place and bring the cooker up to full pressure over high heat. Reduce heat to medium-low, just to maintain even pressure, and cook for 7 minutes. Remove from heat and release pressure quickly.

4. Stir in cheese, green onions and lemon zest. Season to taste with pepper. Serve immediately.

Italian Sausage Risotto with Peas

Serves 4

Mild Italian sausage and green peas make this homey risotto a meal in a dish. Make sure you start with good-quality lean sausage.

1 tbsp	unsalted butter	15 mL
1 tbsp	extra-virgin olive oil	15 mL
1	onion, finely chopped	1
2	cloves garlic, chopped	2
8 oz	mild Italian sausage (bulk, or with casings removed)	250 g
1 cup	Arborio or other short-grain white rice	250 mL
¼ cup	dry white wine	50 mL
2 cups	chicken or vegetable stock	500 mL
1 cup	baby green peas (thawed if frozen)	250 mL
½ cup	shredded Asiago cheese	125 mL
	Salt and freshly ground black pepper	

1. In the pressure cooker, heat butter and oil over medium-high heat. Add onion and sauté for 5 minutes, until softened but not brown. Add garlic and sausage; sauté for 5 minutes, until sausage is no longer pink. Stir in rice, coating well with butter. Stir in wine and cook until it is absorbed. Stir in chicken stock.

2. Lock the lid in place and bring the cooker up to full pressure over high heat. Reduce heat to medium-low, just to maintain even pressure, and cook for 7 minutes. Remove from heat and release pressure quickly. Stir in peas and cheese. Season to taste with salt and pepper.

Risotto with Mushrooms and Shrimp

The pressure cooker is brilliant for risotto — the creamy rice dish cooks by itself in 6 to 7 minutes. This version makes an elegant dinner for two with a salad to start, or a great first course for four.

● TIP

Use homemade chicken stock (see recipe, page 283) for the best flavor. Otherwise, use a good-quality commercially prepared stock.

2 tbsp	extra-virgin olive oil	25 mL
1 tbsp	unsalted butter	15 mL
2	cloves garlic, minced	2
1 cup	sliced mixed mushrooms (such as brown, oyster, portobello, shiitake, morel)	250 mL
1	onion, sliced	1
1 tsp	chopped fresh thyme	5 mL
1 cup	Arborio or other short-grain white rice	250 mL
2 cups	chicken stock	500 mL
¼ cup	dry white wine	50 mL
12 oz	medium to large shrimp, peeled, deveined and cut into half lengthwise	375 g
½ cup	freshly grated Parmesan cheese	125 mL

1. In the pressure cooker, heat oil and butter over medium heat. Add garlic, mushrooms and onion; sauté for 5 minutes or until softened (but not brown). Stir in thyme and rice; sauté for 1 minute. Pour in stock and wine.

2. Lock the lid in place and bring the cooker up to full pressure over high heat. Reduce heat to medium-low, just to maintain even pressure, and cook for 7 minutes. Remove from heat and release pressure quickly.

3. Stir in the shrimp; cover (but do not lock) and let stand for 10 minutes until shrimp are opaque. Stir in the Parmesan. Serve immediately.

Wild Rice Casserole with Mixed Mushrooms and Chestnuts

This side dish makes a great addition to Thanksgiving or Christmas dinner. Use it as a stuffing for roast chicken, game hens or whole baked salmon. To accompany richer meats such as goose or duck, try replacing the mushrooms with currants, apricots or cranberries.

● **TIP**

The pressure cooker makes peeling chestnuts fast and easy. Cut an X in the base of each nut and place in the cooker; cover nuts with plenty of water, lock the lid in place, and cook at full pressure for 6 minutes. It's easy to peel off the shells and the bitter brown skin. Or use your pressure cooker to speed-soak the smoky dried chestnuts sold in Italian and Asian markets. Allow 2 minutes of cooking under pressure and 10 minutes of natural pressure release to rehydrate the dried chestnuts.

2 tbsp	unsalted butter	25 mL
2	cloves garlic, minced	2
1	onion, finely chopped	1
1 cup	sliced mixed mushrooms (such as portobello, oyster, shiitake and white)	250 mL
1 cup	wild rice	250 mL
1 cup	cooked and crumbled chestnuts or ½ cup (125 mL) toasted pecans	250 mL
2	sprigs thyme (or 1 tsp/5 mL dried)	2
2 cups	chicken stock	500 mL
	Salt and freshly ground black pepper	

1. In the pressure cooker, melt butter over medium heat. Add garlic, onion and mushrooms; sauté until they start to brown. Stir in wild rice, chestnuts, thyme and stock. Bring to a boil.

2. Lock the lid in place and bring the cooker up to full pressure over high heat. Reduce heat to medium-low, just to maintain even pressure, and cook for 20 minutes. Remove from heat and allow pressure to drop naturally. The rice should be tender, with many of the grains broken and curled. If not, return to full pressure and cook for 2 to 3 minutes longer. Remove from heat and allow pressure to drop naturally.

3. Drain off any excess liquid. Discard thyme sprigs. Season to taste with salt and pepper.

Barley for Breakfast

Hot oatmeal makes a healthy breakfast, but how about hot barley with dried fruit and cinnamon for a change of pace?

● TIPS

The candied pecans can be stored in an airtight container for several weeks.

The barley can be prepared through step 3 and stored in an airtight container in the refrigerator for up to 3 days. Warm in the microwave or on the stovetop, then continue with step 4.

- ● Preheat oven to 350°F (180°C)
- ● Baking sheet, lined with parchment paper

1 cup	pecan halves, coarsely chopped	250 mL
¼ cup	liquid honey	50 mL
¾ cup	pearl barley	175 mL
3 cups	water	750 mL
½ tsp	salt	2 mL
¼ cup	chopped mixed dried fruit (apricots, apples, prunes, figs, cranberries and/or raisins)	50 mL
¼ cup	pure maple syrup	50 mL
½ tsp	ground cinnamon	2 mL
½ cup	vanilla-flavored yogurt or whipping (35%) cream	125 mL

1. In a bowl, toss together nuts and honey. Spread nuts on prepared baking sheet and toast in preheated oven for 10 minutes. Let cool.

2. Meanwhile, in the pressure cooker, toast barley over medium heat, stirring constantly, for 4 to 5 minutes, until fragrant. Stir in water and salt.

3. Lock the lid in place and bring the cooker up to full pressure over high heat. Reduce heat to medium-low, just to maintain even pressure, and cook for 15 minutes. Remove from heat and release pressure quickly. Drain any excess water from the barley and stir in dried fruit, maple syrup and cinnamon.

4. To serve, stir yogurt or cream into the barley mixture and top with candied pecans.

Barley with Mint and Root Vegetables

Barley is a healthy whole grain that makes a nice substitute for rice. Prepared in the pressure cooker, it's fast, toothsome and never sticky. Adding grated Parmesan to this dish gives it a flavor that's reminiscent of risotto. Be sure to caramelize the vegetables until they're nice and brown — that's what gives this savory root vegetable dish it a full, rich flavor.

¼ cup	unsalted butter	50 mL
2	carrots, cut into small cubes	2
2	parsnips, cut into small cubes	2
1	sweet potato, peeled and cubed	1
1	onion, chopped	1
1 cup	pot or pearl barley	250 mL
3	cloves garlic, minced	3
3 cups	chicken or brown stock	750 mL
2 tbsp	chopped fresh mint	25 mL
2 tbsp	chopped fresh parsley (optional)	25 mL
1 cup	finely grated Parmesan or Asiago cheese (optional)	250 mL
	Salt and freshly ground black pepper	

1. In the pressure cooker, heat butter over medium heat. Add carrots, parsnips, sweet potato and onion; sauté until vegetables start to caramelize. Add barley and garlic; cook, stirring, for 5 minutes to toast the grains. Pour in stock.

2. Lock the lid in place and bring the cooker up to full pressure over high heat. Reduce heat to medium-low, just to maintain even pressure, and cook for 20 minutes. Remove from heat and release pressure quickly. The barley should be tender. If not, cover (but do not lock) and simmer over low heat until tender.

3. Stir in mint, parsley and Parmesan (if using). Season to taste with salt and pepper.

Barley with Boursin and Spinach

A bit of creamy Boursin cheese turns a plain pot of barley into an elegant side dish. The spinach adds bright color and extra vitamins.

2 tbsp	unsalted butter	25 mL
1	onion, chopped	1
1½ cups	sliced mushrooms	375 mL
2	cloves garlic, minced	2
1 cup	pearl barley	250 mL
1 cup	dry white wine	250 mL
1 cup	water, vegetable stock or chicken stock	250 mL
3 cups	finely chopped spinach	750 mL
¼ cup	Boursin cheese, crumbled	50 mL
	Salt and freshly ground black pepper	

1. In the pressure cooker, melt butter over medium heat. Add onion and sauté for about 5 minutes, until softened. Add mushrooms and sauté for about 5 minutes, until they release their liquid. Stir in garlic, barley, wine and water.

2. Lock the lid in place and bring the cooker up to full pressure over medium-high heat. Reduce heat to medium-low, just to maintain even pressure, and cook for 18 minutes. Remove from heat and allow pressure to drop naturally. Add spinach, stirring until bright green and wilted. Stir in Boursin. Season to taste with salt and pepper.

Kasha with Mushrooms and Dill

The smoky grains of toasted buckwheat that go into traditional kasha make for a simple peasant dish that's delicious alongside pot roast or grilled fish and works perfectly as a filling for vegetarian cabbage rolls (see page 120 for a traditional cabbage roll recipe).

1 cup	buckwheat groats (kasha)	250 mL
1	egg, lightly beaten	1
3 tbsp	unsalted butter, divided	45 mL
1 tbsp	extra-virgin olive oil	15 mL
1	onion, finely chopped	1
2 cups	chicken stock or water	500 mL
½ tsp	salt	2 mL
2 cups	chopped mushrooms	500 mL
½ cup	chopped red bell pepper	125 mL
2 tbsp	chopped fresh dill	25 mL

1. In a bowl, combine buckwheat and egg.

2. In the pressure cooker, heat 1 tbsp (15 mL) of the butter and the oil over medium heat. Add onion and sauté for about 5 minutes, until softened. Stir in buckwheat mixture and cook, stirring, for about 2 minutes, until egg is set and grains are separated. Stir in chicken stock and salt.

3. Lock the lid in place and bring the cooker up to full pressure over medium-high heat. Reduce heat to medium-low, just to maintain even pressure, and cook for 8 minutes. Remove from heat and allow pressure to drop naturally.

4. Meanwhile, in a skillet, melt the remaining butter over medium heat. Add mushrooms and sauté for about 10 minutes, until they release their liquid and start to brown. Add red pepper and sauté for about 5 minutes, until softened.

5. Fluff the kasha with a fork and stir in the sautéed mixture and dill.

Wheat Berries Carbonara

Here's a great way to enjoy the flavors of a creamy Italian sauce with a healthy serving of whole grain.

● TIP

Substitute whole raw buckwheat for wheat berries; reduce water to 4 cups (1 L) and cooking time to 15 minutes.

2 cups	whole wheat berries or whole-grain rye	500 mL
1 tsp	salt	5 mL
6 cups	water	1.5 L
3 tbsp	extra-virgin olive oil, divided	45 mL
2	onions, finely chopped	2
8 oz	Canadian back bacon, slivered	250 g
1 cup	frozen peas, thawed	250 mL
1 cup	whipping (35%) cream	250 mL
1 cup	freshly grated Parmesan cheese	250 mL
	Salt and freshly ground black pepper	

1. In the pressure cooker, combine wheat berries, salt, water and 1 tbsp (15 mL) of the oil. Lock the lid in place and bring the cooker up to full pressure over high heat. Reduce heat to medium-low, just to maintain even pressure, and cook for 35 to 40 minutes. Remove from heat and release pressure quickly. The wheat berries should be tender. If not, return to full pressure and cook for 3 to 5 minutes longer. Remove from heat and release pressure quickly. Drain well.

2. Meanwhile, in a large sauté pan, heat the remaining oil over medium-high heat. Add onions and bacon; sauté until onions are golden brown. Add peas and heat through. Stir in cream and cooked wheat berries, stirring to coat.

3. Reduce heat to medium-low and cook just until heated through. Stir in Parmesan cheese. Season to taste with salt and pepper. Serve immediately.

Spelt with White Beans

This Tuscan dish uses an ancient grain called spelt, an early ancestor of modern wheat. The large grains are loaded with fiber and B vitamins but are low in gluten, so they can often be tolerated by those with gluten sensitivity. Spelt has a wonderful nutty flavor and, when combined with white beans, creates a healthy meatless stew.

● **TIP**

To make quick work of chopping the vegetables, combine them in a food processor and pulse until finely chopped.

¾ cup	dried small white beans	175 mL
1½ cups	whole-grain spelt or wheat berries	375 mL
2 tbsp	extra-virgin olive oil	25 mL
3	cloves garlic, minced	3
3	stalks celery, finely chopped	3
1	large onion, finely chopped	1
1	carrot, finely chopped	1
4	tomatoes, chopped (or 1 cup/250 mL chopped canned tomatoes)	4
4 cups	chicken stock	1 L
1 cup	dry white wine	250 mL
2 tsp	chopped fresh sage or rosemary	10 mL
	Salt and freshly ground black pepper	
	Extra-virgin olive oil (optional)	
	Freshly grated Parmesan cheese (optional)	

1. Soak beans overnight in water to cover or using the quick pressure-soak method (page 208). Drain and set aside.

2. Meanwhile, soak spelt in cold water to cover for at least 2 hours or overnight. Drain and set aside.

3. In the pressure cooker, heat oil over medium heat. Add garlic, celery, onion and carrot; sauté for 5 minutes, until onions are softened and fragrant. Stir in tomatoes, chicken stock, wine and sage. Stir in beans and spelt.

4. Lock the lid in place and bring the cooker up to full pressure over high heat. Reduce heat to medium-low, just to maintain even pressure, and cook for 30 minutes. Remove from heat and allow pressure to drop naturally. The spelt should be tender but chewy. If not, return to full pressure and cook for another 5 minutes. Remove from heat and allow pressure to drop naturally. Season to taste with salt and pepper.

5. Spoon into shallow bowls and, if desired, drizzle with oil and sprinkle with Parmesan cheese.

Desserts

Espresso Chocolate Cake

This is a dense, flourless cake — like a big adult-style brownie, with a shot of coffee to boost the dark chocolate flavor. Serve it with a dollop of sweetened whipped cream or a scoop of good-quality coffee ice cream and a chocolate-covered espresso bean on top. Or, in summer, try this decadent dessert with fresh strawberries or raspberries on the side.

- 7-inch (18 cm) springform pan, buttered
- Rack or trivet to fit bottom of pressure cooker

4 oz	bittersweet chocolate, chopped	125 g
4 oz	semisweet chocolate, chopped	125 g
1/3 cup	brewed espresso	75 mL
1/4 cup	granulated sugar	50 mL
3 tbsp	unsalted butter	45 mL
4	eggs, separated	4
1 tbsp	granulated sugar	15 mL
	Confectioner's (icing) sugar or unsweetened cocoa powder	
	Sweetened whipped cream or ice cream	
	Chocolate-covered espresso beans	

1. In a saucepan, combine bittersweet and semisweet chocolate, espresso, 1/4 cup (50 mL) sugar and butter; heat over medium heat, stirring, until chocolate is melted and mixture is smooth. Remove from heat and stir for 5 minutes to cool.

2. In a bowl, using an electric mixer, beat egg whites until almost stiff. Add 1 tbsp (15 mL) sugar and beat until stiff peaks form. Set aside.

3. In a large bowl, lightly whisk egg yolks. Whisk in a little of the chocolate mixture. Gradually whisk in the remaining chocolate mixture. Fold in beaten egg whites until well mixed but still fluffy.

4. Wrap the base of the springform pan with foil. Pour batter into the pan and cover with a piece of buttered foil, making sure pan is well sealed.

5. Set rack in the bottom of the pressure cooker. Pour in 2 cups (500 mL) water for steaming. Fold a 2-foot (60 cm) long piece of foil several times to make a strip strong enough to lift the pan. Center pan on midpoint of strip and fold the ends together to make a handle. Lower the pan into the cooker.

6. Lock the lid in place and bring the cooker up to full pressure over high heat. Reduce heat to medium-low, just to maintain even pressure, and cook for 20 minutes. Remove from heat and allow pressure to drop naturally. Using foil handle, lift pan out of the cooker onto a cooling rack. Remove foil lid and let cake cool completely.

7. Release cake from pan and dust with icing sugar. Cut into wedges and serve with whipped cream and an espresso bean on top of each wedge.

● **TIP**

If you don't have an espresso machine, look for instant espresso powder to use in this recipe or substitute extra-strong brewed coffee.

Steamed Lemon Poppy Seed Cake

You won't find a moister poppyseed cake than this one. The recipe is based on Sue Spicer's favorite family cake and one of my quick coffee cake glazes. You'll need to use a low pressure setting and a longer cooking time to get this cake to rise properly.

- 4-cup (1 L) soufflé dish or Bundt pan, greased and floured
- Rack or trivet to fit bottom of pressure cooker

½ cup	unsalted butter, softened	125 mL
1 cup	granulated sugar	250 mL
2	eggs, separated	2
1 tsp	vanilla extract	5 mL
	Grated zest of 2 lemons, divided	
	Juice of 2 lemons, divided	
1¼ cup	all-purpose flour	300 mL
1 tsp	baking soda	5 mL
1 tsp	baking powder	5 mL
½ tsp	salt	2 mL
⅔ cup	milk	175 mL
⅓ cup	poppy seeds	75 mL

Glaze

½ cup	confectioner's (icing) sugar	125 mL

1. In a bowl, with an electric mixer, beat butter with sugar until light and fluffy. Beat in egg yolks and vanilla. Beat in half of the lemon zest and lemon juice.

2. In a separate bowl, combine flour, baking soda, baking powder and salt. Beat dry ingredients into butter-sugar mixture, alternating with the milk, making three additions of dry and two of milk. Fold in poppy seeds.

3. In another bowl, beat egg whites until stiff. Gently fold into batter until just combined. Pour into prepared dish. Cover with a piece of foil, making sure dish is well sealed.

4. Set rack in bottom of cooker. Pour in 2 cups (500 mL) water for steaming. Fold a 2-foot (60 cm) long piece of foil several times to make a strip that will be used to remove dish. Center dish on midpoint of strip and fold the ends together to make a handle. Use strip to lower dish into the cooker.

5. Lock the lid in place and bring the cooker up to low pressure over high heat. Reduce heat to medium-low, just to maintain even pressure, and cook for 40 minutes (or cook at full pressure for 20 minutes). Remove from heat and allow pressure to drop naturally. Using foil handle, lift dish out of cooker onto cooling rack. Remove foil lid. Let cool completely.

6. *Glaze:* Whisk remaining lemon zest and lemon juice together with confectioner's sugar. To serve, turn the cake out onto a serving platter and drizzle with glaze.

● TIP

Like a rich pound cake, this dessert is even better if you wrap it well and store it for a day or two before serving.

New York–Style Cheesecake

Serves 8 to 10

This is the basic cheesecake you grew up with — dense, creamy and ready for any kind of fruit topping, from strawberry or blueberry sauce to gingered peaches (see variation, below).

● **TIP**

Cheesecake can be wrapped and refrigerated for up to 3 days or frozen for up to 3 months.

● 7- to 8-inch (18 to 20 cm) springform pan
● Rack or trivet to fit bottom of pressure cooker

Crust

3 tbsp	unsalted butter, softened	45 mL
6 tbsp	crushed graham wafers	90 mL

Filling

1 lb	cream cheese, cubed	500 g
1 cup	granulated sugar	250 mL
2 tbsp	all-purpose flour	25 mL
3	eggs	3
1/3 cup	plain yogurt or sour cream	75 mL
2 tbsp	vanilla extract	25 mL

Topping

1/3 cup	sour cream	75 mL
2 tbsp	granulated sugar	25 mL
	Blueberry or strawberry preserves or sauce (optional)	

1. *Crust:* Thickly butter the bottom and sides of springform pan. Sprinkle crushed graham wafers inside pan, tilting to coat sides, and press the crumbs into the soft butter. Wrap the outside of the pan with foil to seal. Set aside.

2. *Filling:* In a food processor, process cream cheese, sugar and flour until smooth. With the motor running, add eggs, one at a time. Add yogurt and vanilla; process for 10 seconds, until well combined. Pour into prepared pan and cover with a piece of buttered foil, making sure pan is well sealed.

3. Set rack in the bottom of the pressure cooker. Pour in 2 to 3 cups (500 to 750 mL) water for steaming. Fold a 2-foot (60 cm) long piece of foil several times to make a strip strong enough to lift the pan. Center pan on midpoint of strip and fold the ends together to make a handle. Lower the pan into the cooker.

4. Lock the lid in place and bring the cooker up to full pressure over high heat. Reduce heat to medium-low, just to maintain even pressure, and cook for 30 minutes. Remove from heat and allow pressure to drop naturally for 7 minutes. Release remaining pressure quickly. Let cheesecake cool in cooker for a few minutes. Using foil handle, lift pan out of the cooker onto a cooling rack. Remove foil lid. Cheesecake should be set around the edges, but still slightly loose in the center. If center is still liquid, seal with foil and return to the cooker. Bring up to full pressure and cook for 5 minutes longer. Remove from heat and allow pressure to drop as above. When cheesecake is cooked, remove foil. Use a paper towel to mop up any water pooled on top of cake.

5. *Topping:* In a small bowl, whisk together sour cream and sugar. Spread evenly over cheesecake, smoothing top. Let cool to room temperature. Cover and refrigerate for at least 8 hours or overnight.

6. Serve topped with berry preserves or sauce, if desired.

• VARIATION

Instead of the berry preserves, serve the cheesecake with gingered peaches. In a saucepan, combine 2 peaches, chopped, $\frac{1}{4}$ cup (50 mL) granulated sugar, 1 tsp (5 mL) ground ginger and a splash of orange-flavored liqueur; heat over medium heat until bubbly. It's the perfect foil for this rich, creamy dessert.

Layered White and Dark Chocolate Cheesecake

What could be more tempting than your favorite dark and white chocolate cheesecakes — together? The layers look lovely, and you can top the whole thing with a decadent layer of sweetened sour cream (which also masks any cracks that may have formed in the top of your cake during cooking).

- 7- to 8-inch (18 to 20 cm) springform pan (use smaller size if necessary to fit inside pressure cooker)
- Rack or trivet to fit bottom of pressure cooker

Crust

2 tbsp	unsalted butter, softened	25 mL
¼ cup	chocolate cookie crumbs	50 mL

Filling

2 oz	semisweet chocolate, chopped	50 g
2 oz	white chocolate, chopped	50 g
1 lb	cream cheese	500 g
½ cup	granulated sugar	125 mL
2 tbsp	all-purpose flour	25 mL
4	eggs	4
½ cup	sour cream or yogurt	125 mL
½ tsp	vanilla extract	2 mL

Topping

½ cup	sour cream	125 mL
2 tbsp	granulated sugar	25 mL
	Fresh strawberries	

1. *Crust:* Thickly butter bottom and sides of springform pan. Sprinkle cookie crumbs inside pan, tilting to coat sides. Leave excess crumbs on bottom. Wrap outside of pan with foil to seal. Set aside.

2. *Filling:* In a heatproof bowl set over hot (not boiling) water, melt semisweet chocolate. In a separate bowl, melt white chocolate. Let both chocolates cool slightly.

3. In a food processor, purée cream cheese, sugar and flour. With motor running, add eggs, one at a time. Add sour cream and vanilla; purée for 10 seconds or until smooth. Divide batter evenly between the two bowls of melted chocolate. Stir both to combine well. Pour dark chocolate filling into prepared crust. Gently pour white chocolate filling over top. Cover with a piece of buttered foil, making sure pan is well sealed.

4. Set rack in the bottom of pressure cooker. Pour in 2 cups (500 mL) water for steaming. Fold a 2-foot (60 cm) long piece of foil several times to make a strip that will be used to remove pan. Center pan on midpoint of strip and fold the ends together to make a handle. Use strip to lower pan into the cooker.

5. Lock the lid in place and bring the cooker up to full pressure over high heat. Reduce heat to medium-low, just to maintain even pressure, and cook for 20 minutes. Remove from heat and allow pressure to drop naturally for 7 minutes. Release remaining pressure quickly. Let cheesecake cool in cooker for a few minutes. Using foil handle, lift pan out of cooker onto cooling rack. Remove foil lid. Cheesecake should be set around edges, but still slightly loose in center. If center is still liquid, seal with foil and return to the cooker. Bring up to full pressure and cook for 2 minutes longer. Remove from heat and allow pressure to drop as above. When cheesecake is cooked, remove foil. Use a paper towel to mop up any water pooled on top of cake.

6. *Topping:* In a small bowl, whisk sour cream and sugar. Spread over cheesecake, smoothing top. Let cool to room temperature. Refrigerate for at least 8 hours or overnight before serving.

7. Serve garnished with strawberries.

● **TIP**

Cheesecake can be wrapped and refrigerated for up to 3 days or frozen for up to 3 months.

Lemon-Lime Cheesecake

This classic, dense, citrusy cheesecake is wonderful served with a fresh or lightly cooked fruit sauce. Try it topped with Saskatoon or blueberries that have been simmered with a little water and sugar, or drizzle with a tart lemon syrup made by boiling ¼ cup (50 mL) freshly squeezed lemon juice with ⅓ cup (75 mL) sugar for a couple of minutes, then chilling.

- 7- to 8-inch (18 to 20 cm) springform pan (use smaller size if necessary to fit inside pressure cooker)
- Rack or trivet to fit bottom of pressure cooker

Crust

3 tbsp	unsalted butter, softened	45 mL
3 tbsp	crushed vanilla wafers	45 mL
3 tbsp	ground pecans	45 mL

Filling

	Grated zest and juice of 1 lemon	
	Grated zest and juice of 1 lime	
1 lb	cream cheese	500 g
1 cup	granulated sugar	250 mL
3 tbsp	all-purpose flour	45 mL
4	eggs	4
¼ cup	plain yogurt or sour cream	50 mL
1 tsp	vanilla extract	5 mL

Topping

½ cup	sour cream	125 mL
2 tbsp	granulated sugar	25 mL
	Mixed fresh fruit and berries for topping (sliced peaches, blueberries, sliced strawberries, etc.)	

1. *Crust:* Thickly butter the bottom and sides of springform pan. In a bowl combine crushed wafers and pecans; sprinkle inside pan, tilting to coat sides. Leave excess crumbs on bottom. Wrap outside of pan with foil to seal. Set aside.

2. In a bowl combine lemon zest and lime zest. Reserve 1 tsp (5 mL), covered and refrigerated, for garnish.

3. *Filling:* In a food processor, purée remaining lemon and lime zest together with lemon juice, lime juice, cream cheese, sugar and flour. With motor running, add eggs, one at a time. Add yogurt and vanilla; purée for 10 seconds or until smooth. Pour into prepared pan and cover with a piece of buttered foil, making sure pan is well sealed.

4. Set rack in bottom of pressure cooker. Pour in 2 cups (500 mL) water for steaming. Fold a 2-foot (60 cm) long piece of foil several times to make a strip that will be used to remove pan. Center pan on midpoint of strip and fold the ends together to make a handle. Use strip to lower pan into the cooker.

5. Lock the lid in place and bring the cooker up to full pressure over high heat. Reduce heat to medium-low, just to maintain even pressure, and cook for 20 minutes. Remove from heat and allow pressure to drop naturally for 7 minutes. Release remaining pressure quickly. Let cheesecake cool in cooker for a few minutes. Using foil handle, lift pan out of cooker onto cooling rack. Remove foil lid. Cheesecake should be set around edges, but still slightly loose in center. If center is still liquid, seal with foil and return to the cooker. Bring up to full pressure and cook for 2 minutes longer. Remove from heat and allow pressure to drop as above. When cheesecake is cooked, remove foil. Use a paper towel to mop up any water pooled on top of cake.

6. *Topping:* In a small bowl, whisk sour cream with sugar. Spread over cheesecake, smoothing top. Let cool to room temperature. Refrigerate for at least 8 hours or overnight before serving.

7. Serve garnished with fresh fruit and sprinkle with reserved zest.

● **TIP**

Cheesecake can be wrapped and refrigerated for up to 3 days or frozen for up to 3 months.

Orange Espresso Cheesecake

Serves 6 to 8

It's still amazing to me that cheesecake "bakes" far better in the pressure cooker than it does in the oven. But the high temperature and steam result in a cake that's infinitely creamier and has less crust (and therefore far less fat). It's a winning method — try it.

- 7 to 8-inch (18 to 20 cm) springform pan (use smaller size if necessary to fit inside pressure cooker)
- Rack or trivet to fit bottom of pressure cooker

Crust

3 tbsp	unsalted butter, softened	45 mL
1/3 cup	graham wafer crumbs	75 mL

Filling

	Grated zest and juice of 1 large navel orange (about 1/2 cup/125 mL juice)	
2 tbsp	instant espresso	25 mL
1/4 cup	warm water	50 mL
1 lb	cream cheese	500 g
1 cup	granulated sugar	250 mL
3 tbsp	all-purpose flour	45 mL
1/4 tsp	ground cloves	1 mL
1/2 tsp	ground cinnamon	2 mL
2 tbsp	Grand Marnier or 1 tbsp (25 mL) brandy and 1 tbsp (15 mL) Triple Sec	25 mL
4	eggs	4

Topping

1/2 cup	sour cream	125 mL
2 tbsp	granulated sugar	25 mL
1 tbsp	Grand Marnier or Triple Sec	15 mL
	Fresh orange segments	

1. *Crust:* Thickly butter bottom and sides of springform pan. Sprinkle graham crumbs inside pan, tilting to coat sides. Leave excess crumbs on bottom. Wrap outside of pan with foil to seal. Set aside.

2. *Filling:* Wrap and refrigerate 1 tsp (5 mL) of the orange zest for garnish. In a small bowl, dissolve the instant espresso in the warm water.

3. In a food processor, purée remaining orange zest, orange juice, cream cheese, sugar and flour until smooth. Add espresso mixture, cloves, cinnamon and Grand Marnier; purée until smooth. With motor running, add eggs, one at a time, and purée for another 10 seconds, until well combined. Pour into prepared pan and cover with a piece of buttered foil, making sure pan is well sealed.

4. Set rack in the bottom of pressure cooker. Pour in 2 cups (500 mL) water for steaming. Fold a 2-foot (60 cm) long piece of foil several times to make a strip that will be used to remove pan. Center pan on midpoint of strip and fold the ends together to make a handle. Use strip to lower pan into the cooker.

5. Lock the lid in place and bring the cooker up to full pressure over high heat. Reduce heat to medium-low, just to maintain even pressure, and cook for 20 minutes. Remove from heat and allow pressure to drop naturally for 7 minutes. Release remaining pressure quickly. Let cheesecake cool in cooker for a few minutes. Using foil handle, lift pan out of cooker onto cooling rack. Remove foil lid. Cheesecake should be set around edges, but still slightly loose in center. If center is still liquid, seal with foil and return to the cooker. Bring up to full pressure and cook for 2 minutes longer. Remove from heat and allow pressure to drop as above. When cheesecake is cooked, remove foil. Use a paper towel to mop up any water pooled on top of cake.

6. *Topping:* In a small bowl, whisk together sour cream, sugar and Grand Marnier. Spread over cheesecake, smoothing top. Let cool to room temperature. Refrigerate for at least 8 hours or overnight before serving.

7. Sprinkle cheesecake with reserved orange zest and serve with orange segments.

● **TIP**

Cheesecake can be wrapped and refrigerated for up to 3 days or frozen for up to 3 months.

Poached Pears in Spiced Red Wine

You can serve this easy but elegant fall dessert warm from the pan or chilled, with a dollop of lemon yogurt. Be sure to use slightly underripe pears and leave them whole, with stems intact, for a dramatic presentation.

● **TIP**

Choose a nice light red wine, such as Beaujolais, Grenache, Pinot Noir or a young Chianti, for this recipe.

6	firm, slightly underripe pears (preferably Bosc or Comice)	6
1	lemon	1
½ cup	granulated sugar	125 mL
3	whole cloves	3
1	cinnamon stick (3 inches/7.5 cm)	1
2 cups	light red wine	500 mL
	Lemon yogurt (optional)	
	Mint leaves (optional)	

1. Peel pears and, using an apple corer or small melon baller, remove cores from bottoms, leaving stems intact and pears whole. Cut a thin slice from the bottom of each pear so it will stand upright. Using a vegetable peeler, remove zest from lemon in large strips. Reserve lemon for another use.

2. In the pressure cooker, combine lemon zest, sugar, cloves, cinnamon and wine; cook over medium heat until sugar is dissolved. Stand pears in pot.

3. Lock the lid in place and bring the cooker up to full pressure over high heat. Reduce heat to medium-low, just to maintain even pressure, and cook for 4 minutes. Remove from heat and release pressure quickly.

4. Remove the lid and let pears cool in their liquid. With a slotted spoon, carefully transfer pears to a shallow dish. Boil poaching liquid over high heat until reduced, glossy and syrupy. Spoon syrup over pears and cool slightly, or chill them overnight.

5. Serve pears whole (or sliced lengthwise up to the stem and fanned) on individual dessert plates with some of the syrup drizzled over them. If served cold, garnish with a dollop of lemon yogurt and a mint leaf.

Poached Winter Fruit Compote

Serve this light and healthy fruit dessert with a dollop of lemon yogurt or crème fraîche. It also makes a nice treat for brunch or spooned over pound cake. *Crème fraîche* is made by combining 2 cups (500 mL) whipping (35%) cream with ½ cup (125 mL) sour cream, and letting the mixture stand at room temperature for 12 to 24 hours to thicken. Refrigerate the crème fraîche up to 2 weeks.

3	firm cooking apples (such as Northern Spy or Rome Beauty)	3
3	firm, underripe pears (Bosc variety holds its shape best; or use Bartlett)	3
1	seedless orange	1
1 cup	apple juice	250 mL
1 cup	dry white wine	250 mL
2 tbsp	buckwheat honey (or other dark honey)	25 mL
1	cinnamon stick (3 inches/7.5 cm)	1
¼ tsp	ground nutmeg	1 mL
	Grated zest of 1 lemon, minced	
½ cup	dried cranberries or dried cherries	125 mL
½ cup	vanilla or lemon yogurt	125 mL
	Ground cinnamon	

1. Peel and core apples and pears; cut into wedges. Set aside. Remove zest from orange; set aside. Cut peel from orange and cut out segments. Cover and refrigerate until serving.

2. In the pressure cooker, combine apple juice, wine, honey, cinnamon stick and nutmeg; bring to a boil. Reduce heat and simmer for 1 minute. Add apples, pears, orange zest and lemon zest.

3. Lock the lid in place and bring the cooker up to full pressure over high heat. Reduce heat to medium-low, just to maintain even pressure, and cook for 1 minute. Remove from heat and release pressure quickly.

4. Using a slotted spoon, transfer fruit to a bowl. Bring remaining syrup to a boil; continue boiling to reduce and thicken. Pour syrup over the fruit and stir in dried cranberries. Cover and refrigerate overnight. Stir in orange segments. Serve in individual bowls, each with a dollop of yogurt or crème fraîche (see note, at left) and a dusting of cinnamon.

Lemony Lavender Creams

Make these lemony puddings in old-fashioned custard cups for that retro feel, then dust them with lavender-infused icing sugar and pop a tiny sprig of lavender on top for a pretty presentation. Lightly caramelizing the sugar gives the pudding an extra layer of flavor and a rich golden color.

- Four ½-cup (125 mL) or six ⅓-cup (75 mL) ovenproof custard cups or ramekins

1½ cups	whipping (35%) cream	375 mL
¼ cup	Grated zest of 1 lemon	50 mL
½ tsp	culinary lavender blossoms	2 mL
¾ cup	granulated sugar	175 mL
¼ cup	water	50 mL
6	egg yolks	6
¼ cup	freshly squeezed lemon juice	50 mL
Pinch	salt	Pinch

Lavender Sugar

¼ tsp	culinary lavender blossoms	1 mL
2 tbsp	confectioner's (icing) sugar	25 mL

Culinary lavender sprigs

1. In a small saucepan, combine cream, lemon zest and lavender; bring to a boil over medium heat. Remove from heat, cover and let stand for 15 minutes to infuse. Strain cream, discarding solids, and set aside.

2. In another saucepan, combine sugar and water; heat over medium heat, stirring until sugar is dissolved. Increase heat to medium-high and bring to a boil. Boil for 1 to 2 minutes, just until sugar begins to change color and caramelize. Remove from heat and carefully whisk in the infused cream.

3. In a large bowl, whisk together egg yolks, lemon juice and salt. Gradually whisk in cream mixture. Divide custard evenly among custard cups and cover each with foil, making sure cups are well sealed.

4. Set rack in the bottom of the pressure cooker. Pour in 2 cups (500 mL) water for steaming. Place custard cups on rack. Lock the lid in place and bring the cooker up to full pressure over high heat. Reduce heat to medium-low, just to maintain even pressure, and cook for 12 minutes. Remove from heat and release pressure quickly. Lift the cups out of the cooker onto a cooling rack. Remove foil lid and let cool completely. Cover and refrigerate until chilled, or for up to 24 hours.

5. *Lavender Sugar:* In a food processor or blender, blend lavender and confectioner's sugar to a powder.

6. Dust each pudding with lavender sugar and garnish with a lavender sprig.

● **TIP**

Use a Microplane grater to grate the lemon zest.

Cool Lemon Custard with Berry Compote

You can also make this pudding in a straight-sided 5-cup (1.25 L) soufflé dish. Cook under pressure for 20 minutes if using a larger mold.

For the mixed berries, try blueberries, Saskatoon berries, cranberries and raspberries.

If desired, dust the top of each dessert with confectioner's (icing) sugar.

- Six ½-cup (125 mL) custard cups
- Rack or trivet to fit bottom of pressure cooker

½ cup	granulated sugar	125 mL
1 tbsp	cornstarch	15 mL
2½ cups	milk or cream	625 mL
2	eggs	2
2	egg yolks	2
	Grated zest of I lemon	
¼ cup	freshly squeezed lemon juice	50 mL

Berry Compote

½ cup	granulated sugar	125 mL
¼ cup	water	50 mL
1 cup	mixed berries	250 mL
2 tbsp	brandy or orange brandy	25 mL

1. In a bowl whisk together sugar, cornstarch, milk, eggs, egg yolks, lemon zest and lemon juice. Pour into custard cups. Cover each with foil, making sure cups are well sealed.

2. Set rack in bottom of cooker. Pour in 2 cups (500 mL) water for steaming. Place custard cups on rack, stacking if necessary. Lock the lid in place and bring the cooker up to full pressure over high heat. Reduce heat to medium-low, just to maintain even pressure, and cook for 12 minutes. Remove from heat and release pressure quickly. Carefully lift cups out and place on a wire rack. Remove foil. Let cool to room temperature. Chill overnight in the refrigerator.

3. *Berry Compote:* In a saucepan, combine sugar and water; bring to a boil over medium heat. Add berries and cook until they begin to break down and release their juices. Most of the berries should remain whole. Remove from heat, stir in brandy and chill.

4. To serve, run a sharp knife around edge of puddings and invert onto individual dessert plates. Top with berry compote.

Cold Rhubarb and Strawberry Soup

On a hot summer day, this soup makes a lovely dessert, served with a scoop of the best vanilla ice cream or gelato you can find. Use red (not green) rhubarb for the most intense ruby color. Star anise adds an exotic flavor, but you can also use a cinnamon stick.

● **TIP**

For the light red wine, try a Gamay, Rosé or Pinot Noir.

Soup

4 cups	chopped red rhubarb stalks	1 L
⅔ cup	granulated sugar (approx.)	150 mL
1	vanilla bean, split lengthwise (or 1 tsp/5 mL vanilla extract)	1
1	whole star anise or cinnamon stick	1
1	1-inch (2.5 cm) strip lemon zest	1
4 tsp	freshly squeezed lemon juice	20 mL
2¾ cups	cold water	675 mL
1 cup	light red wine	250 mL

Garnish

2 cups	chopped red rhubarb	500 mL
¼ cup	water	50 mL
2 tbsp	granulated sugar	25 mL
1 cup	chopped strawberries	250 mL
	Premium vanilla ice cream or gelato	

1. *Soup:* In the pressure cooker, combine rhubarb, sugar, vanilla bean, star anise, lemon zest and lemon juice. Pour in cold water. Lock the lid in place and bring the cooker up to full pressure over medium-high heat. Reduce heat to medium-low, just to maintain even pressure, and cook for 20 minutes. Remove from heat and allow pressure to drop naturally. Strain soup through a fine-mesh sieve into a bowl, discarding solids. Taste soup and add more sugar, if necessary. Stir in wine. Cover and refrigerate until chilled, or for up to 24 hours.

2. *Garnish:* Meanwhile, in a saucepan, combine rhubarb, water and sugar; bring to a boil over medium heat. Boil for 1 minute, until rhubarb is soft but not mushy, then remove from heat. Transfer to a bowl and stir in strawberries. Cover and refrigerate until chilled, or for up to 24 hours.

3. Divide soup among shallow soup bowls. Top each bowl with some of the garnish and a scoop of ice cream.

Coconut Crème Caramel

This variation on a classic dessert makes the perfect ending to a spicy Thai or Szechuan meal. Serve it with slices of ripe mango, papaya and star fruit, or a drizzle of passion fruit coulis.

- 6-cup (1.5 L) soufflé dish (use smaller size if necessary to fit inside pressure cooker)
- Rack or trivet to fit bottom of pressure cooker

1 cup	granulated sugar	250 mL
¼ cup	water	50 mL
1 cup	milk	250 mL
1	can (14 oz/398 mL) coconut milk	1
1	can (10 oz/300 mL) low-fat sweetened condensed milk	1
½ tsp	vanilla extract	2 mL
3	eggs	3
2	egg yolks	2
	Sliced tropical fruits (such as papaya, mango, star fruit, etc.)	

1. In a saucepan, combine sugar and water. Bring to a boil, without stirring, over medium-high heat. Continue to boil, swirling pan occasionally to prevent burning, for about 7 minutes or until syrup is a deep caramel colour. Carefully pour into soufflé dish, swirling to coat bottom and sides with caramel. Set aside.

2. In another saucepan, whisk together milk, coconut milk and condensed milk. Heat over medium heat until bubbles form around edge of pan and mixture is steaming. Stir in vanilla. In a bowl, whisk eggs together with egg yolks. Whisk in a little of the hot milk mixture. Gradually whisk egg-milk mixture back into saucepan. Cook over low heat, stirring constantly, for about 4 minutes or until mixture is slightly thickened. Do not boil. Pour into soufflé dish; cover with a piece of foil, making sure dish is well sealed.

3. Set rack in the bottom of pressure cooker. Pour in 2 cups (500 mL) water for steaming. Fold a 2-foot (60 cm) long piece of foil several times to make a strip that will be used to remove dish. Center dish on midpoint of strip and fold the ends together to make a handle. Use strip to lower dish into the cooker.

4. Lock the lid in place and bring the cooker up to full pressure over high heat. Reduce heat to medium-low, just to maintain even pressure, and cook for 30 minutes. Remove from heat and allow pressure to drop naturally for 30 minutes. Using foil handle, lift dish out of cooker onto cooling rack. Remove foil lid. The custard should be just set in the middle. If center is still loose, seal with foil and return to the cooker. Bring up to full pressure and cook for 2 minutes longer. Remove from heat and allow pressure to drop as above. When custard is cooked, remove foil.

5. Let cool to room temperature. Cover with plastic wrap and chill for at least 12 hours or for up to 24 hours. To serve, run a sharp knife around edge of custard to loosen. Invert on a rimmed plate. Slice into wedges and garnish with fresh fruit.

● VARIATION

If you wish to make individual puddings, use eight $1/2$-cup (125 mL) straight-sided soufflé dishes; wrap each well with foil after filling and stack on the trivet or in the steamer basket of your pressure cooker. These smaller crème caramels need only about 12 minutes under pressure. Let pressure drop naturally after steaming, then chill for several hours. The puddings can be turned out on individual dessert dishes for serving.

Sticky Toffee Pudding

Serves 6 to 8

This is a cross between a heavy cake and a steamed pudding. Serve it warm with caramel sauce, vanilla ice cream or a classic crème anglaise sauce (see Steamy Chocolate Pudding, page 266). Using the low pressure setting ensures that the cake will rise properly.

● TIPS

If you cook at full pressure in step 6, reduce the cooking time to 15 minutes.

Wrap cooled pudding tightly in plastic wrap and store at room temperature for up to 1 week. Slice it into wedges and warm each wedge for a few seconds in the microwave before serving.

- 7-inch (18 cm) springform pan, buttered
- Rack or trivet to fit bottom of pressure cooker

1¼ cups	finely chopped dates	300 mL
¾ cup	boiling water	175 mL
¼ cup	blackstrap molasses	50 mL
1¼ cups	all-purpose flour	300 mL
1 tsp	baking powder	5 mL
¼ tsp	salt	1 mL
¾ cup	packed dark brown sugar	175 mL
⅓ cup	unsalted butter	75 mL
1	egg	1
1 tsp	vanilla extract	5 mL

Caramel Sauce

⅔ cup	packed dark brown sugar	150 mL
⅓ cup	whipping (35%) cream	75 mL
¼ cup	unsalted butter	50 mL
1 tsp	vanilla extract	5 mL

1. In a heatproof bowl, combine dates, boiling water and molasses; let cool.

2. In a small bowl, combine flour, baking powder and salt.

3. In a large bowl, using an electric mixer, cream brown sugar and butter until fluffy. Beat in egg and vanilla. Add the flour mixture alternately with the date mixture, making two additions of each and beating well after each addition.

4. Wrap the base of the springform pan with foil. Pour batter into the pan and cover with a piece of buttered foil, making sure pan is well sealed.

5. Set rack in the bottom of the pressure cooker. Pour in 2 cups (500 mL) water for steaming. Fold a 2-foot (60 cm) long piece of foil several times to make a strip strong enough to lift the pan. Center pan on midpoint of strip and fold the ends together to make a handle. Lower the pan into the cooker.

6. Lock the lid in place and bring the cooker up to low pressure over high heat. Reduce heat to medium-low, just to maintain even pressure, and cook for 30 minutes. Remove from heat and allow pressure to drop naturally. Using foil handle, lift pan out of the cooker onto a cooling rack. Remove foil lid and let cool for 15 minutes, then release from the pan to continue cooling.

7. *Caramel Sauce:* Meanwhile, in a small saucepan, combine brown sugar, cream, butter and vanilla; bring to a boil over medium-high heat, stirring until sugar is dissolved. Reduce heat and simmer for 5 minutes, until sauce is smooth and slightly thickened. Remove from heat and keep warm.

8. Serve pudding while still warm, drizzled with warm caramel sauce.

● **VARIATION**

You can also use 8 ramekins, buttered, for individual desserts. Divide batter evenly among ramekins and cover each with a piece of buttered foil, making sure ramekins are well sealed. Arrange on the rack in the cooker (they can be stacked). Individual puddings will cook in 15 minutes at low pressure or 8 minutes at full pressure.

Steamy Chocolate Pudding with Vanilla Crème Anglaise

This decadent chocolate pudding is like a big, dense, steamy brownie. Serve it warm out of the pressure cooker in a pool of heavenly vanilla crème anglaise or with a scoop of frozen vanilla yogurt for a wonderful temperature contrast.

- 4-cup (1 L) pudding mold, soufflé dish or Bundt pan, buttered and floured (use smaller size if necessary to fit inside pressure cooker)
- Rack or trivet to fit bottom of pressure cooker

3 oz	bittersweet chocolate, chopped	75 g
½ cup	unsalted butter, softened	125 mL
¾ cup	granulated sugar	175 mL
2	eggs, separated	2
1 tsp	vanilla extract	5 mL
1 cup	all-purpose flour	250 mL
1 tsp	baking powder	5 mL
1 tsp	baking soda	5 mL
Pinch	salt	Pinch
⅔ cup	milk	150 mL

Vanilla Crème Anglaise

¾ cup	confectioner's (icing) sugar	175 mL
1 tsp	cornstarch	5 mL
2	egg yolks	2
2 tbsp	unsalted butter, melted	25 mL
1 cup	milk	250 mL
2 tsp	vanilla extract (or other flavoring, such as rum or coffee liqueur)	10 mL
1 cup	whipping (35%) cream, whipped	250 mL

1. In a heatproof bowl set over hot (not boiling) water, melt chocolate. Let cool. In a bowl, with an electric mixer, beat butter with sugar until fluffy. Beat in egg yolks and vanilla.

2. In a separate bowl, combine flour, baking powder, baking soda and salt. On low speed, beat dry ingredients into butter mixture alternately with milk, making three additions of flour and two of milk. Beat in chocolate.

3. In another bowl, beat egg whites until stiff peaks form. Gently fold into chocolate mixture. Pour into prepared mold. Cover with lid or a piece of foil.

4. Set rack in bottom of pressure cooker. Pour in 2 cups (500 mL) water for steaming. Fold a 2-foot (60 cm) long piece of foil several times to make a strip that will be used to remove mold. Center mold on midpoint of strip and fold the ends together to make a handle. Use strip to lower mold into the cooker.

5. Lock the lid in place and bring the cooker up to low pressure over high heat. Reduce heat to medium-low, just to maintain even pressure, and cook for 40 minutes (or cook at full pressure for 20 minutes). Remove from heat and allow pressure to drop naturally for 8 to 10 minutes. Release any remaining pressure quickly. Using foil handle, lift the mold out of cooker onto a cooling rack. Remove foil lid. Let cool for 30 minutes on rack. Run a sharp knife around the edge of pudding to loosen and invert onto a plate to cool completely.

6. *Vanilla Crème Anglaise:* In a bowl, whisk together confectioner's sugar, cornstarch, egg yolks and butter. In a double boiler, heat milk until steaming. Whisk a little of the hot milk into the sugar mixture. Gradually whisk back into the double boiler. Cook over simmering water, whisking constantly, until thick enough to coat a spoon. (Do not let the sauce boil or it will curdle.) Remove from heat and stir in vanilla. Whisk for 5 minutes to cool. Fold whipped cream into custard. Keep chilled in refrigerator. To serve, slice pudding and present in a pool of crème anglaise, or with frozen vanilla yogurt on the side.

● **TIP**

To ensure that puddings have a cake-like texture, it's best to have a dual-pressure machine. The lower pressure setting (8 psi) requires more cooking time, but this allows the puddings to rise. Under high pressure, steamed puddings remain very dense. And while these compacted desserts are still quite delicious, I prefer the lighter results you get using the low-pressure setting.

Steamed Carrot Pudding

This pudding is a Christmas tradition in our family, but you can serve it anytime — the pressure cooker makes this rich, steamy winter dessert fast and fabulous. Make sure to cut off and discard the stems of the figs.

● TIP

If you cook at full pressure in step 5, reduce the cooking time to 30 minutes.

- 6-cup (1.5 L) pudding mold or soufflé dish, buttered
- Rack or trivet to fit bottom of pressure cooker

¾ cup	all-purpose flour	175 mL
1 tsp	baking powder	5 mL
½ tsp	ground cinnamon	2 mL
½ tsp	ground cloves	2 mL
1 cup	packed dark brown sugar	250 mL
½ cup	unsalted butter or lard, softened	125 mL
1	egg	1
1 cup	grated carrots	250 mL
1 cup	grated apples	250 mL
1 cup	raisins	250 mL
1 cup	dried black Mission figs, stems removed, chopped	250 mL

Caramel Sauce

1	can (12 oz or 370 mL) evaporated milk	1
1	can (14 oz or 300 mL) sweetened condensed milk	1
2 tbsp	unsalted butter	25 mL

1. In a small bowl, combine flour, baking powder, cinnamon and cloves. Set aside.

2. In a large bowl, using an electric mixer, beat brown sugar and butter until fluffy. Beat in egg. Stir in carrots and apples. Fold in flour mixture, raisins and figs, stirring until just combined.

3. Pour batter into prepared mold and cover with a piece of buttered foil, making sure mold is well sealed.

4. Set rack in the bottom of the pressure cooker. Pour in 2 cups (500 mL) water for steaming. Fold a 2-foot (60 cm) long piece of foil several times to make a strip strong enough to lift the mold. Center mold on midpoint of strip and fold the ends together to make a handle. Lower the mold into the cooker.

5. Lock the lid in place and bring the cooker up to low pressure over high heat. Reduce heat to medium-low, just to maintain even pressure, and cook for 50 minutes. Remove from heat and allow pressure to drop naturally. Using foil handle, lift mold out of the cooker onto a cooling rack. Remove foil lid and let cool for 10 minutes.

6. *Caramel Sauce:* Meanwhile, in a heavy saucepan, combine evaporated milk, condensed milk and butter; bring to a boil over medium heat. Boil, stirring frequently, for 20 to 30 minutes, until sauce is thick and caramel-colored. Keep warm.

7. Run a sharp knife around edge of pudding to loosen and unmold onto a plate. Serve warm wedges of pudding drizzled with caramel sauce, or wrap pudding in foil and refrigerate for up to 1 week. Reheat pudding, covered with plastic wrap, in the microwave on High for 5 minutes and serve warm with caramel sauce.

● VARIATION

You can also use 6 individual pudding molds, buttered. Divide batter evenly among molds, filling two-thirds full, and cover each with a piece of buttered foil, making sure molds are well sealed. Arrange on the rack in the cooker (they can be stacked). Individual puddings will cook in 20 minutes at low pressure or 11 minutes at full pressure.

Pumpkin and Date Pudding

Serve this dense, steamy cake after a fall supper. It has more fiber and less fat than traditional pumpkin pie, but it's best topped with a scoop of vanilla bean ice cream!

- 8-cup (2 L) pudding mold, heatproof bowl or soufflé dish, well buttered
- Rack or trivet to fit bottom of pressure cooker

2 cups	all-purpose flour	500 mL
2 tsp	baking powder	10 mL
1 tsp	ground cinnamon	5 mL
1 tsp	ground ginger	5 mL
½ tsp	baking soda	2 mL
¼ tsp	ground nutmeg	1 mL
¼ tsp	salt	1 mL
½ cup	packed brown sugar	125 mL
⅓ cup	unsalted butter, softened	75 mL
1	can (14 oz/398 mL) pumpkin purée (not pie filling)	1
2	eggs	2
1 tsp	vanilla extract	5 mL
1 cup	finely chopped dates	250 mL
	Vanilla ice cream or sweetened whipped cream	

1. In a bowl, combine flour, baking powder, cinnamon, ginger, baking soda, nutmeg and salt. Set aside.

2. In a large bowl, using an electric mixer, cream brown sugar and butter until fluffy. Beat in pumpkin. Beat in eggs, one at a time. Stir in vanilla. Fold in flour mixture and dates, stirring until just combined.

3. Pour batter into prepared mold and cover with parchment paper and foil, making sure mold is well sealed.

4. Set rack in the bottom of the pressure cooker. Pour in 2 cups (500 mL) water for steaming. Fold a 2-foot (60 cm) long piece of foil several times to make a strip strong enough to lift the mold. Center mold on midpoint of strip and fold the ends together to make a handle. Lower the mold into the cooker.

5. Lock the lid in place and bring the cooker up to full pressure over high heat. Reduce heat to medium-low, just to maintain even pressure, and cook for 40 minutes. Remove from heat and allow pressure to drop naturally. Using foil handle, lift mold out of the cooker onto a cooling rack. Remove foil lid and let cool slightly. Run a sharp knife around edge of pudding to loosen and unmold onto a warm serving plate.

6. Serve slices of warm pudding topped with ice cream or whipped cream.

● **TIP**

An easy way to finely chop sticky dates is to spray the knife blade with nonstick cooking spray or rinse the knife in warm water from time to time as you work. Whole pitted dates and other dried fruits are less sticky if you toss them with a little flour before chopping.

Classic Christmas Plum Pudding

This is the only way to produce a plum pudding — moist and ready so fast, you'll never steam your Christmas pudding in a conventional steamer again! You can use a 6-cup (1.5 L) heatproof bowl or pudding mold that fits easily into your pressure cooker to make the classic-shaped holiday pudding, but the pudding cooks most evenly in a 7- to 8-inch (18 to 20 cm) springform pan or ring mold. Happy holidays!

- 7- to 8-inch (18 to 20 cm) springform pan (or heatproof bowl or pudding mold), buttered (use smaller size if necessary to fit inside pressure cooker)
- Rack or trivet to fit bottom of pressure cooker

2 cups	currants	500 mL
1 cup	dark raisins	250 mL
1 cup	dried cranberries	250 mL
1 cup	minced candied lemon peel or citron	250 mL
½ cup	brandy or rum	125 mL
1½ cups	all-purpose flour	375 mL
1 cup	dry bread crumbs	250 mL
½ cup	chopped pecans	125 mL
1 tbsp	chopped candied ginger	15 mL
1 tsp	baking soda	5 mL
1 tsp	ground cinnamon	5 mL
½ tsp	salt	2 mL
¼ tsp	ground nutmeg	1 mL
¼ tsp	ground cloves	1 mL
¾ cup	unsalted butter, very cold or partially frozen	175 mL
3	eggs	3
1 cup	packed brown sugar	250 mL

Brandy Sauce

1 cup	packed brown sugar	250 mL
1 cup	whipping (35%) cream	250 mL
¼ cup	unsalted butter	50 mL
¼ cup	brandy or rum	50 mL

1. In a bowl, combine currants, raisins, dried cranberries, candied lemon peel and brandy. Cover and let stand at room temperature for 8 hours.

2. In a large bowl, combine flour, bread crumbs, pecans, ginger, baking soda, cinnamon, salt, nutmeg and cloves. Using a cheese grater, grate butter into bowl; add marinated fruit. With your hands, toss to mix. In a separate bowl, beat eggs together with brown sugar; pour over the batter. Using hands, combine well.

3. Wrap base of springform pan with foil and pack the batter into pan, pressing to eliminate any air pockets. Cover with a piece of buttered foil, making sure pan is well sealed. Use kitchen string to tie foil tightly in place.

4. Set rack in the bottom of pressure cooker. Pour in 3 cups (750 mL) water for steaming. Fold a 2-foot (60 cm) long piece of foil several times to make a strip that will be used to remove pan. Center pan on midpoint of strip and fold the ends together to make a handle. Use strip to lower pan into the cooker.

5. Lock the lid in place and bring the cooker up to full pressure over high heat. Reduce heat to medium-low, just to maintain even pressure, and cook for 1 hour. Remove from heat and allow pressure to drop naturally. Using foil handle, lift pan out of cooker onto a cooling rack. Remove foil lid. Let cool for 15 minutes. Run a sharp knife around edge of pudding to loosen and unmold onto a plate. Let cool to lukewarm.

6. *Brandy Sauce:* In a saucepan over medium-low heat, combine brown sugar, cream, butter and brandy. Simmer, stirring, for about 10 minutes or until sauce coats the back of a spoon. Serve pudding warm with brandy sauce.

● **TIP**

While this dense fruit pudding can be prepared and eaten on the same day, it's best made in advance and refrigerated for 2 to 4 weeks, wrapped in a brandy-soaked cheesecloth. You can then resteam the pudding for 10 minutes in the pressure cooker or reheat it in the microwave before serving with the warm brandy sauce.

Apricot Bread-and-Butter Pudding with Brandy Cream Sauce

Dried winter fruits and brandy add a unique flavor to this rich and comforting dessert. Make it in a 6- to 8-cup (1.5 to 2 L) soufflé dish that will fit easily into your pressure cooker.

- 6- to 8-cup (1.5 to 2 L) soufflé dish (use smaller size if necessary to fit inside pressure cooker)
- Rack or trivet to fit bottom of pressure cooker

Pudding

½ cup	dried apricots, slivered	125 mL
½ cup	raisins	125 mL
½ cup	slivered almonds	125 mL
½ cup	pecans, toasted	125 mL
¼ cup	diced candied orange peel	50 mL
½ cup	melted unsalted butter	125 mL
1	large loaf of dense white bread, sliced, crusts removed	1
	Brown sugar	
4	eggs	4
¾ cup	granulated sugar	175 mL
½ tsp	ground nutmeg	2 mL
1 tsp	ground cinnamon	5 mL
1 cup	milk	250 mL
2 tbsp	cognac or rum	25 mL
1 tbsp	vanilla extract	15 mL

Brandy Cream Sauce

1 cup	whipping (35%) cream	250 mL
½ cup	2% milk	125 mL
¼ tsp	vanilla extract	1 mL
¼ cup	granulated sugar	50 mL
Pinch	salt	Pinch
3	egg yolks	3
½ cup	brandy	125 mL

1. *Pudding:* In a bowl, combine apricots, raisins, almonds, pecans and orange peel. Set aside.

2. Brush bottom and sides of soufflé dish with some of the melted butter; sprinkle with enough brown sugar to coat bottom and sides. Put one-third of bread slices in bottom of dish; sprinkle with half of the fruit mixture. Drizzle with some of the remaining butter. Repeat with remaining bread, fruit mixture and butter, ending with a layer of bread.

3. In another bowl, beat eggs; add sugar, nutmeg, cinnamon, milk, cognac and vanilla. Pour slowly into soufflé dish, gently pressing to ensure bread has absorbed the custard. Let soak in refrigerator for 15 minutes. Cover with a piece of buttered foil, making sure dish is well sealed.

4. Set rack in the bottom of pressure cooker. Fold a 2-foot (60 cm) long piece of foil several times to make a strip that will be used to remove dish. Center dish on midpoint of strip and fold the ends together to make a handle. Use strip to lower dish into the cooker. Pour in enough water to come halfway up sides of dish.

5. Lock the lid in place and bring the cooker up to full pressure over high heat. Reduce heat to medium-low, just to maintain even pressure, and cook for 45 minutes. Remove from heat and release pressure quickly. Using foil handle, lift dish out of cooker onto a cooling rack. The pudding should be set and a toothpick inserted in the center should come out clean. If not, seal with foil and return to the cooker. Bring up to full pressure and cook for 2 minutes longer. Remove from heat and release pressure quickly. Remove foil lid. Serve warm or let cool on rack.

6. *Brandy Cream Sauce:* In the top of a double boiler, combine cream, milk and vanilla; bring just to a simmer. In a bowl, whisk sugar, salt and egg yolks; slowly whisk in some of the hot cream mixture. Whisk egg mixture gradually back into double boiler and cook over medium heat, stirring constantly, until thick. Let cool in refrigerator. Stir in brandy.

7. Reheat pudding in microwave or steamer. Slice and serve with the brandy sauce.

● TIP

If desired, after step 5 you can cover the pudding and refrigerate until chilled.

Banana Bread Pudding

Use a soufflé dish that will fit comfortably inside your pressure cooker for this comforting steamed pudding, a decadent variation on the classic bread pudding. Serve it with a dollop of vanilla or coconut ice cream.

- 8-cup (2 L) soufflé or casserole dish, buttered
- Rack or trivet to fit bottom of pressure cooker

1	loaf day-old French bread, cubed (about 4 cups/1 L)	1
2	ripe bananas, mashed	2
½ cup	white chocolate chips	125 mL
½ cup	finely chopped toasted pecans	125 mL
2	eggs	2
⅔ cup	milk	150 mL
2 tsp	rum or vanilla extract	10 mL

1. Arrange one-third of the bread cubes in the bottom of prepared dish. Top with half the banana, half the white chocolate chips and half the pecans. Repeat layers and top with the remaining bread cubes. Press lightly to pack.

2. In a bowl, whisk together eggs, milk and rum. Pour evenly over bread, pressing gently to ensure that the bread absorbs the custard. Cover with a piece of buttered foil, making sure dish is well sealed.

3. Set rack in the bottom of the pressure cooker. Fold a 2-foot (60 cm) long piece of foil several times to make a strip strong enough to lift the dish. Center mold on midpoint of strip and fold the ends together to make a handle. Lower the dish into the cooker. Pour in enough water to come halfway up the sides of the dish.

4. Lock the lid in place and bring the cooker up to full pressure over high heat. Reduce heat to medium-low, just to maintain even pressure, and cook for 45 minutes. Remove from heat and release pressure quickly. Using foil handle, lift dish out of the cooker onto a cooling rack. Remove foil lid and let cool slightly.

5. Scoop pudding out of the dish with a serving spoon and serve warm, or cover and refrigerate for up to 3 days. Reheat in the microwave, if desired, or unmold the cold pudding and cut into wedges to serve.

Creamy Rice Pudding with Sun-Dried Cranberries

Serves 4 to 6

The pressure cooker is ideal for making risotto. And here we have a sweet version of the rice dish that, combined with milk and dried fruit, makes a deliciously comforting dessert. Don't worry if the pudding looks soupy when you remove the lid; the rice will absorb more liquid as it cools.

2 tbsp	unsalted butter	25 mL
1 cup	Arborio or other short-grain white rice	250 mL
2 cups	water	500 mL
1	can (14 oz/385 or 398 mL) 2% evaporated milk	1
½ tsp	ground cinnamon	2 mL
¼ tsp	freshly grated nutmeg	1 mL
½ cup	dried cranberries, dried cherries or raisins	125 mL
½ cup	low-fat sweetened condensed milk	125 mL
1 tsp	vanilla extract	5 mL

1. In the pressure cooker, melt butter over medium heat. Stir in rice, coating the grains with butter. Stir in water, evaporated milk, cinnamon and nutmeg; bring mixture to a boil over medium heat, stirring to make sure the milk doesn't burn.

2. Lock the lid in place and bring the cooker up to full pressure over medium-high heat. Reduce heat to medium-low, just to maintain even pressure, and cook for 6 to 7 minutes. Remove cooker from heat and allow pressure to drop naturally for about 7 minutes. Remove lid.

3. Stir in dried cranberries, condensed milk and vanilla. Let stand, covered (do not lock), for 5 minutes. Spoon pudding into individual dishes and serve warm, or cover with plastic wrap and chill to serve cold.

Cranberry and Apricot Barley Pudding

Serve this creamy barley pudding for dessert, or even for breakfast. Switch up the dried fruit with whatever you have on hand — it's great with chopped dried apples, currants or even prunes.

2 tbsp	unsalted butter	25 mL
¾ cup	pearl barley	175 mL
2 cups	water	500 mL
2 cups	milk or half-and-half (10%) cream	500 mL
½ cup	packed brown sugar	125 mL
1 tsp	vanilla extract	5 mL
½ tsp	ground cinnamon	2 mL
½ cup	dried cranberries or raisins	125 mL
½ cup	chopped apricots	125 mL
Pinch	salt	Pinch
	Additional milk or whipping cream (optional)	
3 tbsp	pure maple syrup	45 mL

1. In the pressure cooker, melt butter over medium-high heat. Add barley and sauté for 1 to 2 minutes, until lightly toasted. Stir in water, milk, brown sugar, vanilla and cinnamon; bring to a boil, stirring until sugar is dissolved. Stir in cranberries, apricots and salt.

2. Lock the lid in place and bring the cooker up to full pressure over medium-high heat. Reduce heat to medium-low, just to maintain even pressure, and cook for 20 minutes. Remove from heat and release pressure quickly. Stir in a little extra milk (or cream), if desired, and serve warm, drizzled with maple syrup.

Stocks, Sauces and Condiments

Tips for Making Stocks

With a pressure cooker, you can make fast and healthy stocks from scratch in less than an hour.

Instead of discarding vegetable peelings, meat and poultry trimmings, fish bones, turkey carcasses and other kitchen scraps, freeze them in plastic bags until you're ready to make the stock.

You can use almost any vegetable in a stock, but avoid strong-tasting members of the cabbage family, turnips and leafy greens. Unless you're making borscht, avoid red beets, which will turn your stock a deep magenta color. If you use vegetable peelings for stock, make sure that the vegetables are well scrubbed.

Browning vegetables and meats before simmering will yield a darker, richer-tasting stock. If you're pressed for time — or simply want a lighter stock — simply skip the browning step.

It's usually best to make your stocks without salt, then season the final dish to taste when it's done.

Refrigerate stocks and skim off any congealed fat before using them. Stocks can be refrigerated for up to 3 days or frozen for up to 6 months. Or you can reduce a stock to one-quarter of its volume and freeze it in ice cube trays, then reconstitute it for use in recipes.

Vegetable Stock

● **TIP**

You can also use clean peelings from carrots and parsnips in this vegetarian stock.

2 tbsp	unsalted butter or olive oil	25 mL
4	cloves garlic, peeled	4
3	sprigs parsley	3
2	carrots, scrubbed and chopped	2
2	stalks celery, coarsely chopped	2
1	large onion, quartered	1
1	parsnip, scrubbed and chopped	1
1	tomato, chopped	1
1	bay leaf	1
1	sprig thyme	1
8 cups	water	2 L

1. In the pressure cooker, heat butter over medium heat. Add garlic, parsley, carrots, celery, onion, parsnip, tomato, bay leaf and thyme; sauté for 10 minutes or until softened. Pour in water.

2. Lock the lid in place and bring the cooker up to full pressure over high heat. Reduce heat to medium-low, just to maintain even pressure, and cook for 15 minutes. Remove from heat and allow pressure to drop naturally.

3. Strain stock through a fine-mesh sieve, pressing on the solids to release all of their liquid. Discard the solids.

Brown Stock

Makes 5 to 6 cups (1.25 to 1.5 mL)

You can use this recipe to make stock from beef and/or pork bones, game trimmings, lamb or duck. For lamb stock, augment with garlic. Game stock is improved by the addition of several juniper berries and dried mushrooms. A tart apple adds a nice sweetness to duck broth.

● TIPS

To make a demi-glace from this stock, simmer until reduced to 1 cup (250 mL), then freeze in ice cube trays. Transfer frozen cubes to a zippered freezer bag and use as a base for sauces or soups.

If you are making more than one batch of stock in the pressure cooker, speed up the process by combining bones and oil in a shallow roasting pan and roast in a 400°F (200°C) oven for 1 hour. Drain off fat and transfer to cooker. Proceed with adding vegetables.

The darker the bones, the richer and more deeply colored your final stock will be.

2 tbsp	vegetable oil	25 mL
2 lbs	beef, veal and/or pork bones, cut into 2-inch (5 cm) pieces	1 kg
1 cup	chopped mixed vegetables or trimmings (onion, carrot, celery, leek, parsnip)	250 mL
1	plum (Roma) tomato, seeded and chopped	1
1 tsp	whole black peppercorns	5 mL
6 cups	cold water	1.5 L
1 cup	dry red wine	250 mL
	Fresh herbs (such as thyme, parsley, rosemary, etc.)	

1. In the pressure cooker, heat oil over medium-high heat. Add bones in batches and cook until browned. Drain any excess fat. Return bones to cooker and add vegetables; sauté, until vegetables start to brown. Add tomato, peppercorns, water, wine and herbs.

2. Lock the lid in place and bring the cooker up to full pressure over high heat. Reduce heat to medium-low, just to maintain even pressure, and cook for 30 minutes. Remove from heat and allow pressure to drop naturally.

3. Strain stock through a cheesecloth-lined fine-mesh sieve. Discard remaining solids. Let cool, cover and refrigerate overnight. Remove any excess fat that has solidified on top before using the stock or freezing it.

Chicken or Turkey Stock

Makes about 8 cups (2 L)

This stock is useful for many dishes — including the famously comforting chicken soup, the perfect antidote to a winter cold. Don't throw out the bones after your holiday turkey is picked clean — the carcass is perfect for making flavorful turkey broth. When the stock is cooked, you can salvage any meat from the chicken or turkey and add it, along with some small egg noodles, to the broth and boil until tender. Look for tiny imported egg noodles in European delis — they make the best chicken soup.

2 to 3 lbs	chicken bones, a small stewing hen or 1 turkey carcass	1 to 1.5 kg
5	whole black peppercorns	5
5	sprigs fresh parsley	5
2	stalks celery	2
2	carrots, scrubbed	2
1	parsnip, scrubbed	1
1	large onion, quartered	1
1	sprig fresh thyme	1
1	bay leaf	1
8 to 12 cups	cold water	2 to 3 L

1. In the pressure cooker, combine chicken, peppercorns, parsley, celery, carrots, parsnip, onion, thyme and bay leaf. Pour in as much water as necessary to reach maximum fill level advised by the manufacturer.

2. Lock the lid in place and bring the cooker up to full pressure over high heat. Reduce heat to medium-low, just to maintain even pressure, and cook for 20 to 30 minutes (depending on the amount of chicken used). Remove from heat and allow pressure to drop naturally.

3. Strain stock through a cheesecloth-lined fine-mesh sieve, pressing on the solids to release all of their liquid. Discard remaining solids.

4. Allow stock to cool, then cover and refrigerate overnight. Remove any excess fat that has solidified on top before using the stock or freezing it.

Fish Fumet

Good fish stock is the basis for many soups and chowders. Ask your fishmonger for fish heads and bones (both are good for stock), or save your own fish scraps in the freezer. Shrimp and lobster shells also make good fish stock. Be sure to use non-fatty fish, such as halibut, sole and turbot; salmon scraps are not good for stock.

1 lb	fish bones and trimmings	500 g
5	whole black peppercorns	5
2	stalks celery, cut into chunks	2
1	carrot, quartered	1
1	small onion, halved	1
1	bay leaf	1
1	sprig fresh thyme	1
1	sprig fresh parsley	1
½ tsp	fennel seeds	2 mL
½ cup	dry white wine	125 mL
8 cups	cold water (approx.)	2 L

1. In the pressure cooker, combine fish bones and trimmings, peppercorns, celery, carrot, onion, bay leaf, thyme, parsley, fennel seeds and wine. Pour in as much water as necessary to reach maximum fill level advised by the manufacturer. Bring to a boil and skim off any foam that rises to the surface.

2. Lock the lid in place and bring the cooker up to full pressure over high heat. Reduce heat to medium-low, just to maintain even pressure, and cook for 15 minutes. Remove cooker from heat and allow pressure to drop naturally.

3. Strain stock through a fine-mesh sieve, pressing on the solids to release all of their liquid. Discard remaining solids. Cool stock and refrigerate or freeze for future use.

Speedy Marinara Sauce

Serves 4

Here's a simple, speedy, authentic and inexpensive sauce — and the kind of "plain" tomato sauce that appeals to most kids, whether you use it on pasta or pizza. It should be a bit chunky, but for really fussy eaters you can purée it in a food processor before serving.

● **TIP**

To save time, you can chop the tomatoes by whirling them in a food processor.

¼ cup	extra-virgin olive oil	50 mL
2	cloves garlic, minced	2
1	small onion, chopped	1
1	can (28 oz/796 mL) tomatoes, chopped, with juice	1
½ cup	dry white wine	125 mL
1 tsp	dried basil	5 mL
½ tsp	dried oregano	2 mL
1 to 2 tsp	packed brown sugar, divided	5 to 10 mL
	Salt and freshly ground black pepper	
¼ cup	chopped fresh basil	50 mL

1. In the pressure cooker, heat oil over medium heat. Add garlic and onion; sauté for 10 minutes, until onion starts to brown. Add tomatoes, wine, basil, oregano and 1 tsp (5 mL) of the brown sugar.

2. Lock the lid in place and bring the cooker up to full pressure over medium-high heat. Reduce heat to medium-low, just to maintain even pressure, and cook for 5 minutes. Remove from heat and reduce pressure quickly. Season to taste with salt and pepper, and stir in the remaining brown sugar to balance the flavors. If necessary, return to medium heat and simmer for 5 to 10 minutes, until thickened. Stir in fresh basil just before serving.

Basic Tomato and Vegetable Sauce for Pasta

Makes 4 to 5 cups
(1 to 1.25 L)

● **TIP**

This versatile pasta sauce will keep 3 days in the refrigerator or up to 3 months in the freezer.

¼ cup	olive oil	50 mL
3	cloves garlic, minced	3
1 cup	chopped onions	250 mL
1	small zucchini, chopped	1
1	large carrot, chopped	1
1 cup	chopped eggplant	250 mL
½ cup	chopped red or yellow bell peppers	125 mL
½ cup	chopped fresh mushrooms	125 mL
1	can (28 oz/796 mL) crushed tomatoes	1
1 tsp	dried oregano	5 mL
1 tsp	dried basil	5 mL
¼ cup	tomato paste	50 mL
1 tsp	granulated sugar	5 mL
¼ tsp	hot pepper flakes	1 mL
	Salt and freshly ground black pepper	

1. In the pressure cooker, heat oil over medium-high heat. Add garlic and onion; sauté until they start to brown. Stir in zucchini, carrot, eggplant, bell peppers and mushrooms; cook for 5 minutes longer. Add tomatoes, oregano and basil.

2. Lock the lid in place and bring the cooker up to full pressure over high heat. Reduce heat to medium-low, just to maintain even pressure, and cook for 8 minutes. Remove from heat and allow pressure to drop naturally.

3. Stir in tomato paste. (If desired, purée some or all of the sauce with an immersion blender or in a food processor.) Stir in sugar and hot pepper flakes. Season to taste with salt and pepper.

Italian Sausage and Tomato Ragù

**Makes 5 cups
(1.25 L)**

Start with a good-quality
sweet or spicy Italian
sausage and you have an
instantly flavorful meat
sauce to serve over
pasta or use in lasagna.
This basic meat sauce
is ideal for any great
Italian-style supper.

● TIPS

*For a Greek-style sauce,
use ¹/₂ tsp (2 mL)
cinnamon instead of
pesto or basil to finish
the sauce.*

*Instead of simmering the
sauce to thicken, mash
together 1 to 2 tbsp
(15 to 25 mL) softened
butter with 1 to 2 tbsp
(15 to 25 mL) all-purpose
flour and whisk into
sauce; cook, stirring, for
about 5 minutes or until
thickened.*

1 tbsp	olive oil	15 mL
1 lb	sweet or spicy Italian sausage, casings removed, meat crumbled	500 g
8 oz	lean ground beef	250 g
4	cloves garlic, minced	4
2	onions, finely chopped	2
1	red or yellow bell pepper, chopped	1
1 cup	finely chopped mushrooms	250 mL
1	carrot, shredded	1
2½ tsp	dried oregano	12 mL
½ tsp	fennel seeds	2 mL
1	bay leaf	1
1 tsp	granulated sugar	5 mL
2 cups	canned plum (Roma) tomatoes, crushed or puréed in blender	500 mL
2 cups	tomato juice	500 mL
½ cup	red wine	125 mL
¼ cup	tomato paste	50 mL
1 tbsp	basil pesto or chopped fresh basil	15 mL
	Salt and freshly ground black pepper	

1. In the pressure cooker, heat oil over medium heat. Add sausage and ground beef; cook, breaking up meat with a spoon, until no longer pink.

2. Add garlic, onions, red pepper, and mushrooms; sauté for 5 minutes. Stir in carrot, oregano and fennel; cook for 1 minute longer. Stir in bay leaf, sugar, tomatoes, tomato juice, wine and tomato paste.

3. Lock the lid in place and bring the cooker up to full pressure over high heat. Reduce heat to medium-low, just to maintain even pressure, and cook for 20 minutes. Remove from heat and release pressure quickly.

4. Simmer, uncovered, to reduce slightly. Stir in pesto and season to taste with salt and pepper. Store in the refrigerator for 2 days or freeze for up to 1 month.

Greek-Style Meat Sauce

Spices like oregano and cinnamon take this meat sauce into Greek territory. Layer it with cooked macaroni, béchamel sauce and cheese for classic pastitsio, or serve it over spaghetti. Use a food processor to mince the onion, green pepper, garlic, mushrooms and carrot to really speed up this simple sauce.

1 lb	lean ground beef or lamb	500 g
3	cloves garlic, minced	3
1	large onion, minced	1
1	green bell pepper, minced	1
1	carrot, minced	1
½ cup	finely chopped mushrooms	125 mL
1	cinnamon stick (3 inches/7.5 cm)	1
1	bay leaf	1
1 tbsp	dried oregano	15 mL
Pinch	ground nutmeg	Pinch
Pinch	cayenne pepper	Pinch
	Salt and freshly ground black pepper	
1	can (28 oz/800 g) tomatoes, puréed in food processor	1
¼ cup	tomato paste	50 mL

1. In the pressure cooker, cook the ground meat over medium-high heat until it is well browned, then drain any excess fat. Add the garlic, minced onion, green pepper, carrot and mushrooms and cook together for 10 minutes longer.

2. Add the cinnamon, bay leaf, oregano, nutmeg, cayenne, salt and black pepper. Stir in the puréed tomatoes and tomato paste.

3. Lock the lid in place and bring the cooker up to full pressure over medium-high heat. Reduce heat to medium-low, just to maintain pressure, and cook for 20 minutes. Quickly release the pressure and remove the lid.

4. Simmer to thicken, if necessary. Discard the bay leaf and cinnamon stick.

My Favorite Barbecue Sauce

**Makes 3½ cups
(875 mL)**

There's nothing to beat
a flavorful, homemade
barbecue sauce. This
one is a little sweet
and spicy, perfect for
brushing on burgers.
If you like your barbecue
bastes even spicier,
torque up this recipe
with some hot pepper
sauce.

3	cloves garlic, minced	3
1	chipotle pepper in adobo sauce, chopped, or 1 jalapeño pepper, chopped, and 1 tsp (5 mL) liquid smoke	1
1	large onion, minced	1
½ cup	packed brown sugar	125 mL
1 tbsp	chili powder	15 mL
1 tbsp	dried basil	15 mL
1 tsp	ground cumin	5 mL
1 cup	dark beer	250 mL
1 cup	ketchup	250 mL
½ cup	canned beef broth, undiluted	125 mL
2 tbsp	Dijon mustard	25 mL
1 tbsp	Worcestershire sauce	15 mL
	Salt and freshly ground black pepper	

1. In the pressure cooker, combine garlic, chipotle, onion, brown sugar, chili powder, basil, cumin, beer, ketchup, broth, mustard and Worcestershire sauce; stir until sugar is dissolved.

2. Lock the lid in place and bring the cooker up to full pressure over high heat. Reduce heat to medium-low, just to maintain even pressure, and cook for 6 minutes. Remove from heat and release pressure quickly.

3. Season to taste with salt and pepper. Simmer, uncovered, over medium heat for about 10 minutes or until reduced and thickened to desired consistency. For a smooth sauce, purée with an immersion blender or in a food processor. Pour the sauce into a clean jar and refrigerate for up to 1 week.

Cowboy Ranchero Sauce

Use this Southwestern
vegetarian sauce over
pasta, spooned over a
meatloaf or enchiladas
before baking, or as a
braising sauce for
chicken.

16	plum (Roma) tomatoes (about 4 lbs/2 kg), cored and halved	16
12	serrano peppers, seeded and halved	12
6	cloves garlic, peeled	6
2	large sweet onions, chopped	2
1 cup	beer	250 mL
2 tbsp	liquid honey	25 mL
	Salt	
1 cup	chopped cilantro leaves	250 mL

1. In the pressure cooker, combine tomatoes, serrano peppers, garlic, onions and beer. Lock the lid in place and bring the cooker up to full pressure over high heat. Reduce heat to medium-low, just to maintain even pressure, and cook for 7 minutes. Remove from heat and release pressure quickly.

2. Strain sauce through a sieve, reserving the liquid. Transfer solids to a food processor and purée until smooth. Return to cooker and add honey to taste. Stir in enough of the reserved cooking liquid to create a smooth sauce. Season to taste with salt. Stir in cilantro just before serving.

Tips for Making Jams and Chutneys

The pressure cooker speeds up the jam-making process in two ways: It quickly softens and cooks fruit to a pulpy purée; and it infuses the mixture with the flavors of added whole spices. Cooking under pressure can reduce preparation time by 50% to 70% in most recipes.

The main rule to keep in mind when making jams and chutneys is never to overfill the pressure cooker. If you are adapting a traditional preserve recipe for pressure cooking, it's always best to be cautious and never fill the cooker more than half full.

Start by preparing fruit preserves in the traditional way — allowing the fruit and sugar to sit for about 1 hour in the pressure cooker, so that the fruits' natural juices are released. Then bring fruit and sugar to a boil, stirring, before locking the lid in place and bringing the cooker up to pressure.

For jams that must reach an acceptable gel point, cook the fruit and sugar together for up to 8 minutes under pressure, then allow pressure to drop naturally and rapidly boil the mixture for an additional 2 to 5 minutes, until a bit spooned on an ice-cold plate, chilled in the freezer, sets up and congeals. You should start checking the gel after about 2 to 3 minutes of cooking, then continue to boil the jam until it is set to your liking. Some mixtures may take up to 20 minutes of cooking if you are looking for a very stiff result, but will reach a softer gel point much sooner. It's up to you.

The recipes in this chapter are for small batches of preserves, which are intended to be refrigerated and served within 3 days or frozen for up to 1 month, although all can be canned conventionally for longer storage.

For complete instructions on canning jams and chutneys for longer room-temperature storage, consult a specialty book like the *Ball Complete Book of Home Preserving, Bernardin Complete Book of Home Preserving, 175 Best Jams, Jellies, Marmalades and Other Spreads* or *The Complete Book of Pickling*.

Strawberry Jam

The pressure cooker makes this smooth-textured jam so quickly, all of the intense strawberry color is preserved. If you have a 6-quart (6 L) machine, you can easily double the recipe.

4 cups	hulled strawberries, halved	1 L
3 cups	granulated sugar	750 mL
	Juice of 1 lemon	

1. In the pressure cooker, combine strawberries and sugar. Let stand for 30 to 60 minutes, until juicy. Using a potato masher, mash fruit, making sure all of the sugar is dissolved. Stir in lemon juice; bring to a boil.

2. Lock the lid in place and bring the cooker up to full pressure over high heat. Reduce heat to medium-low, just to maintain even pressure, and cook for 7 minutes. Remove cooker from heat and allow pressure to drop naturally.

3. Remove the lid. Bring to a rapid boil over high heat; boil, uncovered, for about 3 minutes, or just until jam reaches the gel stage (when a bit spooned onto an ice-cold plate sets up and congeals; see page 291 for details). Skim off any foam and ladle into hot sterilized jars, leaving $\frac{1}{2}$ inch (1 cm) head space. Seal jars. Cool and refrigerate for up to 1 week, freeze for up to 1 month, or process for shelf storage.

Fresh Apricot Jam

This recipe makes a very smooth, softly set apricot jam, perfect for glazing fruit tarts or other desserts. If you prefer a chunkier jam, only purée a portion of the fresh apricots with the orange flesh in the food processor.

6 cups	apricots, halved	1.5 L
1	large navel orange, peeled	1
½ cup	water or apple juice	125 mL
6 cups	granulated sugar	1.5 L

1. In a food processor, in batches if necessary, purée apricots, orange and water. Pour into the pressure cooker. Stir in sugar and let stand for 30 minutes. Bring to a boil, stirring until sugar is dissolved.

2. Lock the lid in place and bring the cooker up to full pressure over high heat. Reduce heat to medium-low, just to maintain even pressure, and cook for 8 minutes. Remove from heat and allow pressure to drop naturally.

3. Remove the lid. Bring to a rapid boil over high heat; boil, uncovered, for about 3 minutes, or just until jam reaches the gel stage (when a bit spooned onto an ice-cold plate sets up and congeals; see page 291 for details). Skim off any foam and ladle into hot sterilized jars, leaving ½ inch (1 cm) head space. Seal jars. Cool and refrigerate for up to 1 week, freeze for up to 1 month, or process for shelf storage.

Spiced Dried Apricot Jam

The aromatic spices in this jam give it a lovely flavor and aroma. While it's delicious on scones for breakfast, it also makes a wonderful accompaniment to pork roast, pâté or cheese.

• TIPS

Look for star anise (a large star-shaped pod) and cardamom seeds at Asian or Indian grocery stores.

The dried fruit in this recipe results in a very firm jam; for a softer set, add more water.

4 cups	dried apricots, coarsely chopped	1 L
2 cups	water	500 mL
6	whole black peppercorns	6
5	whole cardamom pods	5
2	cinnamon sticks (3 inches/7.5 cm)	2
2	whole star anise or 1 tsp (5 mL) anise or fennel seeds	2
	Juice of 2 lemons	
4 cups	granulated sugar	1 L

1. In a bowl, combine the apricots and water. Cover and let soak for 24 hours.

2. In a square of cheesecloth, wrap peppercorns, cardamom pods, cinnamon sticks and star anise; tie into a bag with kitchen string. (Or place ingredients in a tea ball.)

3. Add apricot mixture and spice bag to pressure cooker. Stir in lemon juice. Lock the lid in place and bring the cooker up to full pressure over high heat. Reduce heat to medium-low, just to maintain even pressure, and cook for 10 minutes. Remove from heat and allow pressure to drop naturally.

4. Discard spice bag. Stir in sugar. Bring to a rapid boil over high heat; boil, uncovered, for about 3 to 4 minutes, until gel point is reached (when a bit spooned onto an ice-cold plate sets up and congeals; see page 291 for details). Skim off any foam and ladle into hot sterilized jars, leaving $\frac{1}{2}$ inch (1 cm) head space. Seal jars. Cool and refrigerate for up to 1 week, freeze for up to 1 month, or process for shelf storage.

Mixed Berry and Red Fruit Jam

**Makes 6 cups
(1.5 mL)**

Use fresh or frozen fruit for this rich, inky, mixed-berry jam. If you like, substitute chopped prunes or dark raisins for the currants.

1 lb	cranberries	500 g
8 oz	raspberries	250 g
8 oz	blueberries	250 g
8 oz	strawberries, chopped	250 g
4 oz	rhubarb, chopped	125 g
4 oz	dried currants	125 g
	Grated zest and juice of 1 lemon	
6 cups	granulated sugar	1.5 L

1. In the pressure cooker, combine cranberries, raspberries, blueberries, strawberries, rhubarb, currants, lemon zest, lemon juice and sugar; let stand for 30 to 60 minutes, until juicy. Bring to a boil, adding up to $\frac{1}{4}$ cup (50 mL) water if necessary to dissolve sugar.

2. Lock the lid in place and bring the cooker up to full pressure over high heat. Reduce heat to medium-low, just to maintain even pressure, and cook for 10 minutes. Remove from heat and allow pressure to drop naturally.

3. Remove the lid. Boil jam rapidly for about 3 to 4 minutes, until gel point is reached (when a bit spooned onto an ice-cold plate sets up and congeals; see page 291 for details). Skim off any foam and ladle into hot sterilized jars, leaving $\frac{1}{2}$ inch (1 cm) headspace. Seal jars. Cool and refrigerate for up to 1 week, freeze for up to 1 month, or process for shelf storage.

Pear Mincemeat

Seal filled jars with metal lids and rings, closing until just "finger tip" tight. Carefully lower jars into boiling water using a jar lifter until they are all submerged in a single layer. Cover the pan. When water returns to a full, rolling boil, start timing the processing. Lift processed jars from water and set on a folded towel on the counter to cool. When you hear the lids pop down as the preserves cool, you will know you have a proper seal.

● **TIP**

Use a heavy, covered canner or stock pot for processing preserves. If you don't have a proper canner (with a wire lifting insert) place a metal rack in the bottom of the pot. The canner or pot should be large enough so that, when submerged, jars will be covered by about 1 inch (2 cm) of boiling water.

2½ lbs	pears, peeled, cored and chopped	1.25 kg
1	green apple, peeled, cored and chopped	1
	Grated zest and juice of 1 lemon	
	Grated zest and juice of 1 orange	
1 cup	golden raisins	250 mL
½ cup	dried cranberries or currants	125 mL
½ cup	packed brown sugar	125 mL
1 tsp	ground cinnamon	5 mL
1 tsp	ground nutmeg	5 mL
¼ tsp	ground ginger	1 mL
Pinch	salt	Pinch
½ cup	chopped walnuts or pecans, toasted	125 mL
½ cup	cognac or pear brandy	125 mL

1. In the pressure cooker, combine pears, apple, lemon zest, lemon juice, orange zest, orange juice, raisins, cranberries, brown sugar, cinnamon, nutmeg, ginger and salt. Bring to a boil over medium heat.

2. Lock the lid in place and bring the cooker up to full pressure over high heat. Reduce heat to medium-low, just to maintain even pressure, and cook for 10 minutes. Remove from heat and allow pressure to drop naturally.

3. Simmer, uncovered, for 10 minutes or until mixture is very thick. Stir in walnuts and cognac; cook for 5 minutes longer. Ladle into hot, sterilized jars, leaving ½ inch (1 cm) headspace. Seal jars. Cool and refrigerate, freeze, or process in a boiling water bath for shelf storage.

Index

Library and Archives Canada Cataloguing in Publication

Chavich, Cinda
200 best pressure cooker recipes / Cinda Chavich.

Includes index.
ISBN 978-0-7788-0209-9 (pbk)
ISBN 978-0-7788-0285-3 (bound)

1. Pressure cookery. I. Title. II. Title: Two hundred best pressure cooker recipes.

TX840.P7C44 2009   641.5'87   C2008-907687-7